BEYOND THE RED CURTAIN

AND OTHER PLAYS

BEYOND THE RED CURTAIN

AND OTHER PLAYS

Roger Curtis

Matador
9 Priory Business Park,
Wistow Road, Kibworth Beauchamp,
Leicestershire. LE8 0RX
Tel: 0116 279 2299
Email: books@troubador.co.uk
Web: www.troubador.co.uk/matador
Twitter: @matadorbooks

ISBN 978 1800460 263

British Library Cataloguing in Publication Data.
A catalogue record for this book is available from the British Library.

Printed and bound by CPI Group (UK) Ltd, Croydon, CR0 4YY
Typeset in 10pt Aldine 401 BT by Troubador Publishing Ltd, Leicester, UK

Matador is an imprint of Troubador Publishing Ltd

The author wishes to thank the fellow writers,
actors and others who have contributed
to the drafting and appraisal of these plays

CONTENTS

BEYOND THE RED CURTAIN

Characters:

Sarah Prestwick

Richard Prestwick – her husband

Edward (Teddy) Grainger – Sarah's father

Alice Grainger – Sarah's mother

Robert (16) – Sarah's nephew, son of her sister Pam, wife of Martin

Amelia (15) – Robert's sister

Eric Grainger – Sarah's elder brother

Dr Metcalfe – a general practitioner

Place – An apartment in suburban London

Time – The near future. The action is played out in real time, without a break.

SCENE ONE

The living/dining room. The dining table, approximately centre stage, is flanked by a sofa and chairs on one side and a sideboard and miscellaneous items of furniture on the other. On the walls are prints and paintings appropriate to the 1980s. An opening right stage leads to a hallway serving the main entrance and the bedrooms; left stage is a door to the kitchen. In the background, and separating this part of the room from an area behind, is a deep red curtain, floor to ceiling. A clock on the wall (active) says 7.30. The table has seven place settings, with plates, cutlery, wine glasses, etc., consistent with a celebration. Sarah, looking a little fraught, is removing one place setting, while Richard looks on.

RICHARD	I thought we were seven.
SARAH	We were. Dear Eric's not coming. Just rung.
RICHARD	Not... He's the bloody eldest!
SARAH	As I reminded him.
RICHARD	Well. He's made his views clear enough, so I guess we might have expected...
SARAH	Richard, it's not that. He lost his job today, so he says. I couldn't push him anymore.
RICHARD	Probably deserved it. They'll be disappointed.
SARAH	Mum will. Don't suppose Dad will even notice.
RICHARD	You've told her?
SARAH	Not yet.
RICHARD	They never got on.
SARAH	Him and Mum? Still... I'll say he's delayed – rail strike or something.
RICHARD	Careful, then. She's up with the news.
SARAH	*(Looking at clock)* Look, before we fetch them. You are happy – about all this.

3

RICHARD	Happy? That's a funny choice of word. We've been going round in circles for days. How about resigned?
SARAH	Odd, isn't it – this being their wedding anniversary and all that. Do you think Mum chose the date to coincide…
RICHARD	Possibly.
SARAH	Anyway, that's how we'll play it. *(Pause)* I'm done here, I think.
RICHARD	Shall I get them?
SARAH	No, wait.
RICHARD	Isn't it better to press on?
SARAH	*(Holding back tears)* I've laid it as it was for their fortieth. *(Pause)* What a difference ten years can make. *(Pause)* Richard, be a poppet, uncork the wine – let it breathe a bit.
RICHARD	OK.
	He uncorks the bottle.
SARAH	Remember the flowers? Jasmine, lilies? Well, they're there.
RICHARD	Well done, love. You've been an absolute angel.
SARAH	Oh, just get them.
	Richard exits right stage. Sarah goes to the red curtain and feels it, turning her back on an imaginary audience to hide her tears. Regaining her composure, she turns, as Teddy and Alice appear in the doorway, with Richard following. They are in their finery, with Teddy flamboyantly dressed, a flower in his buttonhole. Teddy looks around and sees the red curtain.
TEDDY	Splendid! When's the cabaret?
SARAH	Well, Dad, tonight we're expecting you to provide the entertainment. Have you brushed up your stories?
TEDDY	As a matter of fact…

ALICE	*(Looking at the table)* Isn't that jasmine? *(Gratefully)* Sarah! *(Seeing plates)* Why are we only six?
RICHARD	Eric rang to say he'd be… delayed. Accident on the M1 or something. Sarah thought an empty setting would look odd.
ALICE	Well, that's Eric for you. Now, Teddy, last time you were sitting… *there.*
TEDDY	Was I?
ALICE	Just sit. *(Pause)* Sarah and I have been busy in the kitchen, haven't we Sarah? But now I'm just going to enjoy…
TEDDY	Where's Pam?
SARAH	Pam and Martin will be here any minute. They're always on time.
ALICE	I was hoping they'd bring the grandchildren, but I see they won't. It's so long since I've seen them.
SARAH	They had their exam results today and wanted to celebrate – with their friends.
ALICE	Priorities! *(Wistfully)* I suppose they don't know.
TEDDY	Know what, dear?
ALICE	What we're… really here for.
TEDDY	Isn't it time for my pills?
ALICE	Well, yes it is, dear, but we thought just now…
SARAH	I know where they are, Dad. I'll get them.
	Sarah goes to a drawer to fetch the tablets.
TEDDY	You did well, Richard, choosing my daughter. Think you've deserved her?
RICHARD	I've tried to make her happy.
TEDDY	Well, she doesn't look too happy now.
ALICE	She's had a trying day, dear. With me in the kitchen. Nothing that a glass of Chateau Pétrus won't put right.

TEDDY	I rather fancy a Guinness.
	Sarah, returning, hears it and she and Richard look at one another.
ALICE	Not with your pills, dear. Remember?
RICHARD	If he'd really like a Guinness…
ALICE	He'll do as he's told. Won't you, Teddy?
TEDDY	Always have. Always done what she said. Will do, up to the last, I expect.
	A telephone rings in the hall off-stage. Sarah goes to answer it.
	Should have left it off the hook.
ALICE	Telephones don't have hooks now, dear.
TEDDY	They used to! On my desk I'd have three: one for clients, one for inside and one for…
RICHARD	*(Amused)* And what was that for, Teddy?
TEDDY	*(Shielding his speech from Alice with his hand)* That would be telling now, wouldn't it?
RICHARD	But surely they replaced them.
TEDDY	With a screen. Could see who you were talking to.
RICHARD	Wasn't that better?
TEDDY	Could scare the shit out of them! *(He makes a face)* Grrr.
ALICE	You weren't really like that, Teddy. You were just a big fluffy bear.
RICHARD	*(With humour)* Still, inappropriate behaviour for a CEO.
	Sarah returns from the telephone, looking anxious.
SARAH	Would you believe? Pam's in labour. Martin's with her in the taxi. Three weeks early.
TEDDY	Whizzo!
ALICE	*(Hurt)* Pregnant? We didn't know she was pregnant. You never told us. How can that be? Amelia's fifteen!

TEDDY	Always the randiest, that one.
RICHARD	Amelia?
ALICE	He means Pamela.
SARAH	*(Guardedly)* It was – well – unexpected and they had to think long and hard about whether to keep it, given her age, and in the end they decided…
RICHARD	They didn't want it advertised until they'd come to terms with it.
SARAH	Anyway, Pam and Martin are devastated not to be here. Pam has made a suggestion.
TEDDY	What's that?
SARAH	That their children… your grandchildren… That Robert and Amelia should take their place.
ALICE	You told us they were celebrating.
SARAH	Apparently not much to celebrate. Robert's baccalaureate anyway. It's do or die with that. Amelia's were just end of term. Pam thought she should be represented.
ALICE	It will be lovely to have them.
RICHARD	*(To Sarah, softly, urgently)* Do they know?
TEDDY	*(Overhearing)* Know what?
SARAH	Nothing, Dad. *(To Richard)* Oh, God. I forgot to ask.
RICHARD	Can you ring her back? Or Martin?
SARAH	I'd better, hadn't I?
	The doorbell rings.
RICHARD	Too late.
SARAH	Play it by ear then. You get them?
	Richard exits to the hall.
	Well, Mum, you've got your wish. Be prepared, eh?
TEDDY	Pretty young thing, isn't she?
RICHARD	Who?
TEDDY	Amelia. Sitting on my lap, always teasing me.

RICHARD	That was years ago, Teddy.
	Sarah returns with the two teenagers. Robert is scruffy, Amelia has green hair and bizarre make-up.
ALICE	*(To Teddy)* Well dear, it seems your cabaret's arrived.
TEDDY	Where's my little angel?
ALICE	Amelia? That's Amelia. Grown up, sort of.
SARAH	*(To teenagers)* Mum and Dad are delighted you could come. Now we're a full house I think we can all sit.
ROBERT	Where's Uncle Eric?
SARAH	Ah. A bit delayed. Said we should start without him.
ROBERT	Strikes me he's not coming.
SARAH	Why?
ROBERT	*(Pointing at place settings)* No room for him, is there?
AMELIA	Clever dick! How'd you fuck up your maths, then?
RICHARD	Easily remedied. Now. You here, Robert. Amelia, you sit opposite.
ROBERT	I'm supposed to look at *that (meaning Amelia)* all evening. That's a fate worse than death.
	Amelia pokes out her tongue at him, but they sit where they're told. Sarah remains standing.
SARAH	Richard, why don't you pour the wine while I fetch the soup. You do that and Robert and Amelia can bring you up to date, Teddy, as you've not seen them for so long. Robert, tell your grandpa where you're at. At... well, school.
ROBERT	You serious? Didn't mum tell you?
SARAH	She said you'd started a boy band.
AMELIA	Keeps him off the streets. I don't think.
ALICE	But onto the road, perhaps?
ROBERT	Yeah, could be.

SARAH	I'll bring the soups.
	Sarah exits to the kitchen.
TEDDY	A band? What do you play?
ROBERT	A thing that hangs round me neck, usually.
AMELIA	He means his guitar.
ALICE	Teddy used to play the guitar, didn't you Teddy? Our first date, remember? You took me back to your place.
TEDDY	I did, didn't I.
ALICE	*(To all)* It was dreadful. I told him to put it away.
RICHARD	Better things to do, eh Teddy?
ALICE	But not by much, if I recall. But it improved.
ROBERT	Must have done, else we wouldn't all be here.
AMELIA	You do believe in setting the tone, don't you?
	Sarah returns with the soups on a tray, sets them out and sits.
SARAH	Mum and I thought it would be nice if we were all to say something. To remember the good things we've all shared together. Like since their fortieth.
ROBERT	Fortieth what?
RICHARD	Years married.
AMELIA	*(To Robert)* Clown!
ROBERT	She's always so clever! Head's so fertile her hair's gone green.
AMELIA	That your joke, was it?
ROBERT	At least I wash my ears out.
	Sarah waves her hands at them to stop, then sits.
SARAH	Richard, you start. Tell us what you remember most.
RICHARD	I guess it's the way we've all rallied round Teddy, like families are supposed to do. It can't have been easy for you, Alice, especially before we got the carer in. You've worked wonders, haven't you.

Look at him now, the smile on his face, *(more seriously)* even now.

ALICE   He's been such a fighter, haven't you, Teddy?

TEDDY   Well…

ALICE   And I'd like to say thanks to you both *(Sarah and Richard)* for being so… attentive. Finding this flat for us, to be near you. And being around to help. That couldn't have been easy, with important jobs to hold down.

SARAH   We've tried our best.

TEDDY   Which is more than can be said for some others I could mention.

ALICE   Teddy, Eric's trying to make it.

TEDDY   Not hard enough, though, is he?

Teddy is beginning to look apprehensive.

ALICE   And Pam's kept in touch.

SARAH   Difficult with a family to manage.

AMELIA   We're not difficult!

ROBERT   Not much.

AMELIA   *You* drive her round the bend.

ROBERT   Why don't you…

Teddy, who has been looking more and more agitated, leans forward and begins to cough blood over the table. Robert, next to him, jumps up.

Bloody hell!

Sarah rises and comes behind Teddy.

SARAH   It's alright, Dad. Let's see if we can clean you up a bit.

She manoeuvres Teddy out of his chair.

ROBERT   That's a good start, innit.

SARAH   Did any go on you?

ROBERT   I don't think so.

SARAH   That's alright, then.

RICHARD	Sit on the sofa, Robert, while I clean this up.
	Sarah guides Teddy from the room. Robert moves to the sofa. Richard lifts the soiled place mat and makes to carry it to the kitchen, but pauses in the doorway.
ALICE	*(Despondent)* I was so hoping he'd make it through.
RICHARD	*(From the door)* It's partly the excitement. If he rests for a while he can still join us later.
ALICE	*(Bitterly)* He'll have to, won't he?
AMELIA	Why, Grandma. What do you mean?
ALICE	Why? Don't you know why you're here? Didn't Pam tell you?
AMELIA	Your wedding anniversary or something.
ROBERT	Married fifty years.
AMELIA	Forty plus ten – the maths wizard strikes again.
ALICE	That's right, we have been. Amazing years, so many good times. But you see, now, Grandpa is not very well.
RICHARD	He's very ill, Robert.
ALICE	A lot has gone wrong inside. He tries not to show it but really he's in great pain.
ROBERT	Is he dying, then?
AMELIA	I thought you could control that now – the pain – with analgesics.
	Robert and Alice look at her in astonishment.
ALICE	You think so? How do you know?
ROBERT	Knows everything, she does.
AMELIA	It was a question in our general paper. *(Confidingly)* We knew it was coming up.
ALICE	So what was the question?
AMELIA	*(Reciting)* Do people suffering unbearably have a right to die?
ALICE	And do they?

RICHARD	Amelia, why don't you and Robert come to the kitchen for a moment. There's something I want to say to you.
ALICE	No, I want to hear what they think.
RICHARD	It's better if I tell them now.
ALICE	*(Holding up her hands)* In a moment. But I want to hear what Amelia has to say. What her teachers have told her.

> *Richard, who has been standing in the doorway, finally disappears into the kitchen.*

AMELIA	That you must do your best to bear it.
ALICE	And when it becomes unbearable?
AMELIA	That's just God's will.
ROBERT	When were you last in church, might I ask?
ALICE	When you saw your Grandpa, when you came in just now. What did you think?
AMELIA	Looked alright to me.
ROBERT	Of course he didn't.
AMELIA	What do you know, imbecile? *(Pause)* Then he was ill, like I get sometimes.
ROBERT	After she's been binge drinking.
ALICE	When you feel really rotten, right?
AMELIA	Right.
ALICE	And if that was your permanent state? You wake up like that, like you on a Sunday morning, feeling dreadful, with no prospect of getting better?
ROBERT	She'd kill herself.
ALICE	She's just said she wouldn't – or implied it.
AMELIA	Then I don't know.

> *Richard reappears in the doorway, listening.*

ALICE	Alright, then. Consider this. Do you think Teddy minded that we saw what happened just now?

ROBERT	Should think it made him feel like shit.
AMELIA	Because he knew it made us feel like shit.
ALICE	It did make him feel like shit. He feels like shit all the time, and it's getting worse day by day. Apart from controlling the pain – and that's not really working – there's nothing anyone can do. *(Softly)* So that's why, a week or so ago, he decided there was no advantage to anyone in going on.
ROBERT	But what can he do about it? He can't exactly kill himself.
AMELIA	Actually he can. One way is to starve yourself to death, or stop drinking. But that's suicide and that's wrong.
ROBERT	Who says?
AMELIA	Anyway, the law changed a year ago and it's OK to get someone to help you.
ROBERT	Like who?
AMELIA	Like a doctor.
ROBERT	Doctors don't kill people.
AMELIA	Who else then?
ALICE	Amelia's right. You need two doctors to agree that the quality of life is so poor and irreversible that it's unreasonable to go on. One must be in attendance when it happens, but it's for the sick person to take the drug that's provided for him… *(cautiously)* or her.
ROBERT	If they're still thinking straight.
	Richard, who has been listening in the doorway, re-enters.
RICHARD	And that's the crux, isn't it? He must be capable of making the decision.
ROBERT	And if he can't? If he's gaga or something?
RICHARD	Then it's more complicated. But fortunately your grandfather is not at that stage yet.

13

ROBERT	So what's stopping him, then?
ALICE	Nothing is stopping him, Robert, and that's why we're here tonight.
ROBERT	Tonight?
ALICE	When Teddy re-joins us we'll say our farewells and... *(emotionally)* the doctor will come and... *(Desperately)* I have to go to him.

Alice rushes out of the room.

ROBERT	Fucking hell!
RICHARD	Now you know the score. I think we should try to make things right again, for when he comes back, don't you?
ROBERT	Pretend nothing's happened.
RICHARD	Not much has happened, that's new at any rate. What you saw is how it's been for the past few days. *(Pause)* The doctor's coming at nine. Do you think we can make it nice again, for when Teddy comes back?
AMELIA	What do you want us to do?
RICHARD	First, finish your soup.
ROBERT	Don't want any more... *(reconsidering)* OK.
RICHARD	Amelia?
AMELIA	OK.
RICHARD	*(Pause)* Perhaps you can remember things from happier days. Holidays. Like when they lived in the farmhouse, if you remember.
ROBERT	That was spooky.
AMELIA	Yeah. Really was. So was Grandpa.
RICHARD	Oh?
ROBERT	Remember hide and seek? In the barn? Hiding in the straw. Bit scary, that, but he never found us there.

AMELIA	*(Slowly, reluctantly)* He did once.
ROBERT	Well, I didn't notice.
RICHARD	*(Deeply concerned)* What happened, Amelia?
AMELIA	*(Hushed)* He made me stay quiet, so you wouldn't hear.
RICHARD	Amelia, why didn't you tell…
AMELIA	*(Angrily)* What point was there? Nobody ever listens. You'd never have believed me.
ROBERT	She always thinks bad about people. Never lets anything rest.
RICHARD	If Grandpa behaved badly…
AMELIA	I didn't say that.
ROBERT	Not much.
RICHARD	So, Robert, what's best then? Pursue it or let it rest?
ROBERT	Let it rest.
RICHARD	You sound very certain.
ROBERT	I know how her mind works.
AMELIA	How, then?
ROBERT	She thinks he's being punished. For things like that. That's what she told me.
RICHARD	Things like what, Robert? No, no, don't answer. Both ask yourselves. Does it matter now?
AMELIA	It might, mightn't it? To him.
RICHARD	A chance to confront the past, you mean? He's never been religious, Amelia.
ROBERT	But *she's* into that sort of stuff.
AMELIA	I'm not! *(Pause)* Only a bit, maybe.
RICHARD	Isn't it reasonable that when we get to the end the goalposts are allowed to shift a little? Let compassion prevail over what we might otherwise see as… well… justice.
AMELIA	Not if it's not the end.

15

ROBERT	Oh, for fuck's sake.
	Footsteps offstage.
AMELIA	Listen. He's coming back.
	Teddy enters with forced military bearing.
TEDDY	Should have warned you at the beginning. Can tell from your faces.
AMELIA	We're sorry.
ROBERT	Yeah. Really sorry, Grandpa.
	Teddy sits, brushing aside Richard's attempt to help him.
TEDDY	So, where were we? The good times. Yes.
RICHARD	*(Noticing)* Where's Alice?
TEDDY	Phoning Eric. God knows why she's bothering. *(Pause)* So where was I?
RICHARD	So what was the best then?
TEDDY	Besides with Alice?
RICHARD	Yeah. The high point of your career. Something like that. To impress these two *(meaning Robert and Amelia)*.
TEDDY	*(Now lucid)* Know anything about architecture, do you? Heard of the Stirling Prize?
AMELIA	No.
ROBERT	Never heard of it.
RICHARD	A very prestigious prize and Grandpa's company won it. When was it?
TEDDY	Nineteen... Wasn't my company then. I was just the project manager.
RICHARD	*(To Robert and Amelia)* It was – and still is – a super modern development near Croydon. Very futuristic. Won hands down apparently, that year.
TEDDY	*(Staring ahead)* Like a mirage, they said it was, when they first saw the drawings. Two hundred and eighty homes, white plastic cladding, flat roofs,

	integral garages, linking walkways. Entirely new way of living. New concept.
AMELIA	*(Disparagingly)* Sounds a dream.
TEDDY	Wasn't easy though. Took years.
AMELIA	To do what?
TEDDY	People living there. Didn't want to move.
AMELIA	And you made them?
TEDDY	Can't halt progress. Paid them well enough.
AMELIA	Should think so too.
TEDDY	*(Suddenly becoming thoughtful)* Except for one. Tattiest house in the row. Hm. Would have made them rich, what we offered. But no, wouldn't budge.
AMELIA	So what did you do?
TEDDY	Built around them. Had to.
RICHARD	The house is still there. Passed it only yesterday. All boarded up.
ROBERT	*(Concerned)* What happened to them, Grandpa?
TEDDY	The couple? *He* went under a train at East Croydon station. Accident of course.
AMELIA	Because you…
RICHARD	We don't know that, Amelia.
	Teddy begins to cough again, but controls it.
TEDDY	*(Again thoughtfully)* It was a common problem then. All over London. Getting land. Getting people out. We had a team. Four people. Two technical, one to support a development, one against it. Then two others to look at the human costs if it happened. Effect on the community, that sort of thing. One for, the other against. Then we'd all argue. Told us what problems we'd run into. Told us what to do.
AMELIA	So which were you?

17

TEDDY	*(Looking at her penetratingly)* In this case? I argued for.
AMELIA	I bet you did.
ROBERT	I've got a question.
RICHARD	We don't need to go there, Robert.
TEDDY	Perhaps we do. What's on your mind?
ROBERT	What happened to his wife.
AMELIA	Yeah. After you killed her husband.
RICHARD	Amelia. That's enough.

Alice appears in the doorway looking anxious, Sarah behind. The others do not see them.

TEDDY	A fair question. *(Pause)* Months later I traced her to a care home in Streatham. Quite gaga, she was. Turned her mind, you see, losing him. *(Pause)* Funny how it's come back to me now. Been with me for a week, wondering what would happen if… to Alice… when I go. *(Pause)* So when Alice said…

Alice steps forward.

ALICE	Well, now Eric knows. I spoke to him.
TEDDY	I told you not to tell him.
ALICE	He's our son, Teddy. We couldn't not tell him.
TEDDY	What'd he say?
ALICE	Not much.
TEDDY	Ask you how you were, did he?
ALICE	Not exactly. *(Pause)* Asked me if I was ready.
TEDDY	Never does.
ROBERT	*(To Amelia)* What're they on about?
AMELIA	No id… *(Pause, realising)* She's going too, isn't she? She's gonna go with him.
ROBERT	You're jokin'.
SARAH	Tell them, Mum. *(Pause)* No, perhaps I'd better.

	(Pause; to Amelia and Robert) You see, it's not just Grandpa that's ill. A few weeks ago Grandma went to the doctor and... they found a lump in her tummy.
AMELIA	Cancer you mean?
SARAH	Cancer of the bowel. And it's spread. Actually – although we don't see anything – it's almost everywhere.
AMELIA	Couldn't she have been treated? Couldn't you, Grandma?
SARAH	She was... up to a point.
TEDDY	*(Tiring, no longer completely lucid)* She's a wonderful woman.
ALICE	That point, Amelia, was when I realised how little time was left for Teddy. I could either have had the treatment... and been sick and lost my hair... or stayed normal, outwardly anyway... for Teddy...
ROBERT	To see him out, like.
ALICE	... *(emotionally)* so we could still love one another, like we always have. *(Pause)* Then, suddenly one day, it seemed a beautiful thing if we would go together. *(Pause)* But it wasn't easy, because... we had children to think of and affairs to settle... and you two... and the doctors to persuade... but in the end Sarah and Pam agreed...
TEDDY	Where's Pam?
SARAH	At the hospital by now, I expect.
TEDDY	She ill, then?
ALICE	No, Teddy. Not ill. She's giving birth.
ROBERT	What about Uncle Eric?
SARAH	Uncle Eric was... abroad. His life's not been easy lately. We thought it best not to trouble him.

AMELIA	Weird. *(Pause)* He's back now though, isn't he?
ALICE	He is, and I was so hoping he could make it this evening. *(Pause)* You don't look too happy, Amelia.
AMELIA	It all sounds a bit selfish to me.
ALICE	Why?
AMELIA	Going before you have to. The law says you need to be suffering unbearably.
ALICE	*(Losing composure)* And do you think I'm not? *(Regaining control)* The law says no such thing. The law says that if the condition's terminal and you expect to die within three months and the doctors agree on that…
SARAH	It's done, Amelia. The doctor's here at nine and there's no going back.
AMELIA	That's not what we were told.
SARAH	*(Losing patience) What* were you told?
AMELIA	That you could say no at the last minute. *(Pause)* We saw a film.
SARAH	What film?
AMELIA	Mr Cribbens in Switzerland. He was lying down with his fingers on the tap. But then the doctor said something to him – you couldn't hear what – and he wouldn't turn it. His fingers just wouldn't move. You should have just seen the doctor's face.
ROBERT	Couldn't he have helped him?
AMELIA	God, no. Not allowed.
ROBERT	Then what happened?
AMELIA	He went home.
ROBERT	The doctor?
AMELIA	*(Giggling)* I suppose. *(Pause)* Mr Cribbens, idiot!
SARAH	*(Angrily)* To what, though? Have you thought about that? Had anything changed for him, do you think?

ROBERT	I think he'd have felt even more rotten, when he got home.
SARAH	There you are, then. So let's stop this nonsense talk, which is only upsetting your grandparents.
ALICE	Actually, it's not nonsense talk. It's about the first time I've heard anyone say what they really think. *(Smiling)* Maybe you two should have been here weeks ago. But I can tell you it wouldn't have changed anything.
TEDDY	Did I have my pills?
SARAH	You had them in your hand when you left the room, remember?
ROBERT	*(Whispering to Amelia)* I don't think he knows what's coming.
AMELIA	He must do. It's the law.
ROBERT	It's the law, it's the law. You're just a fucking parrot.
RICHARD	*(Loudly)* Teddy was telling us about the high points in his career, Alice. Can you remember yours?
ALICE	Oh, my goodness me. There were so many.
RICHARD	Quite a star in your youth, so I believe.
ROBERT	Like when you were on the stage?
ALICE	You know about that?
ROBERT	Saw the photo albums in the study.
AMELIA	Who said you could go in there?
ROBERT	Sorry.
ALICE	That's was before Teddy's time, thankfully.
AMELIA	Why thankfully?
ALICE	Well. One tended to live the high life in those days. Flowers thrown onto the stage. Admirer's queueing at the stage door.
TEDDY	What admirers?
ALICE	All artistes had admirers, Teddy. You knew that.

21

TEDDY	Nobody told me anything.
ROBERT	*(To Alice)* Who was Raymond?
ALICE	Raymond?
ROBERT	Paul Raymond. Behind you in the photo. On the poster. Read it with me magnifying glass.
AMELIA	You little sneak!
ALICE	Ah, yes. Raymond's ticket agency, you must mean. Mr Raymond's long gone.
AMELIA	I thought his daughter…
SARAH	*(Changing subject)* I think it's time we rang Martin again, don't you. See how Pam's getting on.
RICHARD	I'll do it. I feel you might be needed here.
	The telephone rings in the hall. Richard goes to answer it.
TEDDY	These admirers. Did I know them?
ALICE	They were all off the scene, Teddy, when you came along. You were the last, I promise you.
TEDDY	I snatched you away, didn't I? From that awful world.
ALICE	It was how I met you, Teddy. But you did and a day hasn't passed when I haven't been grateful.
TEDDY	And it wasn't just my money?
ALICE	*(Affectionately)* No. It wasn't just your money. Just you.
	Richard returns.
RICHARD	Martin says they're just climbing the hospital steps. Panic over apparently.
SARAH	*(To herself)* Thank goodness for that. So we can all get on with our meal at last.
	Sarah gets up to go to the kitchen.
TEDDY	Where's Bumble?
SARAH	Bumble?

TEDDY	I haven't seen her today. Alice, have you seen Bumble?
ALICE	You gave Bumble her breakfast yourself, dear. Don't you remember?
TEDDY	So where's she now?
SARAH	Well, actually, Dad, Bumble's at home with us.
TEDDY	But you're both here.
SARAH	It's what we agreed. We'd look after her.
TEDDY	I'd like to have said good-bye to Bumble.
ALICE	You did, dear. You gave her extra chunks, as a farewell gesture.
TEDDY	Only because you told me to.
	Sarah finally leaves for the kitchen.
RICHARD	I'll help you.
	He follows her. Alice and Teddy are left with Amelia and Robert.
TEDDY	*(Staring at Amelia)* Why's she got green hair?
ROBERT	*(Snidely)* Last month it was mauve. She thinks she's being independent. She's talking about a ring through her nose. Know why she doesn't?
AMELIA	Because he said he'd thread a piece of string through it when I was asleep and tie it to the bed. He would, too.
ALICE	*(Laughing)* Robert! You wouldn't do such a thing!
ROBERT	Only because she'd get back at me with something worse.
TEDDY	In my day I'd have been expelled with green hair. Can't understand why you'd do that to yourself.
AMELIA	Because I want to.
ALICE	Teddy has forgotten about when he was young. You should ask him about his tattoo.
ROBERT	When, Grandpa?

TEDDY	What tattoo?
ALICE	When you were in the Navy, dear. Before my time, thankfully.
ROBERT	Can you show us, Grandpa?
TEDDY	I've forgotten where it is.
AMELIA	*(Coldly)* It's on your left arm, near the shoulder. Of a woman with no clothes on.
ALICE	How do you know that, Amelia? Did he tell you?
AMELIA	*(Staring at Teddy)* He must have done, mustn't he?
ROBERT	I think he came swimming with us once.
AMELIA	I don't rem... *(Robert kicks her under the table)* Ouch!
ALICE	Well. I have to say it's the least endearing thing about him. It's why he always wears tee shirts on holiday, isn't it Teddy? Even by the pool.
AMELIA	Does he swim in them too?
	Sarah and Richard return with a trolley bearing the food.
SARAH	I've cut your steak up, Dad. Thought it might be easier.
TEDDY	So long as there are lots of chips.
SARAH	Plenty of those.
TEDDY	We must have gone swimming, mustn't we?
SARAH	*(Amused)* What?
TEDDY	On holiday.
SARAH	I haven't the foggiest idea what you're talking about.
ALICE	The grandchildren must have seen Teddy's tattoo when they went swimming.
SARAH	I thought he always covered it up, when we were children. Thank goodness. How embarrassing would that have been for a child.
RICHARD	Does it really matter? Come on everybody, eat up or your food will get cold. *(Pause, to Teddy)* Teddy,

	you don't look very happy. You can have a whole steak if you'd rather.
TEDDY	It's not the steak.
RICHARD	What then?
TEDDY	Nothing. *(Long pause)* We've all made mistakes.
SARAH	Oh my goodness. We do have a touch of the grumps, don't we?
TEDDY	*(To Sarah)* Have you made mistakes?
SARAH	Other than Richard, you mean?
ALICE	*(To Sarah and Richard)* Don't be alarmed. Dr Metcalfe told us that towards the end it's usual to look back over one's life. And things that happened get magnified. That's the advantage of being a catholic, which we're not. It can all come out.
RICHARD	An extravagance denied to most of us.
SARAH	So we can take it as read we've all done things we've regretted.
AMELIA	So what have *you* done, Aunt Sarah?
SARAH	*(Thinking hard)* Well, Amelia, for a start I wasn't very nice to your uncle Eric.
TEDDY	Few people were, with good reason.
RICHARD	*(To Sarah)* So what did you do to him?
SARAH	He was the eldest. Pam and I would... well... torment him.
AMELIA	I should have thought he could have taken care of himself.
SARAH	He did, in a manner of speaking. He left home. Then got in with a bad crowd. Drugs, the lot.
ALICE	But he pulled through. Such a pity he's not here with us. Pam and Eric. *(Pause)* It's all going a bit pear-shaped, isn't it?
RICHARD	Nonsense, Alice. I'm going to put it back on track.

25

TEDDY	Had a train set once. When I was a boy. Hornby Dublo.
ALICE	It's still in the back room somewhere.
ROBERT	We used to play with it.
TEDDY	I'd love to see it.
SARAH	What, now?
TEDDY	Duchess of Atholl, red and black. The best engine I ever had.
ROBERT	*(Enthusiastically)* Shall I go and get it?
RICHARD	You know where it is?
AMELIA	'Course he does. He's into everything, he is.
RICHARD	Right, you do that, Robert.
AMELIA	Then I'm coming too.
RICHARD	Off you go, then.
	Robert and Amelia immediately make for the door and exit.
SARAH	They're well meaning, Dad, but sometimes they can be…
RICHARD	… a bloody pain.
TEDDY	Did I take my tablets?
ALICE	You did, dear.
TEDDY	No more till tomorrow, then.
ALICE	*(Patting his hand)* No, dear.
TEDDY	*(In distress)* The pain's not gone, you see.
ALICE	We all understand that. *(Under her breath)* Especially me.
	Sarah and Richard look at her with concern.
SARAH	Sorry, Mum. If we've…
ALICE	Neglected me?
RICHARD	You can't mean that, Alice. *(Pause)* Here, let me take your plates.

Robert returns clutching an electric train engine, which he puts in front of Teddy.

ROBERT Found it!

Teddy looks at Robert admiringly. Amelia returns.

TEDDY You were always friends with your old grandpa, weren't you?

ROBERT You thought I wasn't?

SARAH You think he had reason not to be? Come on, Dad. There's no point in searching for skeletons that don't exist.

Amelia looks at Sarah angrily, then at Richard quizzically. Richard exits to the kitchen.

The stage darkens and lightens immediately on Sarah and Richard visible in the kitchen through the open door, but out of sight of the others, who are now dimly lit.

SARAH *(To Richard)* So what was all that about?

RICHARD *(Vigorously sorting plates)* What was all what about?

SARAH Something's not right with Teddy.

RICHARD Well, isn't that what's tonight's all about?

SARAH Stop being evasive. And what were those glances between you and Amelia – and Robert trying to distract. I'm not a fool, Richard, and Teddy's my father.

RICHARD A small misunderstanding best forgotten.

SARAH Well, I don't forget quite so easily, so you'd better tell me.

RICHARD Believe me, it's not sensible.

SARAH Tell!

RICHARD *(Long pause)* It's just that... just after Amelia arrived and you were out of the room, she hinted...

SARAH Hinted what?

RICHARD	That Teddy might have behaved... well... improperly – when she was a child. I'm sure there's nothing in it.
SARAH	What are you saying?
RICHARD	Amelia's never liked Teddy. It could be she's being... vindictive.
SARAH	Then shouldn't we ask her?
RICHARD	To what purpose?
SARAH	Because he can't go to his death with a thing like that hanging over him, that's why.
RICHARD	So what's he supposed to do about it?
SARAH	Oh, fuck. Nothing. *(Long pause, realising)* Oh, God!
RICHARD	What?
SARAH	Something Pam once said to me. One day years ago. She came to me, quite tearful, because something had happened to Amelia. Her clothes were torn, apparently, and she was distressed. Could I throw any light on it?
RICHARD	When was that?
SARAH	The year we were all on holiday together. On the farm.
RICHARD	And could you – throw any light on it?
SARAH	Amelia said she'd been climbing in the hay loft and got trapped.
RICHARD	So what did you say?
SARAH	I said Amelia was quite a tomboy then, and no need to disbelieve her.
RICHARD	And there the matter ended?
SARAH	I'm... not sure.
RICHARD	Why not?
SARAH	Because... things were never quite the same, after that holiday. We saw less of Pam – and the

28

grandchildren hardly ever. It could all have been coincidence, but one does wonder.

RICHARD *(Guardedly)* And your mother?

SARAH A closed book. Always has been staunchly loyal to Teddy – have you ever heard her say a word against him?

RICHARD Can't say that I have.

SARAH Maybe that's because she's always been the one in control.

RICHARD Currents run deep with your mother.

SARAH We'd better get back. *(Pause)* There are the mousses, on that tray there. Can you bring them?

Richard goes ahead carrying the tray. He turns at the doorway.

RICHARD Just a thought, what was Teddy's relationship with Eric?

SARAH Who knows?

Sarah shakes her head in disbelief and enters the dining room, now normally lit.

ALICE *(Looking up)* You were talking very earnestly in there. Was it a good thing we couldn't hear you?

SARAH *(With humour)* Quite possibly.

ALICE Try not to be too hard on us. When we're gone and you go through our things, and questions will occur to you…

SARAH I'm sure that won't happen.

They notice that Teddy is almost asleep.

ALICE Now look. Teddy's nearly finished his steak – and all the chips. But he's getting very tired.

SARAH You're both looking tired. What say we take a break, rest a while, smarten you up. Then we'll have the dessert – mango mousse, just what you like, eh Dad? Then another glass of wine…

TEDDY	Or two…
SARAH	As many as you want.
ALICE	You always were the thoughtful one, Sarah.
SARAH	Yes, well… *(Pause)* Come on then, up with you…

Sarah helps Teddy to his feet and Richard pulls back Alice's chair. They leave the room together. Robert and Amelia, still sitting, pull why-are-we-here faces at one another. Reverting to childishness Robert screws up his napkin and throws it at Amelia, who throws it back.

The stage darkens to black momentarily.

SCENE TWO

Robert and Amelia are still sitting at the table, each engaging with a mobile phone. Amelia looks up.

AMELIA	What are you doing?
ROBERT	Saturday night, innit. Results are in. *(Pause)* Oh, fucking hell!
AMELIA	Lost your pocket money, have you?
ROBERT	Nah. Well, not much. What're you doing?
AMELIA	Says here – on the government website – doctors have been jailed for helping people to die.
ROBERT	You're not taking this a bit seriously?
AMELIA	It frigging well is serious. If the new government hadn't got in the law wouldn't have been passed and we wouldn't be here now.
ROBERT	Well, I'm all for it.
AMELIA	You haven't even thought about it.
ROBERT	Enough to know that if I was going gaga or couldn't swallow or peed myself all the time I'd want to go.

It's not just the pain, is it? It's so people remember you as you want them to.

AMELIA   Yeah, well that's all fine, isn't it, if it's just up to the sick person. But you've also got to think of the people looking after them. Not everyone wants to look after sick people. They might put pressure on them to die.

ROBERT   Why'd they do that?

AMELIA   It's obvious, imbecile. To save themselves a lot of bother and money. I mean, look at the trouble Auntie Sarah and Uncle Richard have gone to. Moved them into this flat, called in every day with shopping, done the cooking for them sometimes. And they've got important jobs to go to.

ROBERT   I've not heard them complain.

AMELIA   You've hardly ever been here. How do you know what they're thinking. What they say to each other in bed at night.

ROBERT   I know it was Grandma and Grandpa's decision.

AMELIA   How can you be sure? You can bet your life Grandma discussed it with Auntie Sarah – not sure about our mum or Uncle Eric. And Aunt Sarah would have discussed it with Uncle Richard.

ROBERT   You're not seriously suggesting that Uncle Richard...

AMELIA   Why should he put himself out like he does. He's not really family.

ROBERT   You're twisted you are. 'Course he is.

AMELIA   Not blood-related.

ROBERT   For fuck's sake, once you marry someone that's what they become. That's why when you die your stuff passes to your mate, not your children.

AMELIA   Not always. Not if you make a will.

ROBERT	Anyway, before the law changed I saw a man on the tele. Broke his neck, he did, falling from his motor-bike. Could only move the muscles of his face. Had to blink when he wanted anything. But you could see he was crying, because he wanted to be shot of it all.
AMELIA	So?
ROBERT	But there were people like you trying to stop him because if he'd been allowed to go, they said, so would others not half as bad as he was.
AMELIA	That's right.
ROBERT	And some said that God just wanted to keep him alive.
AMELIA	Some of us do think that life is sacred and should be preserved, however crap it is.
ROBERT	Well, I bloody well think God would have agreed with me, seeing the state that man was in.
AMELIA	Anyway, it's now up to doctors to decide.
ROBERT	Yeah. Doctors like playing God, Mum says.
AMELIA	Doctors have to swear an oath not to harm patients. That keeps them on the right lines. But that's where the new law's got a problem – some doctors think that helping a person to die is the same as harming them.
ROBERT	Well, I wouldn't see it that way. I'd say keeping someone alive who's suffering is more harmful than letting them die a bit earlier than they might have done.
AMELIA	You have thought it through, haven't you?
ROBERT	And another thing. If it had been me, like, in Grandpa's position I could have held on longer if I'd known – when it really got too tough – I could pull the plug.
AMELIA	*(Sarcastically)* Fall off the twig, you mean.

ROBERT	What? Where did you get that from?
AMELIA	Uncle Eric. Heard him say it once. Stuck in my mind.
ROBERT	Not about Alice and Teddy.
AMELIA	Could have been.
ROBERT	Well, thankfully *he's* not looking after them. *(Pause)* I wonder what he'd think about Grandma going.
AMELIA	Same as me, probably. That she's not ready.
ROBERT	Aunt Sarah thinks to go with Teddy is a beautiful thing to do.
AMELIA	Still, if I could I'd stop her. Get her to think again.
ROBERT	So what could you do? Stand in front of those curtains over there. No, Grandma, you can't go in there. And she says, well thank you Amelia, my little angel, I'm so grateful…
AMELIA	I should… do that.
ROBERT	Then tomorrow she'd feel like you do after your bingeing. And so would you…
	The doorbell rings. The teenagers take no notice. The bell rings again, more aggressively. They look up at the same time.
ROBERT	Their door's shut. They've not heard.
AMELIA	You go, then.
ROBERT	Why me?
AMELIA	Because you're the biggest. Fathead. *(Pause)* Probably flowers or something. You wouldn't know what to do with them. *(Reluctantly)* I'll do it.
	Amelia exits to the front door. Robert continues tapping his phone. Seconds later Amelia returns with a neatly dressed man (ERIC) in a suit and loud tie. Although he adopts an apparently aggressive tone towards the teenagers he has some rapport with them, especially Amelia.

AMELIA	It's Uncle Eric.
ROBERT	Can see that.
ERIC	Hello, Robert. Long time, no see. *(Pause)* You've kept yourself out of trouble, then?
ROBERT	Like you, I suppose.
ERIC	That's not very welcoming. *(Pause)* Didn't expect to find you two here. I thought it was just close family.
AMELIA	We are close family.
ERIC	You tearaways? Pam loosened your reins or something?
AMELIA	Mum's at the hospital.
ERIC	So I heard. Twilight pregnancy. A bit of competition coming your way, right?
AMELIA	It won't worry us.
ERIC	No, plenty of spoils to divide.

Eric walks around the room and examines the cards on the mantelpiece.

ERIC	Fiftieth anniversary! That's a good cover, isn't it? *(Pause)* So, seriously for a moment, kids. What's your take on it? This new change in the situation?
AMELIA	Grandma, you mean?
ROBERT	She doesn't think Grandma should do it.
ERIC	And you do?
ROBERT	*(Hesitantly)* Yeah. They both want it.
ERIC	But she *(meaning Amelia)* doesn't think that's enough.
AMELIA	How'd you know that?
ERIC	Because she's a prissy little stick-in-the-mud. *(To Amelia)* Aren't you? Under that green hair.
AMELIA	Do you like it?
ERIC	Not the prissy bit, but the green hair. Um, maybe.

	(Looking at her face closely) Yeah, tempts me in that does. Or would if you were a bit older. *(Pause)* But hey, what're they up to through there? Praying?
AMELIA	They're not religious.
ERIC	Tarting themselves up, then. *(Pause)* But you say not religious. Were once. I remember a time… *(Serious now)* I was the eldest. Confirmed I was – the only one of the three. Can still remember the words. I believe in… But when *Pam* came along behind. Well, there was a challenge! A bridge too far, that. That's when they gave up on me, I think.
AMELIA	Did you believe then?
ERIC	Nah. Thought it was all gobbledegook. Still do.
AMELIA	Not even when they had you in the dock?
ERIC	Wasn't me that done it, though, was it?
AMELIA	Everyone thought so. *(Pause)* Not even a little prayer? Help you out?
ERIC	Maybe a little one. Nothing to lose, was there? Everything against me. If it hadn't been for the DNA test yours truly wouldn't be here now.
AMELIA	*(Joking)* Worth another little prayer, that then. Of thanks?
ERIC	Actually I did oblige.
AMELIA	OK then, why have you come?
ERIC	You need to ask that question?
AMELIA	I know you, Uncle Eric. You don't do anything without a reason.
ERIC	Hah, you're a sharp one, Amy. Isn't she a sharp one, Bob?
ROBERT	Don't call me that.
ERIC	Bobby, then. How about that? *(Pause)* But no, you're right, there are issues. *(Pause)* Ah, I can hear someone coming.

> *Alice and Teddy appear in the doorway, with Sarah and Richard behind. Teddy enters first. Seeing Eric he stops dead, but Alice is delighted to see her son.*

TEDDY   Talk of the devil.

> *Alice moves forward and kisses Eric, who remains impassive.*

ERIC   Too late to get you anything. Shops all closed.

ALICE   Doesn't matter. You is enough.

ERIC   *(Looking at the table)* Well, I see you've not quite done. Room for one more?

SARAH   I'll lay a place. I can heat up the steak.

ERIC   Nah. Already eaten, thanks. What's the dessert?

SARAH   Mango mousse.

ERIC   Fucking hell.

SARAH   A nice wine, though.

ERIC   Now you're talking.

> *Sarah lays a place for him and Richard pulls up a chair. Eric sits.*

Now. *(To Alice)* Your little grand-daughter here. Well, we've been having a little talk, and we think you shouldn't be too hasty, know what I mean? *(To others)* I mean, Mum and I've not seen too much of each other lately. And it would have been nice, for me, to have... well... made up for being... on my part you understand... well... a bit distant.

RICHARD   *(Coldly)* I don't think you were greatly missed, Eric.

ERIC   That's not the lady speaking.

ALICE   Of course you were missed, Eric. Not a day went by...

ERIC   You see? But I was wrong and I need to explain something. Why I've been away. *(Pause, guardedly)* Clearly you haven't read the papers.

RICHARD	You've been banged up again, haven't you?
ERIC	Nah. Nah. Came a bit close, but nah.
RICHARD	So what was it then?
ERIC	A... parking fine.
RICHARD	And you didn't pay it?
ERIC	In Marbella, wasn't I?
RICHARD	Escaping from your previous escapade.
ERIC	Alleged escapade.
RICHARD	Let's not split hairs.
ALICE	Eric happened to be parked on a double yellow line outside that jewellers shop which was raided.
ERIC	Wrong place, wrong time. Story of my life. *(Pause)* Now, Mum, look. You don't need to be hasty... about this thing.
RICHARD	What thing is that, Eric?
ERIC	What she intends to do. *(To Alice)* You don't look ready for the pot, Mum. Sorted out your affairs, have you? Thought about what you want to do with this place?
TEDDY	They've taken Bumble.
ERIC	Oh, the cat. Well, that's a start. But that's an easy one. What about the furniture... and the paintings.
SARAH	We've had more important things to think about, Eric.
ERIC	Course you have. Course you have. But I know how easy it is for things to go. Heirlooms. Like these two *(meaning Robert and Amelia)* would appreciate one day.
SARAH	We've made a list.
ERIC	Too easy to get someone in to flog the lot. Then when the dust settles it's gone. Forever.
RICHARD	So what have you got your beady eyes on?

37

Eric throws up his hands.

ERIC   Me? Not a thing, me. Wouldn't give any of it houseroom.

AMELIA In any case, they must have made wills to say how things are split.

ALICE   Of course we have. A long time ago, though. Not sure about the fine detail. And I know Teddy has. Haven't you, Teddy?

Teddy's expression has been building to express great anger.

TEDDY   He gets nothing from me. It's written in.

ERIC   Charming.

TEDDY   Anyway, it all goes to Alice.

ALICE   Well I'm sure I've divided everything equally.

SARAH   That's that, then. Richard, can you fetch the mousses from the kitchen?

RICHARD In a moment. *(Pause)* But there's an issue here, isn't there? Are wills still valid under... well... these circumstances?

Robert points at Amelia.

ROBERT Better ask *her.* Knows everything, she does.

RICHARD Amelia?

AMELIA The new law says they are. It came up in our lesson.

RICHARD And if people choose to go... together... and their wishes are different?

AMELIA That I wouldn't know.

ERIC   Better set your watches, then. Who goes first.

All eyes are upon Eric.

RICHARD That's why you're here, isn't it? If Mum goes first it's all Dad's, to do with as he likes. You've worked all that out, haven't you?

ERIC   You're talking through the back of your head, you are, Richard. You should be ashamed, spoiling their last evening together with nasty innuendos. *(Pause)* I came to set things straight, Mum. Between us two. Think we could have a few minutes together, private like, before I go? Say goodbye properly, shed a few tears together.

ALICE   I'd like that very much, Eric.

SARAH   Why don't you take Mum to the bedroom, Eric.

ERIC   Good idea. Coming, Mum?

Eric leads Alice out of the room.

RICHARD   That true, Teddy? You written him out?

TEDDY   Can't honestly remember. *(Gleefully)* Got the bugger thinking, though.

AMELIA   That's a wicked thing to do.

RICHARD   Don't tell me you're on his *(Eric's)* side.

AMELIA   No. But you've always been unkind to him.

TEDDY   Bloody deserved it. Chance after chance, we gave him. Could have gone to university. But no. Set him up in business. No, squandered the lot on a Lotus. Pink, of all colours.

ROBERT   Oh, I remember *that*. That was great!

AMELIA   We were in it when it crashed!

RICHARD   Yes. Well. I suspect that was the final straw. Eh, Teddy?

TEDDY   Would have been, but for Alice. *(Pause)* Here, what do you think they're saying to each other. Like to be a fly on the wall in there.

ROBERT   I can hear them coming. You can ask them.

Alice and Eric and re-enter and take their seats.

TEDDY   *(To Alice)* Shaken him off, have you? All done and dusted?

ALICE   Eric's accepted I have a right to decide. There's an end to it.

39

ERIC   Famous last words!

RICHARD   In that case – and seeing we're all here together again – I suggest I refill our glasses while Sarah serves the desserts. We also need to keep an eye on the clock. Dr Metcalfe will be here at 9.00 prompt.

            This causes a coldness to descend on the gathering.

SARAH   Oh! I forgot the candles.

            She takes matches from the sideboard and lights them tentatively.

ERIC   Shouldn't we put the lights out?

            All stare at him, even though the allusion was not intended.

            Sorry.

            Richard gets up and switches off the main ceiling light. He and Sarah retire to the background.

ALICE   Dr Metcalfe is very nice. You thought so, didn't you Teddy?

TEDDY   Who?

ALICE   We saw him together two weeks ago. Have you really forgotten? You loved those plush armchairs.

TEDDY   He asked silly questions.

ALICE   *(To the others)* He did no such thing.

TEDDY   Asked me how old I was.

AMELIA   And what did you tell him?

TEDDY   Can't remember. Upset him though.

ALICE   He was just confirming you were competent to make decisions.

TEDDY   Why'd he want to do that?

AMELIA   *(Sarcastically)* And can you – make decisions?

RICHARD   *(From background)* Let's not go there. Amelia.

AMELIA   But it's important. The law says…

RICHARD	Yes, we know. The law says you must be competent to judge whether to commit yourself. Dr Metcalfe was obviously satisfied.
AMELIA	And the second doctor?
ALICE	We saw Dr Green the week before, with a psychologist. Dr Metcalfe had all the papers.
AMELIA	They spoke, did they? These doctors?
ALICE	Yes, of course.
AMELIA	And that was when…
ALICE	…I made the choice to… go with Teddy.
AMELIA	Dr Green and Dr Metcalfe?
ALICE	*(Getting irritated)* Dr Green *and* Dr Metcalfe.
AMELIA	*(Thoughtfully)* You can't live with the pain… or you can't live without Teddy?
RICHARD	Amelia, this is helping no-one.
ERIC	Hang on there, Richard, the girl's got a point. All very well losing Teddy, but what about the rest of us? My sister – and the grandchildren. Has she properly said good-bye to them? *(Turning to Amelia and Robert)* How you going to remember your granny, eh? Wouldn't you have liked a bit more info? What did you tell me in there, Mum – about it having to be within three months of intolerable pain. You there yet? You told me yesterday you'd been shopping, the day before that having tea with your hen-friends, last weekend feeding ducks in the park. What was on the agenda for next weekend?
RICHARD	A lot can change – will change – within three months.
ERIC	*(Dismissively)* Yeah.
AMELIA	*(To Eric)* We know why you might want to keep her alive.
RICHARD	That's unfair. Apologise to your uncle.

AMELIA   *(Exaggeratedly)* Sorry, Uncle Eric.

            By now Alice is crying into her handkerchief. Teddy is holding her hand.

ALICE   Please stop all this. Tonight was so that Teddy and I could leave you in peace and goodwill, not acrimony.

ROBERT   *(Quietly)* I think you're all missing the point.

SARAH   What's that, Robert?

ROBERT   That it's none of our business.

RICHARD   How's that, then?

ROBERT   That a person should be able to decide whether or not they want to die. Without others interfering.

AMELIA   So you'd support suicide, would you? If I want to throw myself under a train I should be allowed?

ROBERT   As I see it the law doesn't stop you. Yet when you're in pain, or desperate, lots of things are put in your way.

RICHARD   The reason, Robert, is that a person in such a predicament is... well... vulnerable. All sorts of pressures could be put on them. People with something to gain – like children not having to look after them.

AMELIA   Or after their money.

ERIC   Bloody hell, do you never let up?

SARAH   *(Quietly)* Can I say something?

RICHARD   Of course, love.

SARAH   I think what Mum has decided – to go with Teddy – is a beautiful thing. No unbearable grief tomorrow. To depart amongst close family in love and trust, so that's how they will remember you. You feel that, Robert?

ROBERT   Yes.

SARAH   Amelia?

AMELIA	I suppose.
SARAH	So from now on let's try to make the evening the best we can.
RICHARD	I suggest we pick up on some of those memories we were telling about earlier. Alice, what about the young Eric – was he always a tearaway?
ALICE	Well, no. As a child he was quite… well… angelic.
AMELIA	So what went wrong?
ROBERT	Amelia!
AMELIA	Sorry.
ALICE	He was actually the brightest of the three children.
ROBERT	That's why he's kept himself out of trouble.
AMELIA	You serious?
ALICE	I still have the cards he sent me, every year on my birthday. Ones he made himself.

Alice gets up, goes to the sideboard and takes a bundle of envelopes from a drawer. She sits and begins to flick through them.

	Then, sadly, when he was about twelve, they stopped. I never knew why.
AMELIA	Perhaps something to do with my mum coming along behind. A mother-daughter thing. Pam was…
ROBERT	*(Reminded)* Fuck!

They all stare at him.

You've all forgotten about Mum.

The telephone rings in the hall.

ERIC	Talk of the devil!

Sarah leaps up and exits to answer it.

Perhaps we'll have something to celebrate. *(Pause, seriously)* What you said, Mum, about the cards stopping…

ALICE	*(Showing Eric the cards)* Look, aren't they wonderful?
ERIC	Probably just a teenage thing, Mum. Other things to do, like.
	Sarah returns.
SARAH	That was Martin. They've taken Pam to the theatre.
RICHARD	So quickly.
SARAH	A breech presentation – and her blood pressure's shot up.
RICHARD	That puts a different complexion on things. Teddy, do you understand what's happening?
TEDDY	It's not about Bumble is it? Are they looking after her?
SARAH	No, Dad. It's about Pam – she's about to have a baby.
TEDDY	I always said she was the randy one. Right, wasn't I?
AMELIA	That's rich, coming from you.
ROBERT	Oh, for God's sake!
RICHARD	*(Hissing)* Amelia, remember what we agreed.
AMELIA	Sorry.
RICHARD	So, we have a bit of a dilemma – waiting to hear what the outcome will be.
SARAH	Maybe we should telephone Dr Metcalfe.
RICHARD	To say what?
SARAH	Get him to delay.
RICHARD	For what purpose?
ROBERT	I think you should let him come.
AMELIA	Robert's right. Like with that man in Switzerland, nothing need happen until it happens.
	Teddy slumps over the table. Alice and Sarah rise to help him.
ALICE	Oh, Teddy.

SARAH	He'd be better lying down. We can manage him between us.
	They lift Teddy from his chair and guide him from the room.
ERIC	How long do caesarian's take?
RICHARD	Not long. Brenda in our office said less than an hour, I think.
ERIC	So we sit twiddling our thumbs.
ROBERT	You don't sound very sympathetic towards your father.
AMELIA	*(To Eric)* Why didn't you follow them, to check how he is?
ERIC	You really need to ask that question? You of all people?
AMELIA	*(Hushed)* You too?
ERIC	You asked why the cards stopped. It was when I realised... what he was. What happened to you, Amelia, was... *(unable to continue)*
AMELIA	And Grandma couldn't have protected you?
ERIC	Maybe never knew. Alice could never see a fault in him – or chose not to.
AMELIA	*(Tentatively)* And your sisters?
RICHARD	*(Sternly)* That book is closed. For ever. *(He holds up his hands to stop them saying more)*
ERIC	Do you think we could put the lights on?
RICHARD	Of course. Robert, can you.
	Robert gets up to switch on the main light. Richard makes to extinguish the candles, then stops.
	Maybe while it's still dark we should... reflect... a little, perhaps say a prayer.
ERIC	I didn't know you were religious.
AMELIA	*(Cautiously)* I already have done.

ROBERT   Oh. And what did you pray for?

ERIC   Like me in the dock – the best outcome, I suppose.

RICHARD   Which is?

ERIC   Let them both go.

RICHARD   And why would the doctor do otherwise?

AMELIA   Because Teddy can no longer think straight. And that's a condition, isn't it?

ERIC   You think the doctor's going to check at nine on a Saturday evening? *(Boldly)* 'Now Teddy, tell me again when you were born. And by the way, who was our last prime minister but one?' You know what the answer to that would be – if there was one.

ROBERT   But surely what was decided two weeks ago still stands.

AMELIA   But there's a new factor, isn't there. Shouldn't he hear about my mum giving birth? That he's got another grandchild?

ROBERT   The doctor might ask us what we think.

RICHARD   Possibly. So what do we think?

ERIC   Teddy's gaga. He wouldn't understand if you told him.

ROBERT   But surely that's not our decision to make. He's got a right to know. We're not God. We don't know what he's thinking.

RICHARD   Let's sound out Dr Metcalfe when he arrives. Besides, a bigger issue concerns Alice – whether she now really wants to or not.

ERIC   Because of the child?

ROBERT   Shouldn't we check how they are?

RICHARD   You're right. I'll take a look.

                As he gets up the telephone rings in the hall.

                I'll take it on my way.

He exits.

ERIC Well. A steep learning curve for you two. And it hasn't flattened off yet, has it? Have you changed your view, Amelia? Has compassion taken over from principle at last?

ROBERT She never changes her mind.

ERIC Making you the wimp, I suppose, eh Robert? What principle do you work to?

ROBERT What's kindest. That's all.

ERIC So you'd let these things happen, even if it encourages people like me to take advantage, hypothetically speaking, of course. Save the NHS money on treatment and care into old age – and me from paying more taxes – not that I actually… Let people like your grandma – who's not really ready if we're honest – jump the gun.

ROBERT You can guard against those things. The law must have safeguards.

AMELIA Must it really?

ERIC Okay then, Amelia. Suppose it was you with Teddy's condition, no hope of treatment, feeling more bloody awful by the day – like you after your binge drinking – and your brother Bobby here comes along and says what do you want to do Amelia? What sort of brother would you like to have, do you think? One like you?

AMELIA I'd still…

ROBERT Then you're a hypocritical little prat.

Eric sits back in his chair and laughs.

ERIC So much for family unity.

Richard appears in the doorway, Sarah following.

Well?

RICHARD That was Martin. Pam's still in the theatre.

ROBERT	And Grandpa?
RICHARD	Sitting up. Quite lucid actually. He asked when Dr Metcalfe's coming.
ROBERT	So he does know what's what.
RICHARD	It would seem so.
SARAH	They'll be back in a moment. Perhaps I should clear the table.
ERIC	I was so looking forward to a mango mousse.
RICHARD	*(Rounding on him)* When your turn comes, eh? And then we'll join you.
ERIC	It's all getting to you, isn't it?
RICHARD	What's bugging you now?
ERIC	This Metcalfe… *(Pause)* How you going to sleep tonight, Richard?
RICHARD	I don't get you.
ERIC	Like, with a conscience. You've been quiet all evening. But I know. 'Cause I know my sister Sarah here wasn't the one that was pushing…
RICHARD	That's an appalling accusation. You really think I encouraged…
ERIC	Well, I don't believe Sarah did.
RICHARD	How can you say that? You've not had contact with her for… well…
ERIC	Been closer than you think.
RICHARD	*(To Sarah)* What's he saying? I thought…
SARAH	We… have had… some contact, Richard.
RICHARD	Bloody bailing him out, I suppose.
ERIC	*(Sarcastically)* Taken as read. Isn't that what sisters are for? *(Accusingly)* She said you knew Metcalfe.
RICHARD	*(Guardedly)* Only distantly.
ERIC	Same golf club, Sarah said. The odd round together, perhaps? 'Cause I don't believe…

RICHARD	What don't you believe?
ERIC	That Sarah wanted it – what's happening to Mum.
RICHARD	And I did, I suppose.
SARAH	It was Alice's choice, Eric. In the end.
ERIC	And Pam? Couldn't you all have waited for Pam to deliver?
RICHARD	*(Angrily)* We couldn't predict Pam's baby coming early.
SARAH	But it *was* her pregnancy that precipitated this, Richard. Get all this over in time... before... *(Quietly)* So they would never know, die without... even more complications in their lives.
ERIC	*(Sarcastically)* And I thought it was their wedding anniversary that decided the timing. Amelia, doesn't the law say you need to die on an anniversary?
AMELIA	The law says...
ERIC	The law says. The law says. Your needle stuck or something?
AMELIA	Don't get what you mean.
ROBERT	Something about vinyls, innit.
SARAH	Enough! I think we've all said enough.
ERIC	You know the score, then, you two.
	Alice enters with Teddy. She and Sarah place him on his seat.
ROBERT	You feeling better. Grandpa?
TEDDY	Yes thank you, Robert.
RICHARD	Now, you must all keep your eye on the clock. Teddy and Alice, on the sideboard there's a bottle of Chateau Pétrus – the same as you had for your fortieth anniversary, remember?
ALICE	You kept it all this time?
RICHARD	For a very special occasion.

He pours everyone a glass, including the teenagers.

Now, a toast, I think.

ROBERT   To when we meet again.

Amelia looks at him askance (Robert being an unbeliever).

ALL   To when we meet again.

ERIC   Down the hatch, then.

RICHARD   *(Looking at the clock)* Well, it's now five to…

The doorbell rings.

SARAH   I'll get it.

She exits. Everyone sits dead still. After a few seconds she returns with Dr Metcalfe.

SARAH   *(To Dr Metcalfe)* My parents you know…

METCALFE   *(With trace of humour)* I believe so. Good evening to you both.

SARAH   … and my husband Richard, my brother Eric…

METCALFE   *(Showing familiarity)* Hello Richard, Eric.

SARAH   … and Robert and Amelia, my nephew and niece.

METCALFE   Pam's children.

SARAH   Why yes…

METCALFE   Teddy told me about them. All to their credit. *(Pause)* So, I see you all have glasses in your hands. That's good. And you've said everything you want to say?

SARAH   I think so. Our final farewells.

METCALFE   Even so, I'll wait in the hall for a moment or two and if there are any thoughts you may have… Then I'll see Teddy and Alice alone before we go through. Perhaps, Richard, you can tell me when you're done.

Dr Metcalfe exits to the hall and closes the door behind him. (During the following exchanges Teddy falls asleep.)

ERIC	Why's he left us, do you think?
ALICE	*(Tentatively)* Because I asked him to.
ERIC	I didn't hear you.
ALICE	Before that. When we took Teddy to the bedroom.
SARAH	You telephoned him?
ALICE	From Teddy's study.
SARAH	Why, Mum?
ALICE	Because you doubted what I was doing.
RICHARD	*(Gently)* That's not true, Alice.
ALICE	It was for Amelia.
AMELIA	Grandma, it's OK. Robert persuaded me.
ROBERT	That's right, Grandma.
ALICE	But I can still see it in your eyes. Amelia, what is it that's so… difficult… for you?
AMELIA	It's just that… well… the Church says it's wrong.
ROBERT	*(Dismissively)* The Church?
ALICE	So that's why I wanted to tell you something I hadn't mentioned before.
ROBERT	Tell us, Grandma.
ALICE	I went to communion last Sunday. I hadn't done that for years – never felt a need. And afterwards I asked the priest for his… well… guidance.
SARAH	What did he say, Mum?
ALICE	That in spite of the law being changed, in the eyes of some in the church it was still a sin to take one's own life. And that threw open the whole question – what we'd agreed. The wound opened up again.
RICHARD	So what made you…
ALICE	… Come back to this? *(Long pause)* I left him at the altar and wandered back down the aisle. And the interior of that church was as silent and desolate as a graveyard, dark and grey – and I saw in it the

unbearable loneliness I would face without Teddy. *(Her face brightening)* Then, something strange happened. Just as I was about to leave, there behind the door was a painting of Jesus – a bit modern and out of place, so I think they'd hung it in the darkest spot they could find – but it caught my eye. I said to him – Jesus – what would you do? And the thought came to me that he'd known what his fate was going to be – even at the last supper – and he could have averted it, but chose that course. That he should die.

SARAH   And that was the message for you? If *he* could…

ALICE   Yes. And then I looked at the title of the painting – quite difficult to see in the gloom. And it said simply: *Compassion*. And that summed it up for me. *(Pause)* I thought you should know, that's all.

ROBERT   That's beautiful, Grandma.

AMELIA   I hadn't thought about it that way. It never came up in class.

ALICE   I shouldn't think it did. But thank you, Amelia.

RICHARD   Shall, I go and fetch Dr Metcalfe, then?

ALICE   It will be a pity to wake Teddy, but yes, I think the time has come.

Richard exits and returns with Dr Metcalfe. Mostly silently, kisses are exchanged with Teddy and Alice and the others leave the room. Dr Metcalfe invites Teddy and Alice to sit and he follows.

METCALFE   Try to relax. There's nothing to fear. It will be exactly as we discussed. Alice will hold your hand, Teddy, and remain like that when she too takes the medicine. There's absolutely no hurry, no compulsion, and if you have any final questions…

They realise that Teddy is emotionally distressed.

You don't have to go through with it, Teddy. Not if you don't want to.

TEDDY	The world's best rid of me.
METCALFE	Would you like a priest to come? Alice told me she…
TEDDY	*(Waving hands)* No… no.
ALICE	What is it then, Teddy?
TEDDY	*(Forcing himself, meaning Amelia)* That girl – what she remembered.
ALICE	Amelia? *(Very concerned)* That was such a long time ago.
TEDDY	Seems like yesterday. I just want to say… sorry.
	Metcalfe looks on, uncomprehending.
ALICE	You want to tell her that?
TEDDY	Shouldn't I?
METCALFE	Can I help?
ALICE	Just by giving us a moment or two longer. It's something from the past, you see. *(To Teddy)* Do you want me to get her?
TEDDY	I think so.
ALICE	*(To Dr Metcalfe)* I won't be a second.
	Alice leaves the room.
METCALFE	I don't know what that's about, but it looks to me as if you're doing a very brave thing, Teddy. Ah, here they come.
	Alice returns with Amelia, who is looking anxious. She stands in front of Teddy.
TEDDY	I just wanted to say… that I… every day…
AMELIA	*(Placing her hand on his shoulder)* It's all right, Grandpa. The Bible teaches us forgiveness.
TEDDY	Am I… [forgiven]
AMELIA	You can put your mind at rest.
TEDDY	It's not too difficult for you?
AMELIA	It would have been. But tonight's shown me… You're forgiven.

There is a scuffling noise in the hall.

TEDDY   What's that?

AMELIA   Do you want to see?

TEDDY   A surprise?

AMELIA   Yes, it really is.

She goes to the door and beckons. Eric enters sheepishly clutching a cat.

ERIC   I went to look for her round the corner at Sarah's and bugger me there she was on the doorstep.

AMELIA   I think she wanted one last stroke. *(Pause, not quite convincingly)* It was Eric's suggestion.

Eric holds the cat out to Teddy at arm's length and Teddy strokes her.

TEDDY   *(Now tiring)* It's Bumble.

ALICE   Thank you, Eric. Thank you, thank you.

Amelia also strokes Bumble and kisses Teddy on the forehead. She and Eric depart.

METCALFE   What a send-off, eh Teddy? *(With hint of impatience)* Now, shall we go through?

As they pass through the curtain the telephone is heard distantly though the now-closed door. On hearing it Alice's expression changes to one of doubt, but she passes through nevertheless. There is muffled conversation and the sound of vessels on surfaces, then profound silence. Suddenly the living room door flies open. Robert enters frantically, pursued by Richard and Sarah with the others following.

ROBERT   *(Shouting)* Grandma, Grandma, it's a baby boy!

He pauses in front of the curtain, uncertain what to do. Dr Metcalfe appears through the gap, his expression angry.

METCALFE   Robert, this is quite out of order. Your grandma needs to be with your grandfather.

AMELIA   Has she taken the…

METCALFE   *(Peering behind the curtain)* I must get back to them.

> *Metcalfe goes behind the curtain. There are several seconds of silence. Then Alice emerges, holding a glass containing a colourless liquid. She begins to cry.*

ALICE   I've failed him.

METCALFE   *(From the gap in the curtains)* Alice, you have not failed him. You were with him to the end. You gave him all the comfort he could possibly have wished for.

ALICE   *(Miserably)* And when we meet again, in the next life?

SARAH   Then you can tell him about your – and his – new grandson. And how you came to know and love him in your final days.

RICHARD   And how you can be with us again. To hear what we've learnt from this evening. Look at us all.

> *She looks at the five faces ringed around her.*

ALICE   You know, that's the first time I've seen you all together like this – all with the same expression. Even you, Eric. *(Pause, then urgently)* I have to leave you.

> *Alice disappears and the curtain snaps shut behind her. Dr Metcalfe, still with the family, nods to himself and quietly leaves them through the curtain. The five family members, believing Alice has followed Teddy into death, slump into chairs.*

ERIC   That's over, then. But this is where it all begins, isn't it?

RICHARD   What's bugging you now, Eric?

ERIC   Well, things won't be the same, will they?

RICHARD   You've protected your assets. No Teddy's will – if ever there was one. So where's the problem?

ERIC	I was thinking of these two *(indicating Amelia and Robert)*.
RICHARD	One of life's lessons.
SARAH	Don't be so cynical, Richard.
ERIC	What must be going through their heads, right now.
SARAH	*(To Amelia and Robert)* You two are okay, aren't you?
ERIC	Doesn't look it to me.
SARAH	Robert, you think Grandma did right, don't you?
ROBERT	I'm… not sure.
AMELIA	You frigging were before. If you'd listened to me she'd still…
ROBERT	Well, if you weren't so fucking bossy…
SARAH	What's troubling you, Robert?
ROBERT	*(Pause, apprehensively)* What happens now.
	There are faint sounds from behind the curtain, suggesting Dr Metcalfe is tidying up.
SARAH	What do you mean?
ROBERT	Well, like do we get to see them? Or do we just walk out of the door?
ERIC	Like a bloody theatrical performance this, isn't it?
SARAH	I'm sure that when Dr Metcalfe's finished…
ROBERT	Finished what?
SARAH	Well… making them all nice again. Then I'm sure…
AMELIA	I don't want to see them.
ROBERT	I think you should.
AMELIA	Why should I?
ROBERT	Because you might learn something…
RICHARD	I think that's enough from you two. Sarah, tell them what will happen.

SARAH	In a while Dr Metcalfe will leave us, and tomorrow morning…
ERIC	*(Cynically)* After breakfast?
SARAH	The undertakers will come and…
ERIC	There's a show for the neighbours. Why not now?
RICHARD	Because we mustn't be hasty. We need to pay our respects if we want to. Have time to reflect.
ERIC	Nah, not my scene. I'd rather remember them like in life. *(Pause)* I'd best be going.
	Eric gets up to go.
SARAH	You'll come with us to see Pam's baby?
ERIC	Sometime. Maybe next week.
SARAH	Pam would appreciate it.
ERIC	I'll give her a ring.
	Eric goes to the door where, unseen by the family, he wipes away a tear.
	Night all. *(Exits)*
RICHARD	Well…
ROBERT	He's upset.
RICHARD	C'mon.
ROBERT	Why can't you see it?
RICHARD	Then he's got a funny way of showing it.
AMELIA	It's all he knows.
RICHARD	And Pam?
ROBERT	He'll go to see her.
RICHARD	You *do* sound sure.
ROBERT	I am sure.
	Dr Metcalfe emerges from behind the curtain.
METCALFE	I had to sort things. Besides, she's still holding Teddy…
SARAH	They went… peacefully, then?

METCALFE   They? Alice is sleeping, can you believe? There's relief, you see, mixed in with the sadness. A huge weight lifted. Then profound tiredness. I've seen it before.

SARAH   You mean she didn't…?

METCALFE   Well no, isn't she a grandmother now?

Alice slowly emerges from behind the curtain.

METCALFE   *(Smiling)* Why, here she is.

Alice looks confused. Dr Metcalfe puts his arm around her shoulders.

I'll be leaving you now, my dear. Try to sleep and don't forget the tablets. I'll call in the morning. *(To the others)* Goodnight to you all.

SARAH   Goodnight Doctor, thank you for everything.

METCALFE   It's a kinder world we now live in, Sarah. We must be thankful for that.

Richard begins to rise.

Don't worry, Richard. I'll let myself out.

Metcalfe exits. Alice sits at the table, facing the others.

ALICE   Such a kind man. *(Pause)* Where's Eric?

RICHARD   He… er… had to catch the last train.

ALICE   I so wanted to see him. But maybe tomorrow at the hospital. *(Pause)* I'm glad he made his peace with Teddy.

ROBERT   And Grandpa with her *(meaning Amelia)*?

ALICE   Yes, that especially. *(Pause)* Now, I think you would all like to see Teddy. He's looking so peaceful… *(crying)* and happy. *(Emotionally)* He was in such pain!

SARAH   Perhaps not all at once, though. If the children go first…

ALICE   Hardly children anymore. *(To Amelia and Robert)* Come with me, then. *(To Sarah and Richard)* You two follow in a moment?

Amelia and Robert, looking apprehensive, follow Alice behind the curtain. Robert is clutching the Duchess of Atholl engine.

SARAH	I didn't expect that.
RICHARD	Nor me.
SARAH	Did I ever know my mother?
RICHARD	As much as anyone.
SARAH	We've got challenges ahead now.
RICHARD	Going through this, you mean? All over again?
SARAH	We'll have to, won't we?
RICHARD	Who knows? Come on. Let's follow them.

They go behind the curtain, leaving the room empty. For several seconds nothing happens. Then the sound of the distant front door opening is heard. Eric enters and sits at the table, deep in thought. As he rises to follow the others the stage darkens to black.

END

SHADOW OF A QUEEN

Characters:

    Alicia – governess to Prince Edward – about 17 years old

    Sir Richard de Redwell – an impoverished knight

    Hagin of Northampton – a wealthy Jew

    Queen Eleanor (Eleanor of Castile, wife of Edward I)

    John de Berewyk – Eleanor's treasurer

    Prince Edward (the future Edward II) – about 6 years old (non-speaking part)

    Edward (King Edward I)

    The Dowager Queen (Eleanor of Provence, widow of Henry III, mother of Edward I)

    Guard at the Tower

    Friar Benedict

    First Servant

    Second Servant

Places and times:

    The Tower of London (1273); Redwell's manor house near Geddington (1273 and 1290); the Royal Hunting Lodge at Geddington (1290)

ACT ONE

SCENE ONE

[1273] A dimly lit passageway in the Tower of London. A guard fidgets outside a closed door. Sir Richard de Redwell, a knight in his late twenties, handsome and rakish, is pacing nervously up and down. There is faint speech from behind the door, which suddenly opens. Hagin of Northampton stands momentarily in the frame, then steps into the passageway. He is about thirty, of serious disposition, with dark hair, and from his dress and the yellow ribbon on his coat is clearly Jewish. Seeing Redwell he is at first amazed, then pleased. As they greet one another the guard disappears into the room.

HAGIN   Richard?

REDWELL   Hagin? You? In the Tower?

HAGIN   Never wonder at that. More Jews have walked these passages than you've seen full moons. *(Pause)* But in truth, I'd hoped to be left in peace – with Eleanor now queen.

                 Redwell puts his finger to his lips to advise caution.

REDWELL   But it can't be chance – can it? – that we've both been summoned.

HAGIN   She wants some of my loans – in exchange for relief from taxes. And that's tempting. Yours for the Manor of Easingbourne is one of them.

REDWELL   *(Alarmed)* You'll not surrender it?

HAGIN   A week to consider.

REDWELL   That's how her predecessor got rich. You know you have no choice.

HAGIN   She's… a gracious enough lady.

REDWELL   *(Under his breath)* Compared with the Dowager Queen, I daresay she is.

           The door re-opens and the guard appears. Seeing Hagin he becomes angry.

GUARD   Still here, Jew? Go on, clear off! *(Changing tone)* Sir Richard, the Queen will see you now.

           Hagin and Redwell touch each other's arm in farewell.

REDWELL   You'd best go. Call by when I'm back in Easingbourne.

           Hagin nods agreement and leaves, looking anxiously behind him as the guard makes as if to pursue him. As Redwell enters the room the door and wall are withdrawn to reveal a more brightly lit, but still forbidding, chamber with only touches of luxury. Queen Eleanor, about thirty, of Spanish complexion and handsome rather than beautiful, is standing by a window, looking out. She turns, smiling, while Redwell falls to one knee. It is obvious that they know each other well.

ELEANOR   Get up, Richard... and welcome. *(With irony)* Look how my circumstances have changed!

REDWELL   I congratulate your majesty on her... elevation.

ELENOR   No thanks to me! *(Indicating room)* I meant this. To put a Castilian in here is like confining you in your ice-pit.

REDWELL   My house *is* an ice-pit.

ELEANOR   So you're in debt again. What was it this time? Horses, the gaming table... women?

REDWELL   All of them.

ELEANOR   Then you're a fool.

REDWELL   I'm a fool.

ELEANOR   And more so for getting into debt to a Jew. Particularly one clever enough to run rings around the Dowager Queen – or so she claims.

REDWELL	Hagin of Northampton is an honourable man.
ELEANOR	And a vulnerable one. *(Pause)* The tide's turning against them, Richard. Be warned.
REDWELL	But that's not why I'm here.
ELEANOR	As you very well know. *(Pause)* It's hardly our fault that your manor adjoins *our* hunting lodge – on which the King insists he's spent a small fortune. You think I'm unreasonable?
REDWELL	If it were the only example…
ELEANOR	It's how I'm advised, Richard. A queen needs security. With Edward rampaging in Wales and crushing the Scots anything can happen. Just look at the Dowager Queen – for all her influence she's destined for a convent. God, how she resents me. *(Pause)* Let's change the subject. How's that fair sister of yours?
REDWELL	She's given birth – but the child may not live.
ELEANOR	Oh, Richard. That is something I have known. I will pray for them.
REDWELL	I'm grateful. Truly.
ELEANOR	*(Pause)* Look, time is short. I… um… know that the loss of Easingbourne is not something you wish to countenance.
REDWELL	It's all I have.
ELEANOR	And still you will not sell to me?
REDWELL	As I said, it's all I have.
ELEANOR	I know.

Eleanor raises her and lightly touches his cheek.

I'm sorry if it will hurt you.

Redwell tries to take her hand, but she withdraws it rapidly.

No!

REDWELL	I haven't seen you since…

ELEANOR	No! Please!
REDWELL	But…
ELEANOR	There are eyes upon me, Richard. You cannot imagine…

The door opens and the guard appears.

Oh, yes, the next petitioner. *(To Redwell)* Well, Sir Richard. If you wish to please me…

REDWELL	I wish for nothing else.
ELEANOR	Then you will not obstruct the Jew. I will pray for the child. *(To guard)* Malgrain, show Sir Richard out.

Redwell bows and leaves, looking bemused. His final glance at Eleanor – who turns away looking miserable – expresses both admiration and resentment.

SCENE TWO

[Five days later] The hall of the manor house of Easingbourne, near Geddington. It is late evening and there are flickering oil lamps on the walls. The room is comfortably furnished. Redwell sits at a desk, with a document in each hand, looking worriedly from one to the other. There is a knock at the door and he slams down the papers in frustration.

REDWELL	Not more bad news…

He rises, walks to the door and opens it. Hagin is standing on the threshold. His coat bears a yellow ribbon. He seems nervous and anxious.

REDWELL	That's a relief.
HAGIN	As bad as that?
REDWELL	Worse. Here, take off your coat. *(Referring to the ribbon)* We'll hide that thing for a start.

Hagin removes his coat and slumps into a chair.

HAGIN	How is your sister?

REDWELL	The child died this morning.
HAGIN	Ohhh.
REDWELL	*(Pause)* You're to London tomorrow?
HAGIN	The Queen wants an answer.
REDWELL	And you'll tell her yes.
HAGIN	I'm inclined to say no.
REDWELL	No?
HAGIN	I've come with a proposition, Richard. But first tell me something. If the Queen takes this debt – with Easingbourne as security – could you remain here, as a tenant perhaps? Given your connections.
REDWELL	She'd send in her bailiffs. Like she has with others.
HAGIN	Sadly it's already dulling her image. *(Pause)* And it would grieve you to go? Would that be so terrible?

Redwell turns to Hagin with an agonised expression.

REDWELL	I have to hold out against her. Can't you see?
HAGIN	Why?
REDWELL	Didn't you see how I was shaking in the Tower? Clearing my debts isn't my only dream, Hagin. Night after night I see her. Sometimes I think it will never end, this… infatuation.
HAGIN	And holding out keeps the bond between you?
REDWELL	Ridiculous as it seems, yes.
HAGIN	That's a hopeless situation.
REDWELL	I know, I know. Pathetic, isn't it?
HAGIN	Then hear my proposition.
REDWELL	Go on.
HAGIN	I… have a child, Richard.
REDWELL	Eh? Well… good. I had no idea your wife was…
HAGIN	No, no, not like that. A different mother. Jewrys and places of easy virtue… side by side. Well, you

	can guess. It's a beautiful child, Richard. One a mother might love and cherish. But I cannot take it home.
REDWELL	*(Amazed)* You want me…
HAGIN	I'm sorry. I should not have presumed…
REDWELL	No… no. There's logic here. But let me straighten my thoughts. The dead child still lies beyond that wall, God rest its soul. And we've had no visitors.
HAGIN	Substitution would deny it a Christian burial, Richard.
REDWELL	Maybe in London I could arrange… That's a detail. Where is the child?
HAGIN	Outside. In the carriage.
REDWELL	Outside? Then bring it in. You can't leave it outside. I'm sure my sister, when she wakes… You know, she prayed so hard.
HAGIN	*(Amused)* Richard, you have asked for nothing in exchange.
REDWELL	Hagin, for what should I ask?
	Hagin takes a document from his pocket and gives it to Redwell.
HAGIN	Well, you might, for example, have asked for this.
	Redwell unfolds the document. His expression becomes incredulous.
	The debt is waived, my friend. I *was* uncertain – but no longer. Come, let me show you the child.
	They move towards the door.
	(Lightheartedly) She has bright sparkling eyes, and already some black hair… and a nose that isn't at all what you might expect…
REDWELL	*That* I have to see.
	They pass through the door and the stage darkens.

ACT TWO

SCENE ONE

[September 1290 – early afternoon] The hall of the manor house of Easingbourne, much as it was in the previous scene, except that the room is drab and the furnishings sparse. Right rear stage is the main door to the exterior and at the back is a large window through which distant trees are just visible. Sunlight illuminates the room. At a table left stage Redwell is examining some papers. Hagin is standing by the window, looking out. Both are soberly dressed. Their appearance is consistent with seventeen years having passed.

REDWELL   Oh! The figures seem to balance, and that can't possibly be right. Can it, Hagin?

HAGIN   Richard, for you it would be a first. But then my friends abroad tell me that foxes can fly, so I'll believe anything. Accept it – just for the moment – and put your papers down.

REDWELL   Any sign of Alice yet?

HAGIN   No. But there's a fellow beyond the gate. He was there when I came in. Know who he is?

REDWELL   An agent of the Crown, I expect.

HAGIN   Not still harassing you? I thought it had all gone quiet.

REDWELL   It had – until the Queen returned from France. Now it's started up again. Or perhaps the fellow's there just to keep a watchful eye on Alice – if she shows up.

                 Hagin walks from the window to the centre of the room. He appears anxious.

                 It'll go alright.

HAGIN   How can we know? Four years ago, wasn't it, she joined the Queen's service. A precocious brat.

	Why should she have changed? Remember how she tormented me. I could take it from others, Richard, *(sadly)* but from *that* child…
REDWELL	Then we'll have to wait and see, won't we? Fortuitous, though, that the Queen's brought her here to Geddington – it being so close, I mean. If you look beyond those oaks you can make out the roof of the Hunting Lodge. It's an opportunity we can't miss, Hagin. Tell me again what the edict said.
HAGIN	All Jew's out of the country by November. Or they die – unless they've converted.
REDWELL	You're sure you want to go through with it, this conversion? The Church will welcome you because the Pope has told it to, but your own people…
HAGIN	Richard, it consumes my whole being. I wish it were otherwise.
REDWELL	And you've heard nothing?
HAGIN	No. But the others have. Those who want to stay.
REDWELL	So the Queen on our doorstep is an opportunity we can't miss. We'll petition her.
HAGIN	Richard, the Queen's coveted this manor of yours for as long as I can remember. You've always said no. Even when the offers were ridiculously generous. How's that going to help my case, um?
REDWELL	It may be all we have to bargain with.
HAGIN	You'd do that? For me?
REDWELL	You're not the only one with a dream, Hagin, but I'm getting old, and mine has almost run its course. It's always been hopeless.
HAGIN	Infatuation with a queen is not just foolish, Richard – it's madness.

From outside comes the sound of a carriage approaching. Hagin's nervousness increases. Redwell looks at him with deep concern.

70

REDWELL   Look, go to the kitchen and compose yourself. Then come to the front door, as if you've just arrived. She'll have seen your horse, but you could have been walking in the grounds.

Hagin exits left stage, into the house.

Secrets, lies, secrets, lies – what an age we live in.

Redwell looks around the room and sees a box on top of a cupboard. He takes it down, puts it on his desk and withdraws from it a toy bear, which he then places on a chair. He returns to the table, picks up one of the papers and stares at it. Then he puts the paper down and holds his head between his hands.

A spoilt fourteen-year-old brat. Why ever did Eleanor accept her into service? Why ever did I offer her in the first place? *(Pause)* Madness!

Footsteps are heard mounting the steps outside, followed by a gentle knock on the door. Redwell rises, walks towards the door and opens it to reveal a beautiful, dark-haired young woman. He is surprised by what he sees and she, in response, smiles broadly.

ALICIA   Uncle Richard, surely you recognise me?

REDWELL   Alice? Have you really changed that much?

ALICIA   *(Imitating the Spanish accent of the Queen)* Not Alice, Uncle – Alicia *(emphasising the middle vowel)* Trusted companion of Queen Eleanor, governess to the young Prince Edward, no less, and consort of kings, etc, etc. *(She begins to giggle, then flings her arms around Redwell's neck)*

REDWELL   Come in, come in. This is truly wonderful.

Alicia enters slowly and perceptively, while Redwell closes the door.

Do you recognise your old home?

71

ALICIA   Uncle, it's as barren as when I left it. Do you still have no money?

REDWELL   Not much.

ALICIA   Should I believe you?

REDWELL   None at all then.

              She wanders around the room, looking at everything, and then sees the bear.

ALICIA   Oh! Bonito bear! You've kept Bonito!

REDWELL   He's been waiting all this time. He's been so sad.

              She picks up the bear and cuddles it.

ALICIA   Have they been kind to you, Bonito? Have you been a good spy for me? Um? Things to tell me? Secrets? When we're alone, eh?

              She replaces the bear gently on the seat and smiles at Redwell.

              You haven't changed, Uncle Richard.

REDWELL   No. But the world about me is spinning.

ALICIA   Because the Queen's returned from Gascony?

REDWELL   And what that entails. *(Pause)* It must be interesting to see it all from the inside.

ALICIA   It is. By the way, Queen Eleanor sends you her greetings.

REDWELL   She knows you're here?

ALICIA   Why ever not? We're very close.

REDWELL   Oh, no reason, but…

              There is a knock at the outside door. Redwell opens it to reveal Hagin, looking apprehensive. He is now wearing the yellow ribbon on his coat.

REDWELL   Hagin of Northampton! I did half expect you. Come in, come in. You remember my niece Alice from the old days.

HAGIN   My very great pleasure.

72

ALICIA	*(Without interest)* Yes, I do remember.
REDWELL	Those tricks you used to play.
HAGIN	Like the toad in my shoe.
ALICIA	Those *were* childish things. I'm surprised you remember them.
HAGIN	Your development... was always... of interest to me, Alice.
ALICIA	But no longer, I'm sure. *(Pause)* Did you have business with my uncle? Perhaps I should leave you two alone.
HAGIN	It was just a social call.
REDWELL	Hagin, how goes your application? *(To Alicia)* Hagin, being Jewish...
ALICIA	That I can guess.
REDWELL	... has applied to become a Christian, as our Church recommends.
ALICIA	Isn't 'recommends' a bit strong?
REDWELL	But so far he's heard nothing. I was wondering if ... well... the Queen might... intercede.
ALICIA	I wouldn't know. You'd have to ask her.
REDWELL	And how should I do that?
ALICIA	Through de Berewyk, her treasurer. *(Pause)* I'd really like to look around the house. May I?
REDWELL	Of course. Your old room's just as it was, apart from the cobwebs. I'll catch you up.
	Alicia exits stage left. Hagin slumps into a chair.
	Oh, dear. I'm so sorry. *(Pause)* But it's early days.
HAGIN	What a year.
REDWELL	Indeed.
	Hagin rises.
HAGIN	You'll want to talk to her. It's best if I go.
REDWELL	We'll talk tomorrow. I'll come to you.

73

HAGIN   That's probably safest.

             Redwell accompanies Hagin to the door, slamming it
             forcefully after he has left. Meanwhile Alicia re-enters
             the room. When Redwell turns he is surprised to see
             her standing behind him.

REDWELL   You were hard on him, Alice.

ALICIA   Uncle, I wasn't trying to be unkind. But if there's a
             delay with his application there may be a reason for
             it. You should tread carefully.

REDWELL   It was presumptuous of me to involve you. *(Pause)*
             Come, let me show you all that I have *not* done to
             the house.

             They exit stage left.

             The stage darkens.

SCENE TWO

[Two weeks later] The reception room of the Royal Hunting Lodge at Geddington.
There are tapestries on the walls and fine pieces of furniture. A closed door at the
rear gives access to a thoroughfare. There is an internal arch right stage and left stage
steps leading to the floor above are just visible. Front stage, a small boy aged about
six (Prince Edward) is lying on the floor, playing with wooden blocks. Rear stage
is a window, beneath which is a small table bearing a chess board, on which the
distribution of pieces is consistent with an unfinished game. Alicia contemplates her
reflection in a wall mirror, then moves to the table, looking intently at the pieces
before shifting her position to see the board from the other side. Meanwhile John
de Berewyk, the Queen's Treasurer, a soberly dressed man of middle age, enters
unnoticed stage left and remains in the shadows watching her.

ALICIA   *(To herself)* Strange.

             Berewyk comes forward, revealing himself.

BEREWYK   What is strange, Alicia?

ALICIA   Oh, de Berewyk, you startled me. The way you
             creep about. It's a good thing you're, well, harmless.

BEREWYK	Although tempted to be otherwise. Sorely tempted. What is it about the game? Did you allow the Queen to destroy you again?
ALICIA	I serve – just like you. But no, this isn't my game.
BEREWYK	The King's then?
ALICIA	He's no patience for games. He can't face losing.
BEREWYK	Well, the Queen's not been herself lately, and sometimes does... well... unexpected things.
ALICIA	I think the fever's returned.
BEREWYK	Perhaps. Well, whatever. I came to tell you that your uncle and the Jew are outside awaiting her return, and she's about to appear. Let's hope for their sakes she's been entertained at the chase.

Edward has been piling up his bricks, but they now come crashing to the floor. Alicia is suddenly angry and makes towards him.

ALICIA	You...! *(Protocol curtails her response)* I've just tidied this room.
BEREWYK	Peace, Alicia. *(To Edward)* Edward, why don't you go and see what Cook's preparing in the kitchen. It smelt rather good to me when I passed.

Edward rises and scuttles from the room. Alicia bends down and begins to pick up the bricks.

ALICIA	That's right, side with him against me.
BEREWYK	*(Wearily)* I side with no-one Alicia. My function in this household is to ensure harmony and favour no-one. I try to dispense light *(looking at her fixedly)* even into the murkiest of corners.
ALICIA	Yes. When you leer at me I'm sure a little illumination helps.
BEREWYK	Don't delude yourself.

Sounds of horses' hooves are heard outside, then footsteps on the gravel path.

I'm away to steel myself for this encounter.

De Berewyk exits. Anticipating the Queen's entry, Alicia walks to the door, judges the moment, and opens it. As the door opens, daylight floods in around the elegant figure of Queen Eleanor, who hands Alicia her gloves, walks to the centre of the stage and turns.

ELEANOR   So. The wily Jew and the stubborn knight. Hagin of Norhampton and the impoverished Sir Richard de Redwell, lord of the Manor of Easingbourne – which, by the grace of God, I will have yet. Are they here?

ALICIA   Ma'am, you told them to be here an hour ago.

ELEANOR   (*Mischievously*) Yes, I did, didn't I. Still, time to consider his position never did Sir Richard any harm. (*Pause*) Why do I bracket them together, those two, like the faces of a handled mask, one always the obverse of the other?

ALICIA   Perhaps they've troubled you in equal measure, Ma'am.

ELEANOR   But it's curious, isn't it? How one can hold in regard quarries so perversely infuriating?

ALICIA   Have they not played fair, Ma'am?

ELEANOR   Silly girl. In games with a queen fairness has no part. How old are you? Seventeen? You wouldn't remember. About the time you were born I had that same Jew brought to the Tower. Uhh (*she shivers at the memory of living there*). (*Imitating herself*) You hold this knight in debt, licensed by the Crown? (*Imitating the Jew*) That is true, your majesty. In the security of Easingbourne Manor? Yes, the wretch replies. Then I will relieve you of this burden in exchange for waiving your tallage dues. Whatever your majesty wishes. (*A long pause*) But he didn't deliver. (*Stamping her foot on the floor*) Why?

ALICIA	Perhaps the debt was repaid.
ELEANOR	It must have been. But with what, I asked myself of the impecunious Sir Richard. And I have asked that question these last seventeen years. Can you imagine how painful that is to my nature?
ALICIA	I think I can.
ELEANOR	And now my lands surround his. Completely. But he won't budge.
ALICIA	You've offered a tempting enough price?
ELEANOR	To no avail. He refuses.
ALICIA	*(Timidly)* People say you... that your men have exerted... great pressure.
ELEANOR	Who says so?
ALICIA	The town. In the market. It's widespread.
ELEANOR	It gives me no pleasure. It is... business. *(Pause)* I see from your face you don't approve. But then you're Sir Richard's niece, brought up in the said manor.
ALICIA	I've never hidden it.
ELEANOR	Then swear to me you know nothing of the matter.
ALICIA	On the tooth of St Barnabus I swear.
ELEANOR	In which case you can look on, or leave when they come, as you please. *(Pause)* By the way, where is Edward? Aren't those his bricks?
ALICIA	Busy in the kitchen – under de Berewyk's instruction, I expect.
ELEANOR	What *would* I do without that man? But Edward. How has it been today, Alicia? Honestly.
ALICIA	He did miss you, Ma'am.
ELEANOR	I neglect him. I shouldn't and I needn't, but I do *(sighs)*.

Eleanor notices the chess-board.

Oh, I was forgetting. Here. Help me with this – carefully!

They move the table forward, close to some chairs. Voices are heard offstage. Too late to escape, Alicia moves to the window and stares out. Berewyk enters.

BEREWYK   My Lady, Sir Richard and the Jew are waiting.

ELEANOR   Then bring them in.

Berewyk goes out and returns immediately with Redwell and Hagin.

Gentlemen, welcome to my humble lodge.

REDWELL   Surely you mean *palace*, my Lady. *(Looking around).* Fineries such as these belong only in *palaces*.

ELEANOR   Am I to be flattered or ridiculed, Sir Richard. Take care to choose wisely.

Eleanor sits.

BEREWYK   Gentlemen, please be seated.

Redwell and Hagin sit. Berewyk follows but Eleanor rises and stands aloof.

You know that my Lady is anxious to settle the matter of Easingbourne. Sir Richard – again – has been offered a fair price and has refused, but that was before Ladyday. Can we therefore accept your presence here as evidence of … reason?

REDWELL   I will not succumb to harassment.

BEREWYK   You accuse the Queen's agents of harassment?

REDWELL   Of misinterpreting the Queen's intentions, for example by resorting to violence… against my men.

BEREWYK   *(Quietly)* That we can pursue elsewhere. Now, concerning Easingbourne…

Berewyk produces a folded paper from his tunic.

Here is the value of your manorial holdings. *(Showing Redwell the paper)* You will see that the source – it's written there – is reputable. *(Pointing)* And there's what the Queen's estate would offer. *(He looks expectantly at Redwell.)*

> *Redwell scrutinises the paper and smiles, then hands it to Hagin, who raises his eyebrows in approval.*

HAGIN   That *is* a generous offer, Richard.

> *Hagin hands the paper back to Redwell, who returns it to Berewyk.*

REDWELL   I'll bear your figure in mind.

> *In exasperation, the Queen turns to Alicia.*

ELEANOR   Your uncle is impossible. Can't you make him see sense?

ALICIA   *(With sarcasm)* My uncle's a gambler. Perhaps he favours lesser returns. Lowering the figure might make it more attractive.

ELEANOR   Sir Richard. You're a gambling man, then? *(Raises hand to silence him)* Don't answer. You wouldn't be in this pickle if you weren't. So here's an opportunity. There *(pointing to the chess-board)* is where the… er… King and I were interrupted. Will you play his position? The winner takes Easingbourne. For you a fair price if I win or to be left in peace if I lose.

REDWELL   Your Majesty is renowned for her skill. I would not wish to harm that reputation.

ELEANOR   Yet you do so with your accusations. Strange. You may reverse the positions if you wish.

REDWELL   Thank you, no.

ELEANOR   I'm disappointed. You will not even look?

REDWELL   No.

ELEANOR   And if I were to order you…

BEREWYK   With respect, my Lady, this is getting us nowhere. Sir Richard, there is another salve for this old wound, perhaps?

REDWELL   It concerns my friend.

All look at Hagin, who appears embarrassed.

HAGIN   My Lady, you may know that I have long thought of embracing the Christian faith.

Eleanor and Berewyk exchange glances.

BEREWYK   Did we know of such a thing?

ELEANOR   *(To Hagin)* Go on.

HAGIN   I...

REDWELL   The day of expulsion approaches. The Church is not hopeful the date can be met.

ELEANOR   So we could lose you, Mr Hagin.

REDWELL   A word from you, my Lady, might just suffice.

BEREWYK   And why should the Queen feel obliged to intervene?

REDWELL   *(Wearily)* To achieve her ends. Should Hagin remain in England, I would hold my position... less tenaciously.

BEREWYK   Meaning he would pay you well.

REDWELL   No.

ELEANOR   No? Then let us hear his case.

REDWELL   It is a matter of...

ELEANOR   Be silent. *(Softly)* Let him speak for himself.

BEREWYK   Jew, was your petition lodged before or after the edict of expulsion.

HAGIN   Before, Sir.

BEREWYK   Then he must have had prior warning.

ELEANOR   No. I knew of it... beforehand.

Berewyk, looking surprised, bows slightly.

We are not... unknown to one another.

HAGIN   I believe there has been mutual benefit.

BEREWYK   Impertinence!

ELEANOR (*Holding up hand*) No. It's true. We have had... dealings. And for that reason I must listen. *(To Hagin)* Your family, your children – they would stay?

HAGIN They would go.

ELEANOR And your wife?

HAGIN She would not survive.

REDWELL She is sometimes... delirious.

BEREWYK Can Christ then cure delerium?

HAGIN My Lady, it is not our intention to test him.

ELEANOR You would be English then?

HAGIN I am already English. Like my father I was born on *English* soil *(faintly implying that Eleanor was not)*.

ELEANOR Ah, yes! But there's one English trait you do not yet possess.

REDWELL The love of persecution!

ELEANOR (*Turning to him, half admiringly*) How can a mere Castilian be expected to know that? But I'm impressed you know my mind. What is the phrase Friar Benedict uses? *Corpus mysterium.* What is not within the body of the Church is its enemy. My, what were the consequences for us all when the laudable Pope Innocent came out with that particular gem. *(To Hagin)* Not even our shared prophets were able to help you then.

BEREWYK My Lady, a word with you aside.

> *Berewyk and Eleanor move to the window to confer. Alicia stands before Redwell and Hagin.*

ALICIA The moment of truth.

REDWELL Alice, we need your support, not your sarcasm.

HAGIN Alice, if only I could explain to you...

ALICIA (*Hissing*) What is it about you that so bewitches my uncle and intrigues the Queen, but leaves me cold. If it was up to me...

Berewyk returns from the window, followed by Eleanor.

BEREWYK The Queen would be saddened if the Church were denied such an illustrious soul. She will think upon it. *(To Redwell)* The other matter is between us. We will speak again.

All rise and the three men bow and exit. Alicia passes the chess game and looks down at the pieces, still puzzled. Eleanor walks thoughtfully to a chair and slumps into it.

ELEANOR The issue has *not* been settled.

ALICIA What more can you want?

ELEANOR It's all so facile. Why now? That Jew's not one for turning. Besides, he has enough friends in France to shelter a whole tribe.

ALICIA Perhaps he has another reason to stay.

ELEANOR Funny. That's what the Dowager Queen said. She thought you might know.

ALICIA Me?

ELEANOR You know this Jew.

ALICIA Only as my uncle's friend.

ELEANOR Then perhaps it was only my imagination that saw him looking at you.

ALICIA Such interest would not be unusual.

ELEANOR *(Amused)* Men in general or just this one?

ALICIA It's just that... I used to see him sometimes, at Uncle Richard's.

ELEANOR But you went there rarely.

ALICIA I've wondered about that. *(Shrugs)* Coincidence, probably.

ELEANOR Perhaps.

Berewyk returns.

82

	(To Berewyk) It seems you have a rival.
BEREWYK	My Lady?
ELEANOR	Hagin. For Alicia's attention.
BEREWYK	My Lady's humour can be fanciful at times.
ELEANOR	Poof! *(Coughs)* We're hardly blind. *(Coughs again)*
BEREWYK	I am pleased to be the butt of Alicia's imaginings should it amuse my Lady, but not if it makes her ill.
ELEANOR	*(Laughing and coughing)* It's nothing. It will pass.
BEREWYK	Then why is there blood on your hand?
ELEANOR	*(Seeing it)* Oh!

> *She moves to the window and stands with her back to the others, wiping her mouth with her handkerchief, which she then examines. She appears too engrossed to hear the following exchange.*

BEREWYK	*(To Alicia)* What mischief now?
ALICIA	No mischief, Sir. *(Giggling)* Men cannot help being men – *(referring to Berewyk)* however their inky fingers might suggest otherwise.
BEREWYK	You dabble your toes in murky water. Be sure not to fall in.
ALICIA	I'm safe enough, I think.
BEREWYK	Assume nothing. That's my advice to you.

> *Berewyk exits, bowing to Eleanor, who returns to centre stage.*

ELEANOR	He's right. You should listen to him.

> *Eleanor moves to the chess table.*

Let's complete the end-game. You take the King's position.

> *They sit at the chess table. Alicia considers the positions, then looks up incredulously.*

ALICIA	But this could be mate against you.

ELEANOR   *(Highly pleased with herself)* I gave him choice of positions. He could have wiped me away forever, had he been less of a mouse. *(Menacingly)* And that lost opportunity has blunted my conscience, Alicia.

ALICIA   You'll still help the Jew?

ELEANOR   We shall see.

They settle back in their chairs.

ALICIA   They say the expulsions will be brutal.

ELEANOR   The King says no. He's forbidden harm to the Jews. Even the fares must be affordable.

ALICIA   And York, and Spalding – what happened to the Jews there?

ELEANOR   Sometimes I think even the King has his doubts. But his mother is so *persistent*. She glories in being the architect of it all. God, sometimes he's so weak. *(Suddenly agitated, putting her hand to her mouth)* Oh, I've forgotten Edward. I've not spoken to him yet. Do you think I'll scare them all to death if I suddenly appear in the kitchen?

ALICIA   I'll stay here then, in case he returns.

Eleanor exits stage right, leaving Alicia to ponder the chessboard and fiddle with the pieces. Voices and footsteps are heard off-stage left. King Edward and the Dowager Queen enter, having passed the visitors leaving. The Dowager Queen wears the austere habit of a nun.

DOWAGER   … and I say he should have been wearing it.

EDWARD   Peace, Mother. It would have been on the coat he gave to de Berewyk.

DOWAGER   You can't be sure.

EDWARD   Mother, if you know and I know he is a Jew what more do you need? Would you have him swathed in yellow ribbon?

DOWAGER	The point is to be punished through humiliation, not to advertise.
EDWARD	In a few weeks you'll be rid of them all. Then what will you do?
DOWAGER	Die in pe... *(Seeing Alicia)* Girl, why are you not with the Queen?
ALICIA	My Lady, the Queen needs her son more than she needs me.
DOWAGER	Ochh!

The Dowager Queen exits, but the King remains behind with Alicia.

EDWARD	Or vice versa. Tell me Alicia, how long have you served the Queen?
ALICIA	Four years, come December.
EDWARD	And you were with us in Gascony. *(A statement, but taken by Alicia as a question)*
ALICIA	You know I was.
EDWARD	Of course. You are happy, looking after Edward?
ALICIA	I'd be happier if he saw more of his parents, Sir.
EDWARD	Then bring him to Clipstone. There is a parlement there in October, then we're to Lincoln.
ALICIA	Is that wise, Sir?
EDWARD	Wise enough I should say.

The King looks around guiltily, then puts his arm around her shoulders in a way that indicates previous intimacy.

Do not be afraid, Alicia.

ALICIA	Please do not test me, Sir.
EDWARD	As you said, it is four years come December. Surely that is something to... celebrate.

He grasps her chin and turns her face towards him. The apparently affectionate gesture carries a hint of threat.

We must join the Queen.

The King withdraws his arm and they leave the room. A few seconds later the Dowager Queen enters pulling Alicia vigorously by the sleeve.

DOWAGER   Back in here, girl.

ALICIA   You were listening.

DOWAGER   It's my business to listen. Who else do you suppose listens – and sees – in this ragbag of a court?

ALICIA   The Queen, de Berewyk.

DOWAGER   The Queen? Can't you feel the changes in the air? Each speck of blood on the floor has everyone scurrying to consider their positions. And mark my words, they should. I should know. How I should know.

ALICIA   *(Calmly)* Why are you still holding my sleeve?

DOWAGER   *(Letting go of sleeve)* I can read you, Alicia. You're feeding too close to the den. You think you can share his meals, but if you're not careful you'll end up as one. *(Pause)* This business with my son…

ALICIA   Nothing's happened.

DOWAGER   But you want it to. Oh how you want it. How often have I seen you preening yourself when you hear his steps. Patting your hair here, straightening your bodice there.

ALICIA   How can you…

DOWAGER   I see from your face that I'm right. Yet… *(looking about her as if addressing a wider audience)* … what if it were to run, um? I'll tell you. Two things can happen. One is nothing, because no one chooses – or dares – to see. The other? The King would not be openly tarnished, Alicia. The action would be to expunge the stain.

ALICIA   You frighten me. There's cunning in your words.

DOWAGER   If rash, you are no fool, Alicia. *(Pause)* Would you say that we're beginning to understand one another? Might understand one another perfectly, if we both appreciated the circumstances. *(Pause)* You love the Queen, yes?

ALICIA   Well I…

DOWAGER   Respect her then. Would not wish to hurt her.

ALICIA   She is my life.

DOWAGER   But increasingly, she's – how shall we say – not quite herself.

ALICIA   I don't understand you.

DOWAGER   Has moments when her judgements are… clouded. For example, there is the… Jewish question.

ALICIA   We all know what you think about the Jews.

DOWAGER   But one in particular.

ALICIA   What's he ever done to you?

DOWAGER   He escaped my late husband's… But that is none of your business.

ALICIA   Then what do you want of me?

DOWAGER   The Queen is inclined to support his application. This knight – oh, I know not how – is persuasive. But when the time comes *(emphasising the next three words)* you will wish *(now beaming at Alicia)* to preserve the equanimity of the court.

           Berewyk enters.

BEREWYK   The Queen reminds us that it is time for dinner.

DOWAGER   We have quite finished, de Berewyk. Alicia and I have even worked up an appetite. Haven't we child? Come.

           All exit and the stage darkens.

SCENE THREE

[Several days later] The reception room of the Royal Hunting Lodge. Eleanor enters. She is in some physical distress and breathing hard. She grips the top of a chair with both hands.

ELEANOR   Is it the curse of a Jew that grips me thus? No, no. He will still trust me to the end, and there are others who hate me more. It must be nature then, and that is frightening. *(Pause)* My physician will do me no harm, but…

        Alicia enters with bottles and a cup on a tray and stands watching Eleanor. The King enters.

EDWARD   *(To Alicia)* Put them down, put them down.

        Alicia puts the tray on a table and withdraws from the room but remains visible to the audience, listening intently.

EDWARD   *(To Eleanor)* Are you unwell?

ELEANOR   No… no! It is my… seasonal problem. The fever's early, that's all.

EDWARD   *(To himself)* So, once again. Autumn steals from summer's gentler hand.

ELEANOR   The weather has changed.

EDWARD   Has it? I hadn't noticed. Be sure to take your syrups then. *(Pause)* We want you well enough for Clipstone.

ELEANOR   Clipstone already? The parlement's not for two weeks.

EDWARD   I fancy a stag or two at Rockingham on the way. It's said they know our wiles less well than here. But if you are unwell… *(Shrugs)* I thought we might take Edward.

ELEANOR   He doesn't need politics.

EDWARD	But he might appreciate you. Or me.
ELEANOR	He's such a handful.
EDWARD	*(Magnanimously)* Alicia will come. He likes Alicia.
ELEANOR	Does he?
EDWARD	Doesn't he? We pay her well enough.
ELEANOR	We pay her very little, but that's beside the point.
EDWARD	Then that's settled. The day after tomorrow.

> *Eleanor sits wearily.*

EDWARD	My dear, you shiver. *(Pause)* Which reminds me. This afternoon, in the kennels. I saw your wolf, Gretel.
ELEANOR	She's due any time. She's so big.
EDWARD	She looked fretful. Not quite right, like I've seen with curs sometimes.
ELEANOR	Then our situations are not so different.
EDWARD	*(Startled by her tone, but choosing not to pursue what he doesn't want to know)* I remember when Hassim gave you the pup – after Aleppo – and you nursed it like a child. And then when we brought her here you could not at first bring yourself to release her.
ELEANOR	And were confounded when she returned to litter.
EDWARD	Were indeed confounded.
ELEANOR	Such freedom she had. Why can animals enjoy what we humans cannot, with all our scheming and design?
EDWARD	What mean you, Eleanor? Men are free. It's my business to see that men are free.
ELEANOR	Oh, not that. The fever's turned my thoughts. A little sleep will soon dispel them.
EDWARD	I had thought... otherwise... this night.
ELEANOR	Then it's cold porridge you would stir, however warm the pot.

EDWARD   That remains my choice. Did that Jew say something to upset you?

ELEANOR   The opposite. He gave me a challenge.

EDWARD   Hah! If Friar Benedict can book you a few square yards at Blackfriars before you're even cold, he can convert a Jew. It's what the Pope would have us do anyway.

ELEANOR   But your mother... has influence. *(Boldly)* You have no conscience do you? Do you know what suffering will result from this expulsion?

EDWARD   My dear wife. Outside our window are stone flags. And under each of them rests a company of ants and God knows what else on six legs. You lift one up and they scurry about like souls in torment. Five minutes later they've gone. Where? Are they now less content, do you suppose? I don't think so. And neither do the people that matter.

ELEANOR   Like your mother?

EDWARD   It's done. There's no going back, even if I wished it. But, as you say, we've done well out of the Jews, and maybe we've been greedy. May the good Lord judge us kindly on that one.

ELEANOR   It's what I fear.

EDWARD   You carry a *conscience*? I hadn't noticed.

ELEANOR   At my time of life one reflects upon such things.

EDWARD   Hah. Melancholy. In another woman I'd say it was passion, not infirmity. Lost dreams before the body sags into puddingness. *(Implied threat)* But you're not just another woman, are you Eleanor?

ELEANOR   *(Bitterly)* Sometimes I wish I were.

EDWARD   *(Indicating that he appreciates the point much more clearly than he has so far chosen to show)* We are all bound by duties, Eleanor. Just as you have been true to me, so I swear that trust has been deserved.

ELEANOR   I have not doubted it. *(Pause, then reluctantly)* You may stir the porridge, if that is what you want.

As the stage darkens Alicia walks thoughtfully away.

SCENE FOUR

[The following morning] A curtain design consistent with a garden obscures the sets of the previous scenes. Distant howls and barks indicate that the kennels are not far away. Eleanor is seated on a wooden bench with some bushes to the side. Her face is drawn but her expression is more philosophical than anxious. Berewyk enters stage left, walking briskly. Seeing her, he stops abruptly, surprised to find her there.

ELEANOR   *(Looking up at him sweetly)* De Berewyk, what haste. Will you not even stop to speak with me?

BEREWYK   *(Flustered)* My Lady, you know that every minute of my time is yours. I was coming to warn you…

ELEANOR   … of the Autumn chill in the air. *(Rubbing her hand along the seat edge, feeling the moisture)* One day it's summer – you remember yesterday how Edward played on this lawn – the next… But the sun should come out to mask our troubles. *(Directly)* What is it you want?

BEREWYK   Friar Benedict has arrived. Frankly, his demeanour is so morbid I thought you might wish to be spared of him. Shall I deal with him?

ELEANOR   *(Laughing)* The decoration of one's sarcophagus is a rather personal matter, unless you think you know me well enough…

BEREWYK   I would not presume that much. But he tells me your chapel at Blackfriars is progressing well. There is no reason to see him.

ELEANOR   I suppose not. But fetch him all the same.

>*The voices of Alicia and Friar Benedict are heard in the distance.*

BEREWYK   No need. He must have found Alicia.

>*Alicia enters with Friar Benedict, who is carrying a rolled up plan. He bows to Eleanor.*

ELEANOR   Friar Benedict, your transactions pursue me like the harbinger of death itself.

FRIAR   My Lady, nothing could be further from my intention. For once may the artists' work go long unrecognised.

ELEANOR   You won't attract true artists then. You have the designs?

>*Friar Benedict spreads the plans on the seat. While Eleanor and the friar pore over them, Berewyk and Alicia take centre stage.*

BEREWYK   How was her night?

ALICIA   Troubled. Thrice I heard her cry out. But whether from pain or lust I cannot say.

BEREWYK   Alicia! The truth surely lies in the number. Be kind, or if you can't be that, be respectful.

ALICIA   That is my nature.

BEREWYK   It is not your nature.

ALICIA   Then it's only you that knows it. And you know why that is.

BEREWYK   *(Angrily)* One day those raven locks of yours will grey to frame a haggard face. Then where will your advantage lie?

ELEANOR   *(Looking up sharply, sensing the discord)* Alicia, where's Edward?

ALICIA   Gone to see Gretel.

ELEANOR   But I can hear the bushes rustling behind me.

ALICIA   I'll get him.

ELEANOR   No, let him be. *(Pause)* She's still delivering, then?

ALICIA	So I was told.
ELEANOR	Then let's go and look. You will see, Friar, that the sun can shine even on a dumb creature.
	She tries to rise, but staggers unnaturally. Alicia and Berewyk move to steady her.
FRIAR	*(Aside, looking at his designs)* Clearly my artists must not delay.
	He turns to the Queen, who is now standing.
	My Lady, de Berewyk tells me there is another issue.
ELEANOR	Ah, yes. The Jew of Northampton.
FRIAR	I thought we spoke before.
ELEANOR	We did. But without result.
FRIAR	*(Patronisingly)* And I explained…
ELEANOR	… that there are things even a queen is not permitted to know.
FRIAR	Would you presume to share the mind of God? I rather think not.
ELEANOR	No matter. If you will not tell me, there's the end of it. *(Pause)* Conversions are a matter for the Church, are they not, with God simply watching to see the quality of the catch?
FRIAR	The hand of guidance is not always explicit. But it is there all the same.
ELEANOR	*(Laughing at him)* I tease you, good friar. Look, the sun comes out. We'll walk to the kennels, to see God's creatures. You like wolves?
FRIAR	No. They come too often in human guise.
ELEANOR	They do! But not Gretel.
	They walk away. Berewyk and Alicia take centre stage, watching them.
BEREWYK	This talk of wolves is no idle matter, as she will find.

ALICIA	You didn't tell her there was a problem?
BEREWYK	No.
ALICIA	Coward.
BEREWYK	But not incompetent.
ALICIA	Incompetent? What do you mean?
BEREWYK	Ask Edward – if you can find him.
ALICIA	Edward? Oh!

She runs off stage, leaving Berewyk alone. As soon as she has gone Edward emerges from the bushes, holding out a large kite for Berewyk to admire.

BEREWYK   *(To himself, as much as to Edward)* Yes, there are extraordinary currents in the air today, young Edward. And riding there – although we mortals cannot see them – are already so many kites, but in colours darker than yours, and with such pretensions. They wheel and dive, up and down, round and round, passing each other, coming together, almost to couple before flying apart to try their luck elsewhere. And then, suddenly – whether by chance or design, it's not for me to say – one of them breaks free. *(Looking down at the boy)* Then what do you think happens? *(Pause)* That's difficult to answer, so I will tell you.

Berewyk's face becomes serious as he realises that the content of his speech has greater significance than he intended. He stands slightly aside, looking sadly after the departing Queen. Alicia returns, stands meekly behind Edward and listens to Berewyk, whose words are now intended for her.

For one exquisite moment, there is a sense of absolute freedom. The tissues move upon themselves, unconstrained, no longer opposing the currents to stay aloft, but travelling with them, in blissful ignorance of anything untoward.

(Sadly) But it cannot last, you see, Edward, because there is no control, no hand or eye to coordinate and direct. And so our lovely kite must come down. Not immediately, not here necessarily, but sometime, somewhere. *(Emotionally)* Let us hope it is a hospitable place, Edward, amongst people who are kind, for that much at least is deserved. *(Smiling at the boy)* Come, let's follow them and see what Gretel has produced.

> *For several seconds Berewyk stares into the distance, then he grasps Edward's hand.*

Your mother has fallen.

> *Berewyk exits, leaving Edward playing with his kite and Alicia standing for a moment deep in thought. Then she follows Berewyk. The stage darkens.*

SCENE FIVE

[The following afternoon] The reception room of the Royal Hunting Lodge. The King is stretched out on one of the chairs, waiting. Footsteps are heard outside the door. He taps the arm of the chair, gets up and goes to the window. As he passes the chess board he looks down at it and an expression of surprise passes his face. He stands at the window looking out broodingly as Alicia enters. Her bearing is cautious, as if she has been summoned.

EDWARD	The leaves are turning.
ALICIA	Their colours are beautiful.
EDWARD	Beautiful, yes, but assuredly they will die and fall, as everything must.
ALICIA	You sound…
EDWARD	Philosophical? *(Turning towards her)* Wouldn't you be, with the court poised to confront itself. *(Miserably)* I've come from the sick room, where my dear wife sleeps.

ALICIA	The bout will pass. It has before.
EDWARD	*(Smiling at her, disbelievingly)* Listen. What do you hear?
ALICIA	It's very quiet. *(Thinking)* Unusually so.
EDWARD	The Queen takes ill and everyone goes to ground. What do you think that signifies?
ALICIA	Their great concern, their…
EDWARD	It's like dogs and cats hearing the storm before we do. Mark my words, it will change us all. And you in particular, Alicia.

The King picks up one of the chess pieces and idly plays with it.

The day after tomorrow she will leave with me for Clipstone. It concerns me, but there is no alternative.

ALICIA	She should not travel.
EDWARD	Your concern is touching. But I sometimes wonder from what source your loyalty springs. Is it the code that binds the actions of servants… or the security of your position – although it has to be said that that looks a bit precarious now. Or could it be affection?
ALICIA	Yes, affection, and because of that, loyalty.

The King puts down the chess piece.

EDWARD	*(Not listening)* Or could it be something else that you wouldn't openly admit, evident only to my mother and sometimes even to me? *(Pause)* But what were we saying? *(Testing)* Travel, yes. I am mindful that Edward is a distraction for her.
ALICIA	So you're not taking me with you?
EDWARD	Perhaps you *should* stay here with Edward. My mother and de Berewyk argued persuasively about that. But… well, we shall see. *(Pause)* Wipe that anger from your eyes, Alicia.

He looks at her searchingly, taking her chin in his hand. She turns her head away.

You flirt with me Alicia, yet when I take your arm or touch your face you withdraw into yourself and I ask myself why?

ALICIA   I don't flirt with you.

EDWARD   But my mother says you do.

ALICIA   She li… is mistaken.

EDWARD   She knows the wiles of women, Alicia.

ALICIA   And scares the wits out of me even more than you do.

EDWARD   How many men have you lain with, Alicia – four, five?

Alicia turns her head away violently.

Answer!

ALICIA   *(Almost inaudibly)* Not so many.

EDWARD   As I know.

Alicia looks surprised. She slumps into a chair facing the audience.

As I make it my business to know. And among them de Clare and de Warenne, eligible both, but not for a lady's maid, Alicia. Do you not know of that line separating affection and loyalty from the necessary demands of the flesh? Those things we males cannot set aside, however hard we might wish them away. What man has wanted you for love, Alicia, tell me that. Ah, yes, I can think of one – poor de Berewyk.

ALICIA   There is never any love in the world. Only lust and jealousy and ownership. Women are just chattels.

EDWARD   True. But not always, Alicia. Sometimes, out of desire, other things develop, encouraged by trust and understanding… and maturity.

The King stands behind the chair and slowly begins to caress her hair, then her neck, making her squirm in an agony of indecision.

You have beautiful hair... and the whitest of skins...

Finally he slowly pushes his hand down the front of her dress.

... and the softest of... breasts...

ALICIA   Please take your hand away.

EDWARD   Why? You don't like it?

ALICIA   *(Anguished)* The Queen might appear.

EDWARD   I told you she sleeps and will not wake yet.

ALICIA   Or de Berewyk, or...

EDWARD   De Berewyk has been instructed to let no one enter. He believes we are discussing your future, Alicia. *(Chillingly)* As indeed we are.

ALICIA   You are trapping me.

EDWARD   *(Laughing)* Shall I describe to you what is happening behind this chair, Alicia. It is almost as if the chair wishes to be pushed forward. By how much, you might ask. I am a tall man, Alicia. Draw your own conclusions.

ALICIA   I don't want to know.

EDWARD   Think hard, Alicia, how you mean to respond.

ALICIA   Please leave me alone.

EDWARD   The stakes are high, Alicia.

ALICIA   I know.

He removes his hand from the front of Alicia's dress and grasps the back of the chair in order to turn it.

EDWARD   I'm turning the chair now.

The Dowager Queen appears from the (unguarded) entrance. Alicia leaps up and makes for the door.

(Calling) Think on it, Alicia.

> *Alicia pauses at the door, looks round, then exits, leaving the King looking shamefaced and his mother with a thin, searching smile on her face.*

> *The stage darkens.*

SCENE SIX

[The following morning] The reception room of the Royal Hunting Lodge. Alicia is tidying objects at a table. Footsteps are heard. She listens for a moment, smiles to herself, casts off her shoes and begins hobbling about. Berewyk enters.

BEREWYK   What ploy is this? If it's sympathy you're after I can tell you you've already had that in full measure.

ALICIA   How gallant! It's a splinter from the floor.

BEREWYK   If you're stupid enough to walk in bare feet…

> *Alicia sits on a stool, pulls her foot towards her and scrutinises it.*

ALICIA   I can't see anything. You have a look.

> *Berewyk hesitates, grimaces, pulls up a chair and sits facing her. Alicia places her foot on his knee, flexing her own knee so that her skirt falls down her thigh. Berewyk is highly embarrassed.*

The foot, de Berewyk. Just concentrate on the foot.

> *Berewyk is torn between keeping his eyes on her foot and letting his gaze wander. He settles down to explore the foot but can find nothing. Alicia bends forward to show him, pointing with her finger.*

ALICIA   Somewhere there.

> *Berewyk pushes with his finger.*

(Deliberately, unconvincingly) Ow!

> *Berewyk, realising he has been duped, slowly raises his eyes to hers. They stare at each other, exploring each*

other's motives. Alicia smiles. Berewyk leans back, still with her foot on his knee, and contemplates the ceiling.

Decisions, decisions. I can see your heart pounding, de Berewyk.

BEREWYK   Don't be ridiculous!

ALICIA   At your temple. Like a little butterfly flapping its wings. Why don't you thrust my foot away if it offends you? *(She looks towards his lap)* Oh! Is that a mole I see surfacing?

Alicia wiggles her foot on his knee. Berewyk slowly advances his hand and attempts to hold the foot. Before he can do so Alicia grasps her stool, shunts it forward, places her foot squarely on Berewyk's chest and propels him backwards. He fails to regain his balance and slides to the floor.

Enough fun for today, don't you think, de Berewyk? Here, let me help you up. *(Without guile)* If the Queen could see you now.

She extends her hand and pulls him to his feet. He stands breathing hard, trying to regain his composure.

BEREWYK   I'll pray for you Alicia. Though – God knows – I'll have to pray hard.

Alicia's expression suddenly turns to one of genuine remorse.

ALICIA   It's what being trapped in this... court... does to you. I don't know how you put up with it, de Berewyk, I really don't.

BEREWYK   Then I'll pray for your release, Alicia.

Berewyk exits. Alicia puts on her shoes and resumes tidying objects on the table.

SCENE SEVEN

[Later that day] The reception room of the Royal Hunting Lodge. Eleanor, now dressed in a nightgown, negotiates the steps left stage, descending slowly and carefully. She walks towards the window, then stops to look down at the chessboard, which is as it was. She touches a knight with her forefinger, then picks it up and stares at it.

ELEANOR   My poor Richard. So many years we have sparred with one another. But for what?

         Eleanor replaces the piece, then takes a sealed paper from her gown and furtively slips it into a drawer in the table. A moment later Alicia enters with a tray bearing a number of bottles.

ALICIA   You shouldn't have left your bed. The King told me to bring you your syrups.

         Alicia sets the bottles on the table.

ELEANOR   Much good they've done me. *(She turns away to look out of the window)* How is my Gretel? Is she done?

ALICIA   There are still… problems.

ELEANOR   She's not…

ALICIA   Friar Benedict says that life is just a preparation for death. Do you think it's the same for wolves?

ELEANOR   Not the wild ones, certainly. But the creatures that befriend us. I believe they take on something that we humans have.

ALICIA   Like?

ELEANOR   Affection, loyalty. Traded against a longing for the wild and the old ways.

ALICIA   The King said she had thirteen in her litter.

ELEANOR   She has finished then?

ALICIA   I believe so.

ELEANOR	I didn't know you discussed such matters with the King.
ALICIA	Not normally, no. It's just that...
ELEANOR	Go on.
ALICIA	It's nothing.
ELEANOR	Go on. You had a thought. I would share it.
ALICIA	Then it's the number of your own children.
ELEANOR	Have you counted them?
ALICIA	Edward, Katharine, Elizabeth, Mary, Alphonso ...
ELEANOR	Go on.
ALICIA	Beatrice, Blanche, Berengaria, Margaret ...
ELEANOR	And the rest?
ALICIA	Joane, Henry. Oh, and Eleanor.
ELEANOR	And the thirteenth?
ALICIA	*(Counting again in her head, looking puzzled)* I must have miscounted.
ELEANOR	So it seems. But then, why thirteen? Why did you say thirteen?
ALICIA	The figure was in my mind. I must have been wrong. I did not mean to be frivolous.
ELEANOR	I did not say you were wrong – or frivolous, Alicia.
	Alicia looks up, startled.
	But thirteen is not a number you bestow upon anything, without reason. Perhaps someone *[implying the King]* suggested it to you.
ALICIA	No! It's just...
ELEANOR	*(Distantly)* There was one other. *(Pause)* They had to prise it from me, you see, because I was so... small. It lived for just two days. *(Viciously)* And a lifetime of death was condensed into those two days. Disbelief, then hope – as people desperate to hide the truth lied and lied... Then the realisation... of

102

the inevitable. I have lost other children, Alicia, but none like that.

There is a distant rumble of thunder.

What's that?

ALICIA   Only thunder.

ELEANOR   Only thunder! There is a sweetness to that sound that I had long forgotten. Soon it will rain and I shall stand at the window and hold out my hand. I haven't done that since childhood. You know, in Castile, in summer, we would make for the mountains and the carriage would take us so very, very high. When we got there, my brother and I, we would climb yet higher, up to the battlements, and look back across the vast plain, and see it as clear as day in the lightning. *(Almost tearfully)* It is my most vivid memory.

ALICIA   *(Curious)* Was it… difficult… for you to leave Castile… so young?

ELEANOR   What do you think?

ALICIA   Me? Oh, for me it would not have been, if I'd married a prince.

ELEANOR   Then that distinguishes us, Alicia.

ALICIA   *(Having never before heard the Queen speak like this)* But you and the King, you've been so close. Everyone says so.

ELEANOR   And it's true. But we've also had our private… thoughts. Just as the beggar and the peasant and… the Jew… all have their own… private thoughts. And do you know what, Alicia?

ALICIA   What?

ELEANOR   I think they're… we're… all the same.

ALICIA   But the advantage, of being a queen, above all others, of all England.

ELEANOR It's a measure of distance, or if you like the thickness of a wall – a barrier that has no purpose but to keep apart... *(Pause)* You have not heard me speak like this, have you?

> *Alicia shakes her head cautiously, not knowing how to respond.*

Child, I have a task for you. Do not fail me.

ALICIA *(Not enthusiastic)* Then ask.

ELEANOR I wish to see the manor house, at Easingbourne.

ALICIA But we... you... leave tomorrow.

ELEANOR I meant tonight.

ALICIA In the rain, even if it were possible?

ELEANOR It is possible. Sir Richard will not refuse you.

ALICIA I have no control over my uncle.

ELEANOR But I have. This once, do it. *(Lightly)* And we'll take Edward. You know how he talks about the creatures of the night.

> *She opens the drawer and holds out the letter.*

Give him this. It will explain.

ALICIA *(Taking the letter)* Has the fever...

ELEANOR ... taken hold of my senses? No. But it's of another kind, running high. *(Stridently)* For the first time in my life I have reached a crossroads. Can you imagine how exciting that can be? To confront the future, such as it is, with choice. It's like... riding a runaway stallion, knowing for certain that you must fall but...

ALICIA *(Looking at Eleanor askance, then at the syrups on the table)* I'm going.

> *Alicia walks briskly from the room.*

ELEANOR Does this euphoria really give me the power to read my own mind, and confront the devil thoughts unleashed there?

She takes one of the bottles and pours some of the contents into a cup.

What's certain – the time for doubt is over. The Jew, Gretel, Friar Benedict and something, even, about the King's demeanour that is best left unexplored. And Alicia. Silly, silly child. And above all else our own days of wretchedness.

She leans forward, sweeping away the chess pieces with her arm so that they are scattered across the floor.

Good Lord, please help me. Please guide me.

The stage darkens.

SCENE EIGHT

[The same evening, well after dark] The room in the manor house at Easingbourne, essentially as in the earlier scene. Moonlight floods through the window. Redwell is standing, disconsolate, looking out. From outside comes the whinnying of a horse and the creaking of a carriage, then footsteps. He opens the door and Alicia enters.

REDWELL	She's with you?
ALICIA	Following. We've left Edward in the cart.

Seconds later Queen Eleanor enters, cautiously, looking about her intently. She motions Redwell to kneel, but he merely bows.

ELEANOR	*(Extending hand)* Sir Richard.
REDWELL	*(Kissing hand)* My Lady.
ELEANOR	You are quite alone.
REDWELL	It is as I agreed with Alicia.
ELEANOR	And you are not afraid?
REDWELL	Of what should I be afraid?
ELEANOR	Oh, that we might permit ourselves a little more, um, harassment. Take advantage of your stupidity.

	Have you eliminated so that we can claim this... well, this ruin. It's hardly likely to become the jewel in my diadem, in spite of what Alice has led me to think.
ALICIA	My praise was of its memory, not of its structure.
ELEANOR	I know, child. It's Sir Richard I am teasing, not you. Richard, you do not speak. Have you nothing to say to me?
REDWELL	*(Miserably)* A lifetime of words, yet nothing comes.
ELEANOR	A sluice that will not budge. *(Suddenly serious)* What will it take to shift it, my good knight? *(Noticing that he shivers)* You tremble.
REDWELL	It is the cold.
ELEANOR	It is cold, but that is not the reason.
REDWELL	Then it's because I fear to pull the handle, *(turning aside)* not knowing... what forces might be unleashed.
ELEANOR	Against me?
REDWELL	No... no, not against you. Within myself.
ELEANOR	Then that is something I would know.
	There is a cry from outside. Alicia is startled but Eleanor at first seems hardly to notice.
ALICIA	It's Edward. He must have woken.
	Alicia flees the room.
ELEANOR	That girl holds a mirror to my mothering. I should hate her for it, but cannot. Richard, what dam would leave its spawn asleep in a cart, at night?
REDWELL	It is a small defect.
ELEANOR	Against what others perceive as avarice, I daresay it is. *(Stands beside him)* But you were going to tell me something. And for that purpose – and for this night only – I would have you call me Eleanor.

REDWELL   *(To himself)* Can this be real? Can reality be fashioned from an age of futile dreams? Or dreams of such unguarded licence fulfil themselves so exactly?

ELEANOR   Oh, it is real enough, Richard. *(Wistfully)* Yet it is not as I would have it.

REDWELL   Something has changed?

ELEANOR   Something has changed.

REDWELL   Would it be…

ELEANOR   Presumptuous to ask? It would have been – but no longer.

REDWELL   *(Suddenly aggressive)* You've always played with me. Why must you continue?

ELEANOR   Richard, can you imagine what it is like to be a queen, the Queen of England, Edward's queen?

REDWELL   Rich and powerful, and by all accounts loved.

ELEANOR   Yes, you're right – all three. But that's the bright side. What of the other? Don't try to answer! It was being a captive, like a rose pruned to keep its shape and force it into bloom.

REDWELL   Who would have wished that?

ELEANOR   Honour. The Church. People like de Berewyk. The King himself even.

    Eleanor sits on a bench.

    Here, sit with me and I will tell you a tale.

    Redwell does so hesitantly.

    There was once a girl – oh, no more than fourteen – betrothed and in the first flush of womanhood. They held a tourney in her honour, and everyone came from far and wide to see just how beautiful she really was, and how her gallant husband could despatch all the other knights with the sure thrust of his lance. And before each joust they would ride up to this young girl, these dashing knights, erect in their saddles, whiskers bristling, horses frisking but in perfect control. And when she smiled at them each face would light up with a purpose that until that moment had been quite unrealised. *(Pause)* But there was one who let his eyes linger – just for a second – and this time she did not smile, but lowered her eyes, and could not stop the pink flush that crept into her cheeks. *(Longer pause)* Then one day the governess took her for a ride. Not the usual canter around the grounds but deep into the forest, further than she had ever been before. They came to a clearing where men were working – rough men with wild faces and thin brown arms, clearing felled wood. Out of the corner of her eye the girl saw something she was not intended to see – her companion raise a finger to her lips. It was as if that finger had been dipped into still water, for from that moment these rough men emptied their hands and moved silently apart, like a ripple. *(Harrowingly, biting her lip)* Except for one, who continued working, quite unaware of what was happening around him. Suddenly the girl was frightened and looked desperately for her companion, but could not see her. For a moment she was alone in a strange hostile and frozen world peopled by one wretched soul. *(Pause)* There was a sudden clap of thunder and the eerie forest light gave way to drops of welcome rain – oh, that rain! – and the governess appeared and they rode on. The girl looked back once, but the men were working, as if nothing had happened.

REDWELL   And then?

ELEANOR   When they got home the girl asked the obvious question: why? The governess replied: did you not see that the man was blind? And I knew then why I had been taken there.

REDWELL	His was a harsh punishment for so little cause.
ELEANOR	Richard, you don't see! It was no punishment, the man's crime was insignificant. It was a warning. To me! *(Quietly)* And all my life, whenever the flame of desire has flickered within me, I would see those sightless eyes...
REDWELL	Eleanor...
ELEANOR	... and remain my husband's dutiful wife.
	She rises and Redwell follows
REDWELL	Then what now gives you courage to... question?
ELEANOR	I will tell you, but bear with me a few moments longer. There are things I would first establish.
REDWELL	Then ask.
ELEANOR	You have held out against me these many years. No one else has been so resolute.
REDWELL	Is that so difficult to understand?
ELEANOR	I thought I did. You had something to lose. You were not alone among men who have looked at me in that way.
REDWELL	I tried hard to conceal it.
ELEANOR	Then why the change? What is it about that Jew that would have you break the tie between us?
REDWELL	Perhaps he offered me money to settle with you.
ELEANOR	I'm sure he did. But it wasn't that.
REDWELL	No?
ELEANOR	No. *(Pause)* You remember the chess board?
REDWELL	Yes.
ELEANOR	And how you refused my challenge?
REDWELL	Yes.
ELEANOR	So what were you frightened of? And don't say my skill as a player.
REDWELL	That I would win.

109

ELEANOR   You could have won! It was set up for it. Yet you were prepared to lose Easingbourne because of the Jew rather on your own account by losing the game to me. Is that not strange?

REDWELL   Eleanor, please don't press me.

ELEANOR   I need to know.

REDWELL   Ask anything of me, but not that.

ELEANOR   I need to know!

REDWELL   Why must you know. Why now?

ELEANOR   Because, Richard, time is short.

REDWELL   Time for what?

ELEANOR   I'm going to die.

Eleanor turns her head and suddenly her despair is apparent. Richard does not know what to do and paces in front of her, then approaches her and touches her face with his hand.

REDWELL   There's a part here I must play. God show me what it is.

ELEANOR   You may comfort me, Richard.

REDWELL   *(Aghast)* Lay hands upon my queen?

ELEANOR   Oh, then give me your hand.

She places his hand on her forehead and holds it there

REDWELL   The fever?

ELEANOR   And here.

She brings his hand sharply to her abdomen.

It is tense, is it not?

Surprised at what he can feel he makes to withdraw his hand, but she holds it there.

REDWELL   It is so.

ELEANOR   Disease and passion, together. What unholy partners in such a little body. Do not despise me, Richard.

REDWELL	Despise you? I cannot despise you.
ELEANOR	Then comfort me.

They draw closer to one another.

REDWELL	But if the King…
ELEANOR	The King has… other…

Alicia enters, agitated and tearful, but then takes note of what she sees. Eleanor and de Redwell break apart.

ALICIA	He's gone again, like he always does.
ELEANOR	He will not be far. Go and look again.
ALICIA	He must be in here somewhere.
ELEANOR	*(Almost shouting)* I assure you he is not! *(Long pause)* Never mind, you had better look. *(To Redwell)* You see, Richard, we are thwarted to the end.
REDWELL	There will be other…
ELEANOR	Opportunities? *(Shaking her head sadly)* Too late. I left it all… too late.

Eleanor rises from the bench and walks wearily away. Then she turns and looks fixedly at de Redwell.

But there is still that other matter.

REDWELL	*(Shaking head)* I cannot.
ELEANOR	You would have taken me, yet can't still my mind over something so trivial?
REDWELL	If it's trivial, why are you so desperate to know?
ELEANOR	The final knot between us – and you cannot bring yourself to tie the strings.
REDWELL	I cannot break an oath, Eleanor.
ELEANOR	Then can you not tell to whom you made this oath?
REDWELL	*(Long pause)* It was Hagin.

For several seconds Eleanor remains deep in thought.

ELEANOR   I see. *(To Alicia)* This meeting never happened, you understand. And Sir Richard here will not speak of it if he knows what is good for him.

REDWELL   Eleanor...

ELEANOR   My Lady.

REDWELL   My dear Lady, whatever may have come between us do not forget your promise to Hagin.

ELEANOR   Promise? Huh.

Eleanor turns on her heal and exits. Alicia follows, perplexed.

The stage darkens.

SCENE NINE

[An hour later] The reception room at the Royal Hunting Lodge, just as it was previously, but candlelit and darker. The door rear stage opens with a crash and Eleanor enters highly agitated with Alicia close behind. She is crying and falls to her knees. Alicia tries in vain to console her.

ALICIA   Why are you behaving like this?

Eleanor holds out her hand, which has blood on it.

ELEANOR   That's why. Can't you see.

ALICIA   Here, let me wipe it off.

ELEANOR   Don't touch me!

Alicia staggers back amazed. The Queen slowly rises to confront her.

Could you not have left us for a few moments longer? Removed for just a second the thorn in the flesh that is my son? And look at you now. Full of pride with your black locks and doe eyes, preening yourself in my husband's favour.

ALICIA   What do you mean?

ELEANOR	You think I'm blind? So occupied with my last days that I don't see what is happening?
ALICIA	I've served you loyally.
ELEANOR	You have not!
ALICIA	So, what if it is true? What could it matter to you now? What use to him is a hot, empty bladder that coughs and spits up blood? *You* might have wasted your youth…
ELEANOR	That isn't true.
ALICIA	So why shouldn't it be my turn?
	Both women realise they've gone too far and slump into chairs. There is a long pause.
ELEANOR	Tell me I'm mistaken.
ALICIA	There *was* temptation. *(Contrite)* But, yes, you were mistaken.
ELEANOR	You said hurtful things.
ALICIA	I had forgotten… your condition. Forgive me.
	Eleanor holds out her hand, which Alicia takes. At this point Berewyk enters.
BEREWYK	Ahem.
	The two women scramble to their feet.
	I hope I'm not intruding.
ELEANOR	Not at all.
BEREWYK	I thought you might wish to be aware that the Dowager Queen is approaching.
	The Dowager Queen enters.
DOWAGER	Dinner was unusually rowdy tonight, don't you think, de Berewyk?
BEREWYK	It can be quite… spirited… when the Queen is absent.
DOWAGER	That's because the King relies upon her to keep order. We all missed you tonight, Eleanor.

ELEANOR   I'm flattered. But beyond that I don't care if I was missed or not.

DOWAGER   De Berewyk tells me that you went out with young Edward. Poor little brat.

ELEANOR   Why poor little brat?

DOWAGER   So enquiring a mind. So little to exercise it.

ELEANOR   We went to hear the wolves baying to the moon, and the boars rooting in the undergrowth. Things you wouldn't appreciate in your… nunnery.

DOWAGER   Of course. It's your last night here, and you had to take… advantage.

BEREWYK   I think the Queen must be tired.

DOWAGER   And so am I. And disappointed. Goodnight to you all.

She exits stage left.

ELEANOR   What's troubling her?

BEREWYK   I believe she is concerned about… relationships.

ELEANOR   With impecunious… knights?

BEREWYK   Or their less impecunious acquaintances.

ELEANOR   Meaning Hagin. *(Grimly)* She needn't worry – he won't succeed. But you may not tell her that.

BEREWYK   *(Alarmed)* I don't quite understand. I've told Sir Richard you have given your support…

ELEANOR   The case is not deserving. The friars have enough to do as it is. Besides, this Hagin has no great ties.

BEREWYK   If my Lady would consider afresh in the morning.

ELEANOR   We shall see. Now leave us, de Berewyk, please.

Berewyk rises, makes to exit, then pauses

BEREWYK   My Lady, there is something I have to tell you.

ELEANOR   Be quick then.

BEREWYK   The wolf Gretel has died.

ELEANOR   Edward will be upset. Now go, please.

Berewyk leaves the room. The stage darkens, to denote the passing of time, but after a few seconds lightens on the same scene, from which Eleanor and Alicia have departed. Suddenly Eleanor in her nightgown runs onto the stage in a state of great anxiety, pursued by Alicia, who is dishevelled and scantily clad.

ELEANOR   How can you do that to me? After what you said. Curse you, curse you, curse you. *(She stands gasping for breath)* You witch!

ALICIA   *(Trying to calm her)* I'm sorry, I'm sorry.

ELEANOR   Keep away from me.

ALICIA   I did not mean to hurt you.

ELEANOR   But you have – and that is the end for us. How could you do it, while I was nearby, sleeping. Curse you!

ALICIA   *(Calmly and coldly)* Your indiscretion with my uncle opened the way for me. When the King comes to you and you can't be still because your fever makes you convulse and sweat and when that's over go to sleep, can you blame him if he comes to me? Can you?

ELEANOR   Oh, my God. I took you in, trusted you with my child, made a friend of you to share my deepest cares. How can you repay me so?

ALICIA   Then you chose wrongly.

ELEANOR   Can you show no remorse?

ALICIA   I can offer you one crumb of comfort.

ELEANOR   Say it!

ALICIA   It will not happen again while you while you live.

Eleanor gathers her clothes about her and flees the room. Alicia remains standing mid-stage then suddenly clutches her head in remorse. After a few moments the Dowager Queen enters.

DOWAGER   As I predicted, the drama unfolds. *(Pause)* I found
it hard to sleep with such commotion. The King,
conversely, has no such difficulty. *(Pause)* I... um...
happened to pass Eleanor's desk and saw there
some unfinished letters... concerning the Jew.

ALICIA   She is in no state to finish them.

DOWAGER   Oh, she will finish them when she's calmed down –
if only to spite me. *(Beaming)* But I'm not vindictive.
(Pause, deadly serious) Should she entrust them to
you I would wish to help... with their delivery.

ALICIA   I could not...

DOWAGER   Could not? What did we agree, Alicia? Tonight you
climbed the mountain, got your first view from
the summit, did you not? *(Pause)* The slopes can be
quite precipitous. Goodnight, Alicia.

The Dowager Queen exits and the stage darkens.

SCENE TEN

*[The same night] The stage brightens to reveal the chapel of the Royal Hunting
Lodge. There is a closed door to the rear and left stage an altar on a dais bearing
lighted candles. Mid-stage are a few token chairs. Eleanor enters as if in a daze
and stops before the altar. She contemplates the candles, one of which is unlit.
She picks up a taper as if to relight the extinguished candle and runs her finger
slowly along its length.*

ELEANOR   *(Breathing heavily and coughing)* My life... has been
a taper such as this – straight and smooth along its
length until... the end is lit. *(Lighting it from a candle)*
And this little flame *(scrutinising it)* – what meaning
does it have? Is it passion long suppressed? Or does
it portend the death to end my troubles? *(Making
to extinguish the flame between finger and thumb but
then hesitating)* What time is left for me, I wonder?

(Coughing uncontrollably; then angrily) What need have I for time. Why not now? Would you, my God, allow that? What if I retch my heart up and scorn to stem the flow? *(Now seriously questioning the possibility)* But what if I were to do it? How would my blemished past stand the passages of death and time? No problem for the Jew – tomorrow I will do as Berewyk suggests and send letters to Archbishop Pecham to intercede. But of that greater issue – that avarice of mine. How many like Richard will rise up to spit their contempt for me after I have gone. I cannot die with that. I cannot. They are wrongs that must be set right for me. *(Pause, then pointing her finger at the flame)* How fast it travels, this tiny flame…

> She closes her hand over flame, extinguishing it, and the stage darkens.

-----INTERVAL-----

ACT THREE

SCENE ONE

[December 1290 – early afternoon] Two servants from the Royal Hunting Lodge are standing at a crossroads (the junction with the Lincoln to Northampton road, one mile from Geddington). One is taking over from the other the duty of watching for Eleanor's funeral cortège. A horse waits nearby [noises off-stage]. It is beginning to snow.

SERV. 1	Thankless bloody task this.
SERV. 2	Should be here soon.
SERV. 1	Who says?
SERV. 2	Alicia said. Left Stamford at nine, here by two.

SERV. 1	On these roads? Glad it's not me what's staying.
	He picks up a bag and begins to walk away.
SERV. 2	But *I've* got the horse. *I'll* be back first.
SERV. 1	Splash me and you're buggered.
SERV. 2	Orders are orders. Ride like hell when you see them. They want to come out to meet her.
SERV. 1	Like a flock of laced-up crows.
SERV. 2	What'd she do for them, for God's sake?
SERV. 1	Snuffed it, didn't she? Wasn't that enough?
SERV. 2	Not so sure. It was safer with her there. *(Pause)* I'd keep clear of old King Long-legs if I was you.
SERV. 1	Always have.
	A shabbily dressed traveller [Hagin] approaches the crossroads.
	Here, where you goin'?
HAGIN	Geddington.
SERV. 1	What d'you want there?
HAGIN	That's my business.
SERV. 2	Don't I know you?
HAGIN	It's possible. Hagin of Northampton.
SERV. 1	A bloody Jew! But there ain't no bloody Jews. They've all gone.
SERV. 2	Unless he's converted.
SERV. 1	*(To Hagin)* Take the easy way, did you?
HAGIN	Our way is never easy. Don't you know that?
SERV. 1	*(Slyly)* For a mark you can walk wiv me.
HAGIN	How if I lent it to you?
SERV. 1	Heh! Heh! That's good. For that I'll let you walk behind, Jew, for free.
	They set off for the Royal Hunting Lodge, leaving the second servant pacing up and down and rubbing his hands together. The stage darkens.

SCENE TWO

[An hour later] The stage lightens upon the reception room in the Royal Hunting Lodge. The previously rich furnishings seem less colourful. Voices outside suggest that a crowd has gathered to greet the funeral cortège.

BEREWYK	It is said, Alicia, that the King is angry.
ALICIA	Angry? At what?
BEREWYK	That on her deathbed the Queen chose to repent. The scales tipped in favour of her conscience.
ALICIA	Just in time then. *(Pause)* Were *you* an agent, de Berewyk?
BEREWYK	No Alicia, not an agent. A mathematician, a conjurer; one who did what was necessary to keep the lady afloat. *That* work was done by others. And the King will make them pay. What tarnishes her image affects the construction of his memory.
ALICIA	I saw my uncle outside. They say he has kept his precious manor.
BEREWYK	Yes, strange the Queen decided not to pursue it. The fever must have dulled her thirst for acquisition. Anyway, Sir Richard will be happy.
ALICIA	On the contrary. He is not.
BEREWYK	Why?
ALICIA	Because the Jew Hagin was deported.
	The clattering of hooves is heard outside. The second servant enters in haste.
SERV. 2	They approach the crossroads, Sir.
BEREWYK	Come, Alicia. It's time to meet them.
ALICIA	I would rather stay…
	Berewyk grabs her arm roughly and pulls her out of the room.
	The stage darkens. After a few moments it lightens

on the same scene. The room is as it was but is now empty. Noises outside, including the neighing of horses, suggest that the funeral cortège has arrived.

There is a sudden clamour outside, building up to a vicious crescendo, which partly subsides. After a few seconds Berewyk enters with Redwell. Both are agitated. They are followed by two servants supporting the bloodied figure of Hagin. Alicia then enters, looking frightened.

REDWELL   *(To Alicia)* They pushed him under the wheels. Animals!

BEREWYK   Here, sit him down.

                The servants lower Hagin into a chair.

REDWELL   Gently, gently.

BEREWYK   *(To Hagin)* Why have you returned from France?

HAGIN   From France? France, you say? *(Incredulously)* You do not know?

BEREWYK   You were deported to France. Why have you returned?

HAGIN   All drowned. All my family.

REDWELL   Ohhh.

BEREWYK   Where were they drowned?

HAGIN   Three hours out of Queenborough.

REDWELL   The boat sank?

HAGIN   It abandoned us.

BEREWYK   Go on.

HAGIN   I swam, for hours, until a boat came by. And then walked. Here.

BEREWYK   A preposterous story. *(To servants, unsympathetically)* Take him to the guardroom and clean him up.

                The servants carry Hagin out of the room.

REDWELL   I'll go with him.

BEREWYK	No, you will not.
REDWELL	I must insist on…
	Berewyk claps his hand and two guards enter.
BEREWYK	Take Sir Richard to the solar and keep him there.
	The guards accompany Redwell from the room.
ALICIA	Why so harsh?
BEREWYK	I will not have the King troubled.
	Raised voices are heard outside.
ALICIA	I think he's arrived.
	King Edward and his party of several courtiers [who have been following behind the funeral cortege] enter.
EDWARD	Why the rabble outside? You look like frightened rabbits. Is something amiss?
BEREWYK	A slight accident, Sire. No-one of consequence.
EDWARD	But is our lady safe?
BEREWYK	In the chapel, Sire. The candles are lit. Your majesty will dine simply before he pays respect?
EDWARD	That was my wish.
	Alicia and the courtiers exit, leaving the King and Berewyk mid-stage.
	That little fracas…
BEREWYK	You may put it from your mind.
EDWARD	We are *all* of consequence, Berewyk. *(Pause)* You remember how the Queen concerned herself with her household down to the lowest gardener? Each one! She treated each one like a younger brother or sister. And her generosity. I used to trip over their carpets because, having none of my own, I was unpractised in that art. How could so rough a man find such a treasure, Berewyk. Tell me that.
BEREWYK	My lady had…
EDWARD	No, let me go on. It eases my mind to talk to

someone who was her... who knew her well. *(Placing his hand on Berewyk's arm)* Things that came to light before she died, Berewyk, vicious things, said by people waiting for the fever to silence her. I would have cursed them, Berewyk, and worse, but for what she told me at that last hateful hour, *(distraught)* before those beautiful eyes closed. What is the truth, Berewyk? No one else will tell me.

BEREWYK   Sire, if fault there was it lay in giving too trusting rein to others. If the zeal of her bailiffs seems excessive now...

EDWARD   But she had incomes for a queen – the estates royal and the queen-gold.

BEREWYK   Hardly enough, Sire, considering...

EDWARD   Enough? Surely!

The King and Berewyk exit and the stage darkens, then lightens again. Alicia is putting something into a cupboard. Redwell emerges from the shadows.

REDWELL   Alice, a word.

ALICIA   Not now. I'm busy.

REDWELL   This is more important.

ALICIA   Than serving the King? That sounds risky. These rooms are like sea-shells against the ear.

REDWELL   Just believe me.

ALICIA   What do you want?

REDWELL   Help Hagin. He's hurt badly.

ALICIA   What's he to me? Go yourself.

REDWELL   They stop me. Just some water... and a cloth... and perhaps...

ALICIA   *(Not unkindly)* Sentimental old fool.

REDWELL   Alice, please! One day you will understand. But one day, not now. Now is too dangerous. *(As an afterthought)* Your mistress would have wished it.

ALICIA	Sounds mysterious. I like mysteries. So, like a good little niece, I obey.

As she exits the stage darkens.

SCENE THREE

[Early evening] A bare room – hardly more than a cell – in which Hagin, still in bloody and torn clothes, is lying on a narrow pallet, beside which is a blanket. Alicia enters carrying a towel and a bowl.

ALICIA	Hagin, can you hear me?
HAGIN	*(Rolling slowly onto his side to face her)* Difficult… to speak.
ALICIA	Then don't try.

> *She offers him water to drink from the bowl, then uses it to wash his face.*

What possessed you to come here?

HAGIN	To find you.
ALICIA	Me?
HAGIN	Yes.
ALICIA	Why me?
HAGIN	To tell you.
ALICIA	Tell me what?

> *Hagin grimaces in pain.*

Jew, don't die on me. Promise you'll not die on me.

HAGIN	You care about me then?
ALICIA	No. Yes. Why should I?
HAGIN	You see no thread between us?
ALICIA	No! My uncle was the only thread.
HAGIN	Think! What colour are my eyes, Alice? And my hair? Not the grey. *(Weakly)* Not the grey.

123

ALICIA   Are you delerious?

HAGIN   *(Grasping her arm)* Answer!

ALICIA   All right. Black. Brown, anyway. I don't know.

HAGIN   And yours?

ALICIA   I'll not have you upsetting yourself.

HAGIN   And yo…?

> *He appears to lose consciousness. She covers him with the blanket. Berewyk appears in the doorway and pauses to assess the situation.*

BEREWYK   Is he asleep?

ALICIA   He sleeps.

> *Berewyk steps forward and looks down upon Hagin*

BEREWYK   The sleep of life – or of death. It makes no difference now.

ALICIA   What do you mean?

BEREWYK   You know the penalty – for disobeying the expulsion. The King will make no exception. I heard him promise that to the Dowager Queen.

ALICIA   Evil witch! I…

> *Berewyk instantly claps his hand over her mouth.*

BEREWYK   God still your tongue, woman.

> *He leads her to the door.*

            It seems he walked all the way from London. A few pieces of root in his coat pocket. Did he speak to you? Say anything at all?

ALICIA   He seemed fascinated by my eyes.

BEREWYK   Aren't we all. *(Softly)* Aren't we all. *(Pause)* Nothing else?

ALICIA   Nothing.

BEREWYK   Then we'll probably never know, will we?

> *He walks towards the door, stops, turns and speaks without looking at her.*

I wish you both peace.

Alicia follows him to the door, confused, then walks back towards Hagin. As she does so Redwell enters warily.

REDWELL   I thought he'd never go.

Seeing Hagin, he walks briskly to him and stoops over him.

Ohh… my poor friend.

Redwell lifts the blanket and part of Hagin's tunic, exposing his wounds.

Alice, you see what the wheel has done. He must be bleeding inside, his face is so pale. Look Alice.

ALICIA   I don't want to look.

REDWELL   You should.

ALICIA   I can't

REDWELL   There's no hope now. *(Rising to his feet)* So… did he speak to you?

ALICIA   A few words.

REDWELL   Was there… an understanding… between you?

ALICIA   No. No… I don't know what you mean.

REDWELL   Yet your eyes tell me differently.

Alicia, tearful, turns away from him. Redwell follows and takes her shoulders. She does not resist.

ALICIA   What would you have me do?

REDWELL   You could… take his hand and squeeze it.

He bends down beside Hagin and takes his hand.

My friend, can you feel your hand?

HAGIN   Mm.

REDWELL   *(To Alicia)* I believe he can.

Alicia approaches Hagin and slowly kneels beside him. She gingerly lifts his hand, as if to comply, but then suddenly thrusts it away and stands up.

ALICIA   No, no, no! I'll have no part of this. You want to
          brand me like an ox for slaughter.

          Alicia rushes towards the door.

REDWELL   Alice! Stop.

          Alicia stops at the door, trembling.

          Stay a moment longer. *(Pause)* This great black
          cloud over us…

ALICIA   Which…

REDWELL   Shhh… Which we cannot speak of and must banish
          for ever from our minds. *(Pause)* Hm. I once met
          a knight returning from the crusade. No ordinary
          knight, this one. Dark, like you. He'd mastered
          the language of Arabia and they'd used him as a
          spy. Sometimes he would encounter another of his
          kind, and would mark the sand at his feet with his
          staff, and the other would respond likewise, then
          they'd scuff it away with their feet. There was no
          need for words, and they'd pass on. It was a token
          of… understanding.

ALICIA   *(Turning away, icily)* There's always been an
          understanding.

REDWELL   Oh?

ALICIA   After Aunt Katharine died, when he and you
          would hide behind the window to watch me play,
          or creep into my room to gloat over me when I
          pretended to be asleep. That was not the behaviour
          of a friend, Uncle.

REDWELL   But you were only a child when Katharine died.

ALICIA   And why did you never marry, Uncle? That might
          have been a solution for us both.

REDWELL   I think you know the answer to that.

ALICIA   *(Slight attempt at humour)* Well, no-one wants a
          wastrel and a drunkard, that's for sure.

REDWELL   You'd be surprised to know that some actually did.

ALICIA	Yet you persisted with your ridiculous fantasy.
REDWELL	How would you have known that?
ALICIA	*(Quoting poem)* 'Your gift of summer light warms the stone/On which your image deep and dear/ Neath lichenous crusts engraved lies/And hidden from unseeing eyes/Awaits...'
REDWELL	*(Alarmed)* Where did you find that?
ALICIA	By chance, amongst your papers.
REDWELL	You had no right...
ALICIA	Then one day, before the Queen left for Gascony...
REDWELL	What?
ALICIA	... I showed it to her.
REDWELL	You did what?

Alicia deliberately stays silent.

What was...

ALICIA	Her reaction? She thought it beautiful. It made her cry.
REDWELL	And then?
ALICIA	I said she should keep it.
REDWELL	Then why didn't she?
ALICIA	I don't know.
REDWELL	She must have said something.
ALICIA	Something about false hopes, and destinies. I was too young to understand.
REDWELL	*(Suddenly becoming distraught)* I can't bear this. How can I live without a dream. I've no family. I've no money, or what I have goes to grasping fraudsters with their unreasonable odds and sky-high interest... *(Pointing to Hagin)* And my only refuge lies dying on the floor...
ALICIA	Then why don't you...
REDWELL	Change? Because gambling's a drug, Alice. An

intoxication that binds my senses and occupies my waking hours, so that those other thoughts can only batter at the cage and for a little while can be held at bay. But when night comes, those bars are prized apart and in they come, like sweet-faced serpents, and entwine themselves into… her image. *(Sobbing)* I've tried, Alice. God knows I've tried. *(Pointing at Hagin)* As he knows. Has always known. Whenever it's gone too far, there he was. Vegetables appearing in the kitchen. Meat in the ice-house when there was none. A horse magicing itself into the stable only hours after mine was to the knackers. And so on and so on.

ALICIA   I had… not realised.

REDWELL   So. You see where the finger of destiny points, Alice. And why death beckons.

ALICIA   But you have no faith, Uncle. What can death offer you?

REDWELL   Oh, I still have faith… in an afterlife.

ALICIA   But there would be… conditions.

REDWELL   Yes! My last great gamble, Alice. For the only prize I ever wanted.

ALICIA   *(Incredulous)* You think that way you'll find her?

REDWELL   Alice, I have nothing further to lose.

> *Alicia turns to face him with her arms held wide, submissively.*

ALICIA   Look, Uncle. Look hard. What do you see?

REDWELL   A beautiful young girl.

ALICIA   As all men do. And compared with her… your dream?

REDWELL   Oh, lovelier by far.

ALICIA   Then draw back from those insane thoughts.

REDWELL   And?

ALICIA   Use *me*. To pull yourself back. Do it whatever way you like. Kindness, lust, my mind, my body. They're all yours. There must be *something* in *me* that can replace her?

REDWELL   And render your life worthless like my own?

ALICIA   Worth? I have no worth. What's passed between these legs *(indicating with her hand)* has seen to that.

Hagin, aware, is seen to be struggling on his litter.

REDWELL   We have all committed… indiscretions.

ALICIA   Not like mine, you haven't. Your dream was that something unattainable might just be grasped. *(Pause)* You want to know what I dreamed of? Every day, until your Eleanor's death broke the cycle? You want to hear?

REDWELL   I don't think I…

ALICIA   No, I'll spare you that. *(Pause)* But when she'd gone I came to dread the emptiness, and those long heavy strides of his night after night stopping at my door. I invented excuses – any excuses – to keep him away. I even…

REDWELL   I don't want to hear.

ALICIA   I even made young Edward sick, by feeding him… Oh, God help me… *(pause)*… so that I did not have to go to *him*. *(Pause)* But you see, I was too late.

Hagin, with great effort, raises himself on an elbow.

HAGIN   Ohhhh.

He falls back into unconsciousness. Redwell and Alicia both stare at him. Redwell bends down and feels Hagin's forehead, then wipes it with the towel and rearranges the blanket.

REDWELL   We should have spared you that. Forgive us our selfishness.

Berewyk appears in the doorway.

BEREWYK   Still here, Alicia? Sir Richard…

               Redwell stands back defensively.

               … don't be alarmed. I'm not quite without
               compassion. *(Pause)* Alicia, the King waits for you at
               table. Sir Richard, I have indicated that… you will
               join us. *(Looking towards Hagin)* Is he comfortable?

REDWELL   We've done what we can.

BEREWYK   Come then.

               *Redwell follows Berewyk, but stops at the door and
               looks back at Alicia, who is still contemplating Hagin.*

REDWELL   *(To Alicia)* Can you not bring yourself…

               *Alicia, in deep torment, slowly turns her head from
               side to side, rejecting his suggestion against her better
               judgement.*

               The stage darkens.

SCENE FOUR

*[Late evening] The interior of the chapel. The Queen's bier rests on a podium
surrounded by candles, before the altar left stage. Centre stage are a couple of
chairs and to their left a wooden bench, which would be for the use of servants.
At the rear is an archway [leading to the Lodge] and through it darkness.
Above the archway is a small balcony. Alicia is kneeling before the podium,
motionless, candle in hand.*

ALICIA   It's so cold! The air enters my lungs like an
               assassin's knife. *(Pulling her cloak about herself)*
               They took your heart, didn't they? And other bits.
               So there's not much left but memories of your
               footsteps on these flags, and your voice to brighten
               my day. *(Pause)* But I still have your child to care
               for. Question is, will old spider-legs trust me with
               his son? *(Pause)* As for Uncle Richard, how hard

he tried, that man. Keeping that wretched manor – for years – and all for fear of losing your attention. *(Pause)* Oh, Ma'am. Why didn't you take greater care, when I told you, and stay here rather than that ice-box of a house at Clipstone. What need had politics of you? What use had the King for you? *(Pause)* But I didn't come to babble at your coffin. *(Almost enthusiastically)* It's this Jew, you see. You wanted to help him, didn't you, and if I hadn't… *(long pause, near to tears)* He's condemned, you see, and old spider-legs will show no mercy. So I need your help. *(Pause)* Uncle Richard tells me to see him and I go. And what do I see but a bloody mess. How can you relate to that? And then he asked me questions, when surely his mind was on other things.

> *Alicia leans forward against a chair in an attitude of prayer. As the stage slowly darkens her body slumps to the ground, as if she has fallen asleep. From almost, but not quite, total darkness the stage lightens. Alicia rises and makes to leave the chapel. She passes the archway at the rear and a voice from its depths addresses her. The light is now sufficient to reveal the King, whom we presume has been standing there awhile.*

EDWARD Alicia, stay.

ALICIA *(Standing still but not turning)* Surely you would rather be alone.

EDWARD Alone! Never wish that, Alicia, on anyone. It is the worst of all torments. The very worst. My father once told me that to kill in war was kindness because it released that very tribulation in so many men. I called him a fool. I would not do so now. *(Pause)* Kneel with me, Alicia, in one last prayer before you go.

> *They kneel*

	I miss her so.
ALICIA	You are not alone in that.
EDWARD	No... no. You were very close.
ALICIA	Very close.
EDWARD	You know the worst thing: no-one mentions her. It's all 'your great misfortune, Sire,' 'our condolencies, Sire, on your grievous loss.' What need have I of their pity? What need other than to hear her name, just once, from normal lips speaking love or respect. Is that so difficult for them?
ALICIA	If they'd heard her last words to me they might...
EDWARD	Words? What words? Say them to me.
ALICIA	That her love for you would continue in heaven.
EDWARD	And then?
ALICIA	And then she fell down coughing, and begged me not to tell anyone she felt death approaching.
EDWARD	Why did she not tell me?
ALICIA	To spare you pain.
EDWARD	But we shared everything. Alicia, you know that.
ALICIA	Certainly most things.
EDWARD	Why only most things?
ALICIA	We are no two of us equal in all things.
EDWARD	In what things were we not equal?
ALICIA	Sire, I spoke out of turn.
EDWARD	You did not. You had something in mind. Tell!
ALICIA	Perhaps... perhaps it was her compassion. It lighted those around her. Like a beacon. None was her equal in that.
EDWARD	Hm, that fool Redwell would not have said so.
ALICIA	Why?
EDWARD	You should have seen his face at dinner.

ALICIA   *(Seeing an opportunity)* What was his problem, then?

EDWARD   The bloody Jew.

ALICIA   Well now, there's an example.

EDWARD   Of what?

ALICIA   Of her compassion. *She* tried to help him.

EDWARD   *(Beginning to see the drift)* I will not retract, Alicia. It was all made clear. If they're found, they die.

ALICIA   The Dowager's very words.

EDWARD   Meaning?

         There are faint sounds from the vicinity of the bier.

         What's that?

ALICIA   Rats.

EDWARD   Then the rat man will suffer.

ALICIA   There. Another example.

EDWARD   Enough of this impertinence. You'd better leave. As you say, it is better to be alone.

         They hear the sound again. The audience, but not the players, see young Edward's head appear above the balcony.

         There it is again *(Looking at the bier, then upwards)* It seemed to come from... But it's not unusual for the night to bring strange manifestations. *(Seeing Alicia shiver)* Child, you are cold. You would be better in bed.

ALICIA   Bed would only worsen the condition.

EDWARD   That supposition might be challenged. But now is not the time.

         Footsteps are heard on the shingle path outside the chapel. The King and Alicia shrink into the shadows. The door of the chapel flies open and Redwell enters unsteadily. He is drunk and looks around with glazed eyes.

REDWELL   A riddle: what is death? Answer: an armful of clothes to be tossed aside, likely to be remembered longer than their owner. Whatever, this place reeks of it. *(Breathing deeply)* Mmm. *(Pause)* What did she do, that girl masquerading as *my* flesh and blood? She would not *accept*, that's what. *(Pause)* Still, it all flies before my greater hurt, my greater purpose.

EDWARD   What is the fool saying? Is he drunk?

ALICIA   Shhh.

REDWELL   Take the King's position, Sir Knight. It is to your advantage, Sir Knight, do you not see?

    He skips on the chequered floor, as on a chessboard.

    One step, two steps and one step and ... psh. I confront the King.

    The manoeuvre has brought him face to face with the King, whom he barely sees and does not recognise.

    And that evening at Easingbourne? Too feeble to take her as a friend and tell. And too proud and stupid to run after her.

EDWARD   I do not like what I do not understand. This has the scent of treachery.

ALICIA   I think it's time to leave.

EDWARD   You'd withdraw now. That smells of complicity.

ALICIA   As you please. Then listen.

REDWELL   *(Unknowingly taking up the suggestion)* Listen? There is no reason on earth for me to listen.

    With tremendous willpower he walks unsteadily to the bier, touching it affectionately.

REDWELL   I wanted to ask you.

    In the following exchanges we hear Eleanor's voice in Redwell's imagination. It is heard by the audience but not, we assume, by the other players.

EL. VOICE   About a blinded knight?

REDWELL	You spoke of a child's infatuation.
EDWARD	*(To Alicia)* Is the fool talking to himself?
ALICIA	Shhh…
EL. VOICE	Infatuation? You think that what stalked half my womanhood can be dismissed as something so trivial as infatuation?
REDWELL	*(Incredulously)* Then what was *my* role?
EL. VOICE	You had his eyes, you see, just as I remembered them at the tourney, and the same rake of the jaw. *(Pause)* And something about the way his body gave itself to the hewn logs, blind as he was.
REDWELL	You transferred that affection to me?
EL. VOICE	No. Do not delude yourself.
REDWELL	Surely, there was no delusion.
EL. VOICE	You must not pursue such thoughts.
REDWELL	Why?
EL. VOICE	You must not!
REDWELL	So that last evening at Easingbourne, when all…
EL. VOICE	The thought of death concentrates a lifetime of memories. Love and guilt – all mixed up, as bubbles rising to the surface of the mire, only to burst… What they contain… *(voice tails away)*

> *Redwell wanders towards the door. As he does so, young Edward's head appears above the balcony, again visible only to the audience.*

REDWELL	*(Turning; loudly, resentfully)* And Easingbourne. Didn't anyone ever tell you that Alice was Hagin's daughter? And that's why the debt was paid. *(In despair)* Ohhh…

> *He staggers out of the chapel.*
>
> *The King rises and goes to the bier, looking at the spot where it was touched, brushing it with his own hand.*

135

EDWARD   Those words, for all their incoherence. They had
              the menace of a cloud of arrows. And no hand
              delivered a more gentle touch than his.

ALICIA   But it seems you had *another* rival.

EDWARD   Oh?

ALICIA   I mean the knight – at the tourney.

EDWARD   (*Long pause, then loudly and emotionally, as if so that
              Eleanor could hear*) His side was pierced – (*indicating
              with hand*) here, but not deeply.

ALICIA   You remember?

EDWARD   As if it were yesterday.

ALICIA   You amaze me.

EDWARD   I followed him to the surgeon's tent.

              *He suddenly grabs Alicia's hair, forcing her head back
              violently while he acts out his words.*

              It's done with needles – fine red hot needles the
              length of your little finger – right to the back of the
              eye.

ALICIA   How could you know such things?

EDWARD   (*Shamefully*) I… had experience.

ALICIA   You have a butcher's mind.

              They slump back into their seats.

EDWARD   So my wife *was* unfaithful to me. Alicia?

ALICIA   Far less than we to her.

EDWARD   Redwell shall die, nevertheless.

              *The King rises abruptly and leaves the chapel. Alicia
              makes to follow. Faint scuffling noises are heard in the
              vicinity of the bier. Alicia stops and turns.*

ALICIA   Who's there?

              *An unidentifiable figure steps forward from the
              shadows. Alicia assumes it is Eleanor's ghost. Only
              later will she see that it is the Dowager Queen.*

DOWAGER   Don't you recognise me, Alicia?

ALICIA   Are you the answer to my prayer?

DOWAGER   Perhaps that is in your mind, Alicia. A product of guilt and remorse. Whether it is or it isn't we are alone. What is it you want?

ALICIA   Forgiveness. That I caused you so much pain, because I was blinded by vanity and ambition.

DOWAGER   Did you not enjoy the King's favour?

ALICIA   At first.

DOWAGER   And then?

ALICIA   From the heights the view was beautiful, until the clouds rolled in. My body was never meant for lust. *(Pause)* Then I…

DOWAGER   Came to your senses?

ALICIA   Yes.

DOWAGER   And now?

ALICIA   The King has… other diversions.

DOWAGER   Were you not warned that the slopes were precipitous?

ALICIA   *(Dimly remembering the Dowager's previous words)* What? What did you say?

DOWAGER   No matter. *(Pause)* We're digressing. Aren't you here because down one of those corridors lies a Jew poised between life and death. *(Lightly)* And all because you stole some letters.

ALICIA   I stole nothing. I just gave them to the Dowager Queen to see and pass on. I meant no harm.

DOWAGER   *So* trusting. *(Pause)*. But there are wider issues, are there not, than the fate of the Jew? There was a rumour…

ALICIA   What rumour?

DOWAGER   That the mistress of easement reported on your waters. It is easily enough done.

ALICIA   And I suppose the flowers stopped.

DOWAGER   There were no more flowers.

ALICIA   So what if I am with child?

DOWAGER   Oh, that's of little moment. The history of kings is littered with bastards. *(Pause)* Those eyes of yours, that black hair. What was it, Alicia, that the Jew asked you, in spite of his pain?

ALICIA   How could you know…

DOWAGER   Did I not once tell you I made it my business to know such things.

ALICIA   *(Confused)* You do not speak like my lady Eleanor. Your mind has coarsened.

> *The figure of the Dowager Queen emerges slowly from the shadows. She moves swiftly towards Alicia as if to embrace her, but as they draw apart a yellow ribbon is seen to be attached to Alicia's gown.*

DOWAGER   *(Laughing)* Perhaps it's time to strike another bargain, Alicia.

> *Alicia sees the ribbon. Screaming, she tries unsuccessfully to tear it off. As she runs from the chapel, she trips over a body (now illuminated for the first time). She runs on, then turns back, realising that it is Redwell. His throat is cut. She approaches slowly and kneels beside him, lifting his head.*

ALICIA   This because of me? Is infatuation held within the mind a capital crime?

EL. VOICE   *(From the direction of the chapel)* It was not the crime, Alicia. His crime was insignificant. It was a warning… *(tails away)*

ALICIA   Ohhh!

> *Alicia slumps to the ground. For several seconds nothing happens. Then she slowly rises, composed and resolute, and looks down.*

Are you with her now, Uncle? I pray that you are, but how I fear for you.

Alicia stands and wipes away a tear. She looks in the direction of the departed Dowager Queen then, realising something, sets off after her.

SCENE FIVE

[A few minutes later] Hagin's cell. The Dowager Queen enters and walks slowly towards him. He looks terrified.

DOWAGER   So. Cheating me still.

HAGIN   As best I can.

DOWAGER   Your eyes scan my vestments. A knife, you think, concealed here? Yes, well it might. But I know death when I see it, Hagin; and I will preserve the blade's shine. *(Pause)* Sir Richard tells me… correction… told me…

HAGIN   He's… dead?

DOWAGER   Like a poleaxed sheep.

HAGIN   Ohhh.

DOWAGER   … told me that you survived the deportation. Would you like congratulations… or…

HAGIN   *(Rallying)* What do you want?

DOWAGER   I want to know *how*!

HAGIN   *(Distantly, speaking with great difficulty)* We caught the noon tide. There were whole families, packed into every cranny and crevice. My wife and family – we were nine. The rest were to follow. But we were in good enough spirits. The sun even shone upon us. We are, if not a forgiving, at least a resilient, people.

DOWAGER   Indeed you are.

HAGIN   The trouble began when we reached open sea. First the children were sick. There were no facilities. And we could see the weather was changing – great black clouds far out to sea. Then we passed some sandbanks. It could even have been our suggestion, but anyhow they took us off, in little boats – oh so careful to keep our families intact – and set us down. What could be more reasonable than to clear up the ship and let us move our legs.

DOWAGER   Too reasonable, I'd say.

HAGIN   Soon little sand-houses began to appear along the water's edge where the children played.

DOWAGER   And then?

HAGIN   I cannot get from my mind that the ship stayed – should want to stay. They had to be sure, I suppose. *(Pause)* As the water rose and the waves lashed our bodies, it stayed. And all our screams were met with ridicule and blasphemies. *(Pause)* I was alone when they set sail.

DOWAGER   But the captain had strict orders…

HAGIN   You knew about it?

DOWAGER   In my realm nothing happens without my knowledge, my control.

HAGIN   Your realm? You still think you are… *(Incredulous)* You ordered it?

DOWAGER   I did what was necessary. You thought you could convert by filling in papers and sinking to one knee in front of… *(contemptuously)* my daughter-in-law. Where in that was Christ and his great mysteries. It was blasphemy! And the Church has no place for blasphemers.

    Alicia emerges from the shadows. She is still wearing the yellow ribbon.

140

ALICIA	Or compassion?
DOWAGER	*(Seeing her)* Ah, the fallen child. And your uncle's… condition?
ALICIA	At least he died with friends.
DOWAGER	A good thing he didn't delay, then, for the chances are *you'll* see no more sunsets. *(Indicating Hagin)* And he certainly won't.
ALICIA	So you've told the King.
DOWAGER	It's a mother's duty to protect her son. Goodnight to you.

> *The Dowager Queen exits. Alicia approaches Hagin and kneels beside him.*

HAGIN	Alice?
ALICIA	*(With teasing humour)* You walked from the Thames to find *me*. You must have been mad.
HAGIN	You would have had me swim to France?
ALICIA	Once, maybe. *(Indicating the yellow ribbon)* Can you see this?
HAGIN	No, Alice, no!
ALICIA	And that I wear it with pride.
HAGIN	Give it to me.

> *Hagin desperately snatches the ribbon and tries to put it under his body.*

ALICIA	Later, then. *(Taking his hand)* Now, here, on my belly. Can you feel it – your grandson?
HAGIN	That is… good, Alice… goo..

> *Hagin slumps back onto his bed and dies.*
>
> *Outside there is a clattering of hooves as a carriage departs. Berewyk enters and rushes to the window.*

ALICIA	What's that?
BEREWYK	The Dowager Queen.
ALICIA	Leaving?

BEREWYK	That surprises you?
ALICIA	Yes.
BEREWYK	*(Looking down at Hagin's body)* Maybe she considers her work is done. Or, looking at you now, senses her efforts have failed.
ALICIA	Mm?
BEREWYK	*(Sniffing)* The air. Is it not already clearer?
ALICIA	You think she was something more than…
BEREWYK	That's not for us to know. *(Pause)* But as for your unborn child – you are in danger, Alicia.
ALICIA	I've accepted my life must end.
BEREWYK	Nonsense. You have everything to live for. A little deception is all that's needed.
ALICIA	And you, de Berewyk? How is it with you?
BEREWYK	Yesterday was my fortieth birthday. And it made me think there were lines to be drawn. Your uncle's infatuation was not an example I should follow. *(Pause)* As for your child, Alicia. If the King should offer you a choice… be receptive.
ALICIA	I should thank you.
BEREWYK	And you can do it by letting me to show you to where you will be safe tonight.

> *Berewyk notices the yellow ribbon beside Hagin's body.*

Strange. How did he come by that?

ALICIA	The Dowager Queen was here.
BEREWYK	Ah, vindictive to the end.

> *Berewyk picks up the yellow ribbon and begins to put it in his pocket, unaware of its history.*

ALICIA	May I… have it?

> *Berewyk shrugs and gives it to her.*

BEREWYK	Now, tomorrow the cortège departs and more

snow could hinder us. We should try, at least, to get some sleep.

They exit and the stage darkens.

SCENE SIX

[The following morning] The reception room of the Royal Hunting Lodge. The windows and door are open and through them we can make out the bustle of preparations for the departure of the funeral cortège. Front-stage, several figures in black, mostly ecclesiastical, are preparing for the departure. They file out through the main door, revealing Alicia, dressed in black and sitting on a chair. She is clutching her bear Bonito and looking disconsolate. Berewyk enters.

BEREWYK   Come Alicia, you have a duty to see your mistress on her way.

ALICIA   A few moments longer, then I'll come.

    Berewyk makes to leave, then turns.

BEREWYK   You did what could for the... for Hagin. That didn't pass unnoticed. And I'm truly sorry about your Uncle Richard.

ALICIA   At least he's spared the pain of seeing her go.

    Berewyk looks at Alicia in puzzlement, which turns to understanding. The King enters.

BEREWYK   *(Touching Alicia's shoulder)* I have to go. They're almost ready and I must leave with them. *(Seeing the King)* Sire.

    The King approaches Alicia and touches the back of the chair next to her.

EDWARD   May I?

ALICIA   Of course.

    He sits beside her.

EDWARD   We've shared many things, haven't we, Alicia?

143

ALICIA	*(Embarrassed, looking down)* Mm.
EDWARD	Many things. *(Pause)* To come to the point. My mother told me there have been no flowers. It is true, then, that you are with child?
ALICIA	It is true.
EDWARD	And a child of a special kind? You understand why I do not speak directly.
ALICIA	*(Fearful and trembling)* It is possible.
EDWARD	You tremble. And rightly. But no, death does not become you, Alicia. Though it is the alternative to what I have in mind. *(Pause)* Besides, death has been so often too facile a solution. I am weary of it.
ALICIA	I am grateful. And the child?
EDWARD	De Berewyk's wife is barren. I saw in that a solution. She must never know its origin. I have told de Berewyk only… that there will be a child.
ALICIA	And me?
EDWARD	You're to Rockingham. A position there with… oh, I forget who. De Berewyk will give you details.
ALICIA	And after?
EDWARD	A burden you will have to bear. *(Rising)* Come, we must go.
	The King exits through the main door. Alicia rises but hangs back. Berewyk enters.
BEREWYK	*(Making excuse)* I was… um… looking for young Edward. He ought to pay his final respects.
ALICIA	I haven't seen him.
BEREWYK	I expect he'll turn up.
ALICIA	*(Attempting humour)* He usually does.
BEREWYK	Yes. *(Embarrassed silence)* You'll follow, then?
ALICIA	Yes.

Berewyk exits. Alicia begins to sob, silently, to herself. After several seconds Berewyk returns, entering cautiously.

BEREWYK   I... um... thought I should tell you... My wife...

ALICIA   I know. She is unwell.

BEREWYK   What I'm trying to say is... well... one day there will be no-one to care for the child. *(Pause)* The future is not without hope, Alicia. Can you can be patient?

ALICIA   But the King would never...

BEREWYK   Let you return? Kings, like us, are mortal. And this one is... well... no longer young.

ALICIA   I can be patient, de Berewyk.

BEREWYK   Good. Come then.

Berewyk puts his arm around her shoulders as they begin to walk towards the door.

(Brightly) Do you remember last summer, when the royal party came to Geddington? Not a single cloud in the sky. How little we knew. *(Pause)* Oh, I'd almost forgotten. The manor of Easingbourne. Am I right in thinking that – besides yourself – your uncle Richard had no near relatives?

ALICIA   I'm sure I'm the only one.

BEREWYK   Good... good... you see, it needs a woman's touch.

They reach the open door.

ALICIA   Look. Sunlight on the snow.

BEREWYK   And the King's already mounted...

Alicia exits but Berewyk lingers. At that moment young Edward enters side stage. He sees Alicia's abandoned bear and picks it up.

BEREWYK   So, young Edward. Have you paid your last respects to your mother?

Edward scuttles to Berewyk's side and on tiptoe whispers into his ear.

You heard her? My, you were privileged. *(Smiling down at the boy, playing along)* Did anyone else, I wonder?

Alicia appears in the frame of the open door, standing motionless, back to the room. Edward points at her accusingly.

Well, Edward, when they've gone you can tell me all about it. Come then.

They exit, the door closes behind them and the stage darkens.

END

THE WOMAN BELOW

Characters:

    Charlie Westcroft – skilled factory worker – thirties
    Nellie Westcroft – housewife – thirties
    Gordon Hogway – upper class – late thirties
    Elaine Bradley – Gordon's elegant partner – thirties
    Sarah Bradley – Elaine's daughter – late teens
    Desmond Finch – local reporter
    Police officers
    Dimitri – Soviet agent

Place – A top-floor (attic) room in a four-storey Victorian house in West London

Time – Early 1950s

ACT ONE

SCENE ONE

[Friday evening] A large but sparsely furnished attic room, sink and cooker in one corner, a single bar electric fire in fireplace against back wall, clock on wall, sofa, table with a table-lamp and a couple of chairs centre stage. Right stage a door (to stairs down) and left stage a door to a bedroom (not visible to the audience). A black telephone of the period sits on a low table beside the sofa. Nellie is staring at it, instructions in one hand, undecided whether to pick up the receiver.

NELLIE   *(To herself)* Oh, Charlie, why weren't you here when it came? He'll ask, have you tried it? You can't just say, no.

> *She looks at the clock, shrugs, walks to the sink, takes a tea towel and covers the telephone with it.*

Let's surprise him. *(Pause)* Friday, though. He'll have racing on his mind. *(Pause)* Lord help us.

> *There is a distant sound of a door closing and muffled footsteps on the stairs, then silence.*

(Long pause) What *are* you doing?

> *Further steps on stairs, then Charlie enters. He is dressed in working clothes, but not untidily.*

You took your time.

CHARLIE   Bumped into Ruby on the stairs.

NELLIE   What'd she want?

CHARLIE   Nothing really.

NELLIE   Must have said something.

CHARLIE   She's not told you then?

149

NELLIE	Never see her. Always lurking in her kitchen. Witch!
CHARLIE	You imagine things. Her lad in Akrotiri – desperate to come home.
NELLIE	Back to this? Thought he'd be pleased to get away, from this. Anyway, your tea's not ready yet.
CHARLIE	Why's that then?
NELLIE	Thought you might have guessed.
CHARLIE	Stop playing games. *(Pause)* What you got there? Ohh, it's come, has it?

Nellie takes away the cloth.

Black as a raven.

NELLIE	Four feet though.
CHARLIE	Calls just as loud, I'll bet. Have you tried it?
NELLIE	Couldn't think of anyone, Charlie.
CHARLIE	You could have rung TIM – for the time.
NELLIE	Oh. *(Pause)* I'll get your tea.

She moves to the oven and takes out a plate.

CHARLIE	I wonder if Mum's got her telephone yet. Be a relief if she has. Did you remember to send our number?
NELLIE	Wrote last week, as soon as we knew it. I told her ring us tonight if hers has come.
CHARLIE	She will then.
NELLIE	I hope Ruby's boy doesn't come back.
CHARLIE	Why?
NELLIE	He never cleaned the toilet. Always in there when you wanted it. Heaven knows what he was doing. And that funny smell.
CHARLIE	There *was* something else Ruby said.
NELLIE	I thought you were a long time coming up.
CHARLIE	She said… we left the light on last night, on the stairs.

NELLIE	How else can we get to the toilet?
CHARLIE	Found it on this morning. She… also said you left the bath dirty on Sunday.
NELLIE	That's a lie. She hates me, that's all. Will say anything… *(Pause)* After all you've done for her. You're always down there, fixing something. Charlie, can't we get out of here? I wasn't made to share. Get a little house somewhere? Doesn't have to be grand.
CHARLIE	I…
NELLIE	Dad may only have had a little shop. But it was ours.
CHARLIE	Be thankful we've a place at all. Everyone's after flats in London. When we've saved…
NELLIE	Saved! Saved! What can we save?
CHARLIE	Perhaps when we start a family…
NELLIE	Two years we've been trying!
CHARLIE	We will…
NELLIE	You promised me… this week… your pay-packet unopened. I'll get my box. We'll just see.

> *Nellie takes a metal money box from the table drawer, puts it on the table and holds out her hand to Charlie.*

CHARLIE	I need to…
NELLIE	What is it this weekend? Kempton… Lingfield?

> *Charlie hands her his wage packet.*

You *have* opened it. Charlie, we agreed.

> *She takes out the money and counts it.*

Two pounds down! What do I put in for the telephone?

CHARLIE	It's a dead cert. Ten to one. Jim said…
NELLIE	That Jim…

> *Nellie begins to cry.*

CHARLIE   But I've got you these.

NELLIE   What are they?

CHARLIE   Look.

Charlie withdraws a packet from his pocket. Nellie takes it and withdraws a pair of silk stockings.

Black market. First time in the factory. Thought you'd like them.

NELLIE   Oh, Charlie. Do you never learn? Can't you see... we can't afford...

The telephone rings. Charlie and Nellie look at each other, astonished.

It'll be your mother.

CHARLIE   Bloody quick off the mark, then.

NELLIE   Perhaps it's the telephone company, checking up on ours.

CHARLIE   At six-thirty?

He picks up the receiver

Charles Westcroft here. *(Pause)* I think you must have the wrong number. I don't know anyone called... how did you... my *mother* gave it to you?... of course we would be pleased to see you... and your daughter... yes, yes, all news when we see you... if you ring twice and wait for one of us to come down... goodbye, Elaine *[Charlie pronounces this 'ee-lane']*.

NELLIE   Who was it Charlie?

CHARLIE   Oh, someone. Before your time.

NELLIE   You've never mentioned an Elaine *[eelane]*.

CHARLIE   Clean forgotten about her. Mum's friend... Great War widow like her... had a girl the same age as me. When she died the child came to live with us. Then one day she went away. We were three kids already and it was difficult to cope. Never knew

152

what happened to her. Mum gave her our number.

NELLIE   That's a coincidence. When do they want to come?

CHARLIE   Tonight. Now.

NELLIE   There's no food in.

CHARLIE   She said they'd eaten.

NELLIE   And the girl. How old's she?

CHARLIE   Fifteen, she said

NELLIE   Where were they calling from?

CHARLIE   I don't know.

NELLIE   Must be nearby if they're going to get home tonight.

CHARLIE   Sorry, I really don't know.

NELLIE   I'll nip next door. See if I can borrow some eggs.

CHARLIE   While I have a wash and a shave. Still got grease all over me.

NELLIE   Charlie?

CHARLIE   Um?

NELLIE   Was she… a friend of yours?

CHARLIE   Played together sometimes. Really don't remember much about her.

> *Nellie goes out leaving Charlie feeling the stubble on his chin.*

SCENE TWO

[Half an hour later] On the radio we hear the beginning of Journey into Space. Nellie is tidying vigorously. Charlie, now smartly dressed, is straightening his tie. The doorbell rings twice.

CHARLIE   Who's going down?

NELLIE   She's your friend.

CHARLIE   Hardly.

                    He leaves the room. Nellie takes off her apron and switches off the radio.

                    Elaine, elegantly dressed, and Sarah, an attractive and bright teenager, enter, followed by Charlie. Elaine appears disappointed by what she sees.

ELAINE   What a long way up. It must keep you fit.

CHARLIE   The wife... Ne...

NELLIE   Nellie.

ELAINE   Nellie. Hello.

CHARLIE   But great views over London – and fantastic sunsets.

ELAINE   Then a pity the window's not bigger.

NELLIE   We can see the flagpole in Kew Gardens.

ELAINE   Well, that's all right then. Kew is somewhere Sarah's always wanted to go.

NELLIE   Won't you sit down, Elaine *[eelane]*?

SARAH   *(Giggling)* We all call her Elaine.

NELLIE   I'll remember.

                    Elaine sits on the sofa.

                 And Sarah?

ELAINE   She'll want to be independent.

SARAH   No I don't.

                    Sarah sits.

ELAINE   So, Charlie. What happened after the war? Your mother said you'd left the Air Force.

SARAH   Did you get shot down?

NELLIE   Charlie worked on Spitfires.

ELAINE   You mean you never flew?

CHARLIE   Not as a pilot, no.

SARAH   Gordon did.

CHARLIE   Who's Gordon?

Elaine glares at Sarah

ELAINE   Yes, I should have mentioned him. Gordon is…
             well… I suppose you'd say my fiancé.

SARAH   Mother!

ELAINE   We do *plan* to get married, dear. But, Charlie, tell
             us what happened. Why didn't you go back to
             Amberfield? Why on earth move to London?

NELLIE   We had to eat, Elaine. There were no jobs on the
             land. There were factories in London.

CHARLIE   I build engines. For buses.

NELLIE   Charlie's very skilled, you know.

ELAINE   Is he really? That's not a trait I recall.

NELLIE   So what do you… recall?

ELAINE   He's never told you?

NELLIE   No.

ELAINE   Well… we were… playmates.

NELLIE   Then how did you lose touch?

ELAINE   Oh, I shan't bore you with all that. Four children
             were too much for Charlie's mother and I was
             moved to a family in Oxford.

SARAH   Where I was brought up.

CHARLIE   Now, yesterday Nellie made a pie and I'm sure
             there's a bit left. Would you two like some? Or
             there are some eggs.

ELAINE   We would… but maybe we should wait just a…

             The telephone rings

SARAH   I bet that's…

ELAINE   It could just be for me.

             Charlie picks up the receiver

CHARLIE   Charles Westcroft… yes, she is.

             He hands the receiver to Elaine

ELAINE   Darling?… yes, yes, charming people… no, no, not

155

one little bit… no, really! You ring twice – but please don't get impatient – there are four flights of stairs… yes… A bientôt, mon ami. *(Puts phone down)*

SARAH   Don't show off, Mummy.

ELAINE   I'm not showing off, darling. It's how we speak to one another.

NELLIE   Where was Gordon calling from?

ELAINE   The nearest phone box, I expect.

CHARLIE   That's just across the road.

ELAINE   Then that's where he'll have been.

The doorbell rings twice.

Are you happy to introduce yourself, Charlie? While I talk to Nellie. It's such a long way down.

Charlie exits. Elaine rises and walks to the window.

ELAINE   Oh! Is that your garden? From the front I'd imagined a sea of concrete. No green at all.

NELLIE   It's shared, but we can all use it.

ELAINE   It's wonderful.

Footsteps on the stairs. Gordon, smartly dressed, enters, followed by Charlie.

GORDON   You know what I like about these old houses, Charles? They exude patience. A hundred and fifty years tolerating the whole spectrum of humanity. By the way, who was the lady that came out as we passed. Not a bad looker, but don't tell Elaine. *(Seeing Nellie)* You must be…

CHARLIE   The wife…

GORDON   Nell, Nellie… Nell.

NELLIE   Nellie.

GORDON   A name redolent of history and… excitement. Nell Gwynn…

ELAINE   Nellie Dean.

SARAH   Eskimo Nell.

ELAINE	No, Sarah, that's disrespectful.
GORDON	*(Quietly humming)* Dead-eyed Dick and Mexican Pete and a whore called…
SARAH	*(Mumbling)* Sorry. I couldn't think of anything else.
GORDON	No matter, I'm sure Nellie's not offended. *(Pause)* What an incredible coincidence, Charles, that Elaine should make contact with your mother just this week.
CHARLIE	Yes, I…
GORDON	Happened to be passing through Amberfield, and Elaine said, *that* is where I once lived.
CHARLIE	How did you find my mother?
GORDON	Elaine?
ELAINE	I didn't stay, Charlie. It was all so long ago.
CHARLIE	And the house was the same?
ELAINE	I… didn't actually go in…
CHARLIE	She's aged. Her memory's going. Did she remember you?
ELAINE	I'm not sure. But she gave us your number.
	Gordon is looking out of the window
GORDON	What splendid dahlias. Your handiwork, Charles?
NELLIE	The chrysants are mine, actually.
GORDON	I say, while there's daylight, why don't we take a look?
NELLIE	You've only just climbed up here.
GORDON	The exercise will do neither of us harm, Nell.
NELLIE	Well, if…
GORDON	And we promise not to disturb… what's her name?… downstairs.
CHARLIE	Ruby.
GORDON	Ruby, yes. We'll tiptoe by. Come then, mes enfants, allons-y!

They exit, but Elaine is hesitant and Charlie blocks her passage to the door.

CHARLIE   Stay a moment?

ELAINE   Of course. You'll have lots of questions.

CHARLIE   Dozens, but where to start?

ELAINE   Where I went?

CHARLIE   No. Why you made no contact.

ELAINE   *(Hesitantly)* I… tried. Nothing ever came back.

CHARLIE   I didn't know.

ELAINE   I wasn't in control. Got in with a different crowd. Then I had Sarah. *(Pause)* Surely you wondering why we're here?

CHARLIE   Well, I…

ELAINE   *(Breaking down)* We're destitute. Gordon is bankrupt. We've nothing. Just what you see. We were evicted, this morning, Charlie. Evicted!

CHARLIE   But we have no money. I bet on losers, Elaine. Didn't anyone tell you?

ELAINE   I know. That's what I've done too. But you see, I love him. *(Pause)* Somewhere to stay… for a couple of nights, while Gordon sorts himself out. He's got contacts.

CHARLIE   But don't you see what we have? Not even a proper bedroom. Look.

Charlie pushes at the bedroom door. Elaine peers in.

ELAINE   Not great. If you have a spare blanket or two we can sleep on the floor.

CHARLIE   No, no. There is an extra bed… in case my mother ever… well, needed it. Though God knows how she'd manage the stairs. *(Pause)* I'll have to talk to Nellie.

ELAINE   Of course. But don't tell Sarah. She's absolutely no idea.

CHARLIE	She seems a very mature child.
ELAINE	*(Pointedly)* Older than her years, people say.
CHARLIE	Elaine?
ELAINE	We'd better follow. *(Pause)* Charlie… why we didn't arrive together… it was something Gordon couldn't bring himself to ask.

> *Elaine touches Charlie's arm momentarily, then they exit.*
>
> *The stage darkens.*

SCENE THREE

[The same night] The room is lit only by the lamp on the table where Charlie and Gordon are sitting. The lamp suddenly catches Gordon's attention.

GORDON	That's a strange construction.
CHARLIE	I made it.
GORDON	Whatever from?
CHARLIE	This and that. Bits of scrap metal.
GORDON	That bit looks like a motorcycle throttle. Tell me you're not a Hell's Angel, Charles.
CHARLIE	No, but you're not far off… with the throttle.
GORDON	Anyway, so much for artistic talent. R.I.P.
CHARLIE	It has… sentimental value.
GORDON	Be that as it may, I think, Charles, that our good ladies have at last drifted from the shores of consciousness. Haven't heard the creak of a bed for at least two minutes.
CHARLIE	Nellie. Head touches the pillow and she's gone.
GORDON	Whereas Elaine. She's a brooder, you know. Always pondering something. Like today – what to bring you. Quality Street or Milk Tray, which to buy.

	Impressed by it when I met her. Keeps her awake usually, but today's been, well, tough. *(Pause)* I'm afraid we ate them.
CHARLIE	Not a problem. Been together long?
GORDON	Hm. Quite a long time. No, I lie, a very long time. Or... so it seems.
CHARLIE	And your girl, Sarah?
GORDON	My girl?
CHARLIE	Isn't she?
GORDON	Goodness no. Origins behind the cobwebs of history, dear fellow. Well before I came along. Not for me to blow them away.
CHARLIE	Like a beer?
GORDON	Nothing stronger? Never mind. Must be cold though.
CHARLIE	It's been on the slab.
GORDON	What?
CHARLIE	The bottle?
GORDON	No, the other.
CHARLIE	The marble slab, in the cupboard.
GORDON	No refrigerator?
CHARLIE	Never seen the point. Never need to keep anything.

Charlie goes to the cupboard and returns with a bottle

GORDON	Target Ale. Well, let's give it a whirl *(pours into glass)*. Just thinking. Those women. Bladders like footballs, sleep to kingdom come. While we... You have to go down all those stairs?
CHARLIE	Well, actually...
GORDON	Yes, I saw one peeping out from under the bed. I'd keep the lid on that one if I were you.
CHARLIE	We never have guests.
GORDON	No family to visit. No siblings?

CHARLIE   Come again?

GORDON   Brothers and sisters.

CHARLIE   Didn't Elaine tell you?

GORDON   May have done. Better to hear it from the horse's mouth.

CHARLIE   Brothers, both gone. One in the Blitz, the other at Dunkirk

GORDON   And you?

CHARLIE   Ground crew. Spitfires. You?

GORDON   Flew the buggers.

CHARLIE   Where?

GORDON   Oh, East Anglia, various places. Try not to remember, downing chaps just like ourselves. Five, I think it was. But you chaps – salt of the earth. Couldn't have done it without you. Always there. *(Long pause)* Look. Charles. I want to explain…

             Nellie, in nightdress, appears from behind the partition carrying a chamber pot covered with a piece of newspaper. She tries to creep past unnoticed.

             My God, what's that? No, don't tell me. *(To Nellie)* Such a charming nightdress, my dear… careful it doesn't spill…

NELLIE   It'd become… rather full.

GORDON   *(Attempting joke)* Whereas you, by contrast…

NELLIE   *(Cracking)* I never wanted it to be like this.

             Nellie exits towards the stairs.

GORDON   Seriously, Charles. You can do better.

CHARLIE   Oh?

GORDON   I know, I know. But I'm already in the future, Charles, brimful of ideas. My problem is just a blip, like previous ones. But I take your point and am contrite.

> *A flushing sound from the toilet below, then steps on stairs and Nellie re-enters.*

All done?

NELLIE   Yes, thank you.

GORDON   Then sleep well, Nellie.

NELLIE   Thank you, Gordon. Good night. *(Turning, to Charlie)* You won't be long, will you?

> *Nellie returns to the bedroom.*

GORDON   Could never understand why those things don't have a lid, can you? *(Pause)* Now, Charles, as I was saying... *(Looking at watch)* Oh, my goodness! It's ten-thirty.

CHARLIE   Um?

GORDON   I... um... promised Ruby...

CHARLIE   Ruby?

GORDON   I'd, um... help her with her... accounts.

CHARLIE   Accounts? She's a spinster!

GORDON   Well... some bills that don't make sense, apparently. Got talking to her on the stairs.

CHARLIE   Can't they wait?

GORDON   I'll just tiptoe down and see if she's still up. Won't be long, but don't wait up. I promise I'll switch the light off.

CHARLIE   I'll leave a torch on the table here. Then no need to disturb the... ladies.

GORDON   That's kind. We can talk more tomorrow. Goodnight Charles.

CHARLIE   Goodnight Gordon.

> *Gordon exits towards the stairs. Charlie picks up the table-lamp, examines it thoughtfully, shrugs, then goes to the sink and takes a toothbrush from the cabinet above.*
>
> *The stage darkens.*

SCENE FOUR

[The next morning] Charlie is at the sink in his vest, wiping his face with a towel, having shaved. Nellie is laying breakfast things at the table, including bowls and a cornflakes packet. There is a pan on the stove.

CHARLIE	Any sign of life?
NELLIE	Not when I opened the window. God, it was stuffy in there.
CHARLIE	If the traffic doesn't wake them, nothing will.
NELLIE	Charlie.
CHARLIE	Um?
NELLIE	I've been thinking. Does it make sense to you?
CHARLIE	What doesn't make sense?
NELLIE	Well, they're… clever people. Not the sort to…
CHARLIE	… get into trouble? No.
NELLIE	You know what time he came up?
CHARLIE	No.
NELLIE	Four o'clock! In the morning!
CHARLIE	With Ruby all that time?
NELLIE	I think he went somewhere. I heard the front door go, then when I looked out he was coming back…
CHARLIE	You're imagining.
NELLIE	… from the phone box across the road. I'd swear.
CHARLIE	Why would he…
	Sarah enters in her nightdress, crying but trying not to show it.
NELLIE	What's up, love? Traffic bother you? How about a nice bowl of porridge?
SARAH	Mm *(No)*.
CHARLIE	Something upset you?
NELLIE	I know, five in a tiny room isn't what you've been

used to, is it?

SARAH	It's not that.
CHARLIE	Can you tell us then?
SARAH	*(Almost inaudibly)* No.
NELLIE	A cup of tea will cheer you up. Here.
SARAH	Don't you have juice?
NELLIE	No. You must have something.
SARAH	It'll do then.
CHARLIE	Tell us when you're ready, eh?
SARAH	*(Smiling weakly)* Mm *(No)*.

Gordon enters, dressed. Sarah glares at him.

GORDON	Good morning! *(Looking round and sniffing)* There's tension in the air. Something the matter?
CHARLIE	No, nothing. We're about to persuade Sarah to try Nellie's porridge. Can we tempt you?
GORDON	For heav… Toast will do fine.
SARAH	Well, I'm having porridge.
CHARLIE	Elaine coming?
GORDON	Putting on her corset. No, I err – her roll-on – as if she needed it. So a while yet.
NELLIE	I'll make some fresh tea.

The telephone rings, startling everyone. Charlie goes to pick up the receiver, but Gordon beats him to it.

GORDON	I'll take it.
CHARLIE	Well I think…
GORDON	I think it's your mother.
CHARLIE	*(Taking phone)* Mum? *(Long pause)* You're at the neighbours? *(Pause)* Well, never mind. Mum, Elaine's here… ee-lane, you've not forgotten already… no, don't worry about it… Tell them I'll pay for the call… Mum, Mum… She's rung off.
NELLIE	Her telephone not arrived then?

CHARLIE   Doesn't know how to use it.

              Elaine enters, looking daggers at Gordon.

ELAINE   If this were anywhere else…

GORDON   It isn't, so sit down and eat your breakfast.

CHARLIE   You look wonderful, Elaine.

ELAINE   Thank you, Charlie. Fortunately I found a mirror
              in your wardrobe. You don't mind, do you?

              Elaine sits.

GORDON   Now, children, here's the good news. I've
              negotiated with Ruby for free use of the bathroom
              – for all of us. I even know how to light the Geyser.
              Sarah, *you* haven't put on make-up to hide the
              grime – how about you first?

SARAH   All right.

              *Sarah looks at Gordon warily and both exit towards
              the stairs.*

ELAINE   Is that porridge? I remember when your Mum
              would put a dob of jam in it. For you, never for me
              though.

CHARLIE   I don't remember that.

ELAINE   Why should you? *(Pause)* Now, before Gordon gets
              back… he asks if he can work here this morning
              – he writes a bit, you know, and it could help to
              bring in… Anyway, Sarah's asked if we could all go
              to Kew, perhaps walk into Richmond to look at the
              shops.

NELLIE   You go, Charlie. I've got shopping to do, and I
              expect Gordon will need some lunch.

ELAINE   Oh he's never fussed about food. *(Embarrassed)* I
              say, do you think the loo's free?

CHARLIE   It's gone three times in the last ten minutes, so it
              must be.

ELAINE   I never was good at mental arithmetic.

Elaine rises and exits.

CHARLIE   There goes my bloody racing.

NELLIE   You'll be able to talk. Without me around.

CHARLIE   What difference does that make?

NELLIE   Oh, old chums and all that.

CHARLIE   Old... Nellie, she could be anybody.

NELLIE   That's not what Gordon said.

CHARLIE   Gordon said?

NELLIE   When we looked at the garden. Last night.

CHARLIE   Gordon wasn't around then. Elaine wouldn't...

         Voices are heard on the stairs.

NELLIE   They're coming back. *(Sarcastically)* Really sorry about your racing, Charlie. Hm, might just save us a bob or two though – if you're not too extravagant with them.

CHARLIE   Well, it's threepence to get into Kew. Shall I treat them... or not?

NELLIE   Whatever you think best.

         Elaine and Gordon enter.

GORDON   Infernal Geyser's gone out and no more matches.

CHARLIE   Over there, by the stove.

         The stage darkens.

SCENE FIVE

[The same morning] Gordon is sitting at the table, writing. Nellie, with hair arranged and more attractively dressed, is cooking at the stove. There is low background classical music on the radio.

GORDON   Smells delicious.

NELLIE   Onion soup. Full of goodness.

GORDON   As are you, Nellie.

NELLIE	Not sure about that.
GORDON	For letting us stay. Putting up with this dysfunctional little trio for no reward – or hope of any.
NELLIE	We must help those in trouble.
GORDON	Trouble, yes. But trouble comes in different guises, Nellie. Some not of our making – like you having us descend upon you – and others we bring upon ourselves. Benign decisions made in innocence can lead us into… unknown territory.
NELLIE	Like me marrying Charlie, then finding out about his gambling.
GORDON	A pertinent example. When one follows one's best inclinations, doing all the time what is right – as one perceives it – yet all the time being led to a precipice one never realised was there.
NELLIE	(With humour) Like that violinist who won a prize, then jumped off Beachy Head.
GORDON	A literal example but yes, an example nevertheless. (Pause) Sometimes I feel that way, Nellie. Look at me. What do you see. An insufferable Oxbridge toff? But I've never harmed anyone, Nellie, yet…

> The music on the radio changes to a Schubert Impromptu.

NELLIE	That's Schubert.
GORDON	It is. How did you know?
NELLIE	I used to play it.
GORDON	But I see no piano.
NELLIE	No.
GORDON	Of course – you'd never get one up the stairs.
NELLIE	We did get it up the stairs.
GORDON	Oh?
NELLIE	Charlie sold it! One weekend I went away and

when I got back… *(bursts into tears)*. *(Vengefully)* One day…

GORDON His gambling?

Nellie nods vigorously

What level, Nellie? The piano.

NELLIE Um… oh, grade eight. Beyond. I would have gone to college…

The music on the radio gives way to the news.

RADIO Here is the News, and this is Alvar Liddell reading it…

GORDON Can we turn it up a bit, Nellie

RADIO Chinese troops are massing on the borders of Pakistan. At home, the Russian businessman Vasili Gregoriev is being questioned by police in connection with the Sokolov spy affair. Bonfires across the country have been lit to celebrate the…

Gordon switches it off.

GORDON I thought we should talk a bit more.

NELLIE If you like. *(Coming closer)* What are you writing?

GORDON Poetry. Isn't it odd that in times of crisis it pours forth. When your head is full of the blackest pitch, yet from the pen comes the most…

NELLIE Can I see?

Gordon hands her the paper.

It's beautiful – but so sad!

GORDON The view from the edge, Nellie. Yet, at our feet are nodding daisies and bees suckling the clover…

NELLIE You could always turn around, away from the precipice, I mean.

GORDON Sometimes that takes more courage than leaping over. And I'm not a brave man, Nellie.

NELLIE I thought that. In spite of what Charlie told me.

| GORDON | About my being a fighter pilot? Hm. What would you say – a pinch of salt needed? Have you got an envelope? |
| NELLIE | Here, on the table. |

Nellie hands him the envelope. Gordon folds the paper, puts it in the envelope and seals it.

GORDON	Now, what's the most trivial and boring thing you can think of?
NELLIE	Hm. Monday's washing.
GORDON	Here's my pen. Write on it 'laundry.'

As she bends over, Gordon puts his arm around her waist.

| NELLIE | Laun… dry. |
| GORDON | It's yours to keep. But hide it. Only open it when you're ready. You'll know when. |

Nellie strokes Gordon's neck and runs her fingers through his hair.

| NELLIE | You poor, poor man. |

Gordon responds with passion.

The stage darkens.

SCENE SIX

[The same afternoon] Charlie is at the sink pouring tea into two cups. He brings them to the table, where Sarah is writing a letter. He puts one cup beside her and stands looking over her shoulder.

CHARLIE	Receive. It's 'ei.' I think.
SARAH	Only think?
CHARLIE	'I' before 'e', except after 'c'. Isn't that what they teach you?
SARAH	They don't teach silly rhymes. Anyway, what does

	it matter? *(Pause)* Mother says you never went to a proper school.
CHARLIE	I left at fourteen – with a family to support, including your mother. The Air Force – and the war – they were my school.

Sarah rubs out the word and replaces it. Charlie sits beside her.

SARAH	Re… ceive
CHARLIE	And there.
SARAH	Oh… yes. Happy now?
CHARLIE	Very happy.

Elaine and Gordon enter from the stairs.

ELAINE	Remarkable. What diligent students.

Sarah and Charlie look up simultaneously.

GORDON	My God!
ELAINE	What?
GORDON	Nothing
ELAINE	Don't be silly Gordon. You don't come out with expletives like that for nothing.
GORDON	Their expressions… they were identical. Just for a second.
ELAINE	Surprise at undeserved praise.
GORDON	What are you writing, Sarah?
SARAH	Why?
GORDON	What are you writing?
SARAH	Why should I tell you? *(Reluctantly)* A letter to Rosie.
GORDON	*(Barely audible)* We had an agreement, remember?
SARAH	I was only telling her where we are.
GORDON	Tear it up.
CHARLIE	Is that really necessary?

GORDON	She will do as she's told, Charles. There are issues you don't understand. Give it to me, Sarah.
SARAH	No!
ELAINE	Then give it to me. We can't argue in front of Charlie and Nellie.

Sarah reluctantly hands over the letter, then rises and makes for the bedroom.

SARAH	I hate you all.

Elaine follows her. Gordon sits in Sarah's vacated chair.

GORDON	Was remarkable, though.
CHARLIE	What?
GORDON	The way you looked. So similar. *(Pause)* Forget it – it's me being fanciful.

Behind the partition Elaine and Sarah can be heard arguing. Nellie enters from the stairs.

NELLIE	That Ruby! All smiles. *(Imitating)* 'And how is Gordon?'
CHARLIE	Doesn't sound like Ruby.
NELLIE	Gordon's obviously special. *(Pause)* Even said we could use her spare room.
CHARLIE	That would be a godsend.
NELLIE	I said we could manage quite well without, thank you.
GORDON	I must thank her then. But it's academic. We won't be staying – it's unfair to trouble you two much longer.

The voices of Elaine and Sarah are now raised.

Oh, those bloody women!

The stage darkens.

SCENE SEVEN

[The same evening] Gordon is sitting alone at the table, eating something from a bowl. Charlie enters from stairs.

CHARLIE	They're window shopping. How can you go window shopping in Chiswick?
GORDON	And in the dark. *(Pause)* Charles, sit down.
CHARLIE	*(Irritated)* I suppose that's allowed… in my own house. *(Pause)* Gordon, I prefer Charlie
GORDON	Dah! For heaven's sake sit down… Charlie.

> *Charlie sits reluctantly. Gordon continues spooning from his bowl.*

	What do you call this?
CHARLIE	*We* call it bread pudding. I wouldn't know what you…
GORDON	A wartime delicacy. I should have known.
CHARLIE	I thought only the working classes…
GORDON	You want to know – what we – *they* – call it?
CHARLIE	Not really.
GORDON	*They* call it… feuilles de pain au lait… sucrées.
CHARLIE	It doesn't surprise me.
GORDON	Difficult to break the habit, Charlie, sorry. Compliment the chef will you. It is delicious.
CHARLIE	The moment she's back from next door.
GORDON	So, what's the attraction next door.
CHARLIE	The Frankensteins.
GORDON	Touché!
CHARLIE	It happens to be their name.
GORDON	And what manner of men are the Frankensteins?
CHARLIE	Men of many parts. As are the women.
GORDON	Charles, I really believe we have something in common.

CHARLIE	A love of spitfires, maybe?
GORDON	Seriously, but we do, Charles. I might have it otherwise, but we do. Common interests. When peoples' lives get entwined... without their wishing it.
CHARLIE	*(Amused)* I don't know what you're on about.
GORDON	You don't. You can't know, yet.
CHARLIE	Gordon, please stop talking in riddles.
GORDON	You're right. I can't keep up the pretence much longer. *(Pause)* You know what I read – studied – at Cambridge, Charles? Marx, Engels, pre- and post-revolutionary thinking. Not in lectures, you understand, but quietly in my room... under the bedsheets, as it were.
CHARLIE	You surprise me.
GORDON	Being a toff, you mean? Well, myself, no less. Squaring the circle is the most difficult of tasks. The libertine squeezing himself into a rigid moral frame. Not easy. But Charles, it had to be. For me, it had to be.
CHARLIE	I can't follow.
GORDON	You will... soon. *(Pause)* It's anger, you see – indignant anger in the face of exploitation. And what drives it we share. Charles. Know what it is?
CHARLIE	No idea.
GORDON	It's injustice... that angers us.
CHARLIE	I'm not an angry person.
GORDON	No? Think back over the week. What's upset you?
CHARLIE	Nothing.
GORDON	Don't believe it.
CHARLIE	Please yourself.
GORDON	Think again.
CHARLIE	Hm. There was one thing.

GORDON There we are.

CHARLIE I'd rejigged the mounting for an engine. Stronger, so better access. They came to see it.

GORDON They?

CHARLIE The Chief Engineer – Gilchrist, plus the foreman and a couple of visitors.

GORDON Recognition then?

CHARLIE You'd think so.

GORDON But?

CHARLIE Gilchrist got out his cigarettes and offered them around.

GORDON Don't tell me – except to you.

CHARLIE Yes.

GORDON Not personal, of course, but an ingrained attitude towards the working man. Those on the shop floor. Right?

CHARLIE Yes.

GORDON So what did you do?

CHARLIE I got out my own packet, very slowly, and lit up.

GORDON Making them all wait.

CHARLIE Yes.

GORDON So whose was the greater social offence, Charles – your's or Gilchrist's?

CHARLIE I should have turned the other cheek, you mean?

GORDON No, I do not mean! If the workers don't respond to injustice they go nowhere.

CHARLIE For a moment you sounded just like our shop steward.

GORDON Should that worry you?

CHARLIE It doesn't. It just seems to me that people who are... how do you say... militant – I'm not one of them, fortunately – either they're have-nots or

174

they're lusting for power.

GORDON The combination can be powerful.

CHARLIE But you seem to be neither. That puzzles me.

GORDON Perhaps there's something else you've forgotten. Sometimes it can be the most powerful of all.

CHARLIE Which is?

GORDON A sense of identity in the morass that is the great scheme of things. You watch soldiers cheerfully marching to their deaths – nothing to do with war, Charles. Women fighting for emancipation, never to travel far from their kitchen sinks. Anti-racists who would cut a black man dead in the street. Students marching... the list is endless. But it still doesn't describe the masses.

CHARLIE Of which I'm one.

GORDON Not sure, but for the moment let's assume yes... What was Nellie telling me about silk stockings in the factory? Incidentally, very pretty they look too. Here, a thousand pounds on the table, now – what do you do? Keep it, spend it, give it to a needy cause?

CHARLIE Ha, I'd probably gamble it away, but that's me. You forget that we – the rest – are capitalists at heart. Obviously what you are not.

GORDON Privileged *and* principled, me... my, my, my. But you're going too far, Charles. They exist, your demons, sure, but they're still the minority. Most yearn for order and justice, not a dubious pathway to wealth and luxury.

CHARLIE You really believe that, don't you?

GORDON Ever heard of the Apostles, Charles? Before the war – some of the most able and intelligent men at Cambridge. They believed it.

CHARLIE Were you...

> *The telephone rings. Gordon just beats Charlie to the receiver.*

GORDON   *(In Russian)* Da, da *[Yes, yes] (Covering mouthpiece, then holding out glass to Charlie)* How about a refill, old chap?

> *Charlie goes to retrieve the bottle from the kitchen area.*

(Into phone, angrily, almost inaudibly, in Russian) Ya skazal tyebye nye zvoneet mnye suda. *[I told you not to ring me here] (Seeing Charlie turning)* … I can't… of course I understand… ring me back in fifteen minutes.

> *Charlie returns with the glass.*

CHARLIE   Anyone interesting?

GORDON   A business contact. He'll ring back in fifteen minutes.

CHARLIE   Your drink.

GORDON   Charles, was there anything… unusual… to you… about that call?

CHARLIE   Should there have been?

GORDON   When he rings back… he, well, insists it's confidential.

CHARLIE   No problem.

GORDON   Where was I, then?

CHARLIE   Being a disciple.

GORDON   What? Ah… yes, an Apostle. *(Pause)* Let's change the subject. What else do we have in common?

CHARLIE   As I said, Spitfires.

> *Without realising it, Gordon begins to fiddle with the table-lamp.*

GORDON   I beg your pardon?

CHARLIE   You never flew spitfires, Gordon.

GORDON	Maybe 'flew' *was* a terminological inexactitude – but not a lie… exactly.
CHARLIE	So when did you…
GORDON	One training flight. I was sick – deemed unworthy of further progression. How did you know?
CHARLIE	The lamp you're fingering.
GORDON	What about it?
CHARLIE	The joystick grip – throttle I think you called it. That button there… is what you press when you want to shoot someone down. Pilots tell me you never forget that feeling.
GORDON	Another subject then?
CHARLIE	Sarah.
GORDON	Ah, I was wondering when we'd get to her.
CHARLIE	She seems a normal enough…
GORDON	Child? Maybe, maybe not. Any teenager would seem normal in the present company.
CHARLIE	And that comment. About us… reacting in the same way.
GORDON	Forget it. Stupid of me.
CHARLIE	And if I can't?
GORDON	Then you have two choices: confront Elaine or search the records. I can tell you already the latter won't help.
CHARLIE	Why?
GORDON	Because I've already looked. Know your adversary, say I!
CHARLIE	Elaine an adversary!
GORDON	Women, Charles. Unpredictable. Never quite know what they're thinking.
CHARLIE	Isn't that a bit sweeping?
GORDON	All women have that potential. Sadly.

CHARLIE	Jesus!
GORDON	All right, let's turn it round? Just suppose there was a connection. Well now, that would interest me too, wouldn't it?
CHARLIE	I don't follow.
GORDON	If, say – for the purpose of argument – Elaine were to become my wife... her history.
CHARLIE	Were to?
GORDON	Yes, yes, of course we can't predict the future exactly, but we can speculate.
CHARLIE	What a strange way of putting it.
GORDON	Look. Until I encountered your mother a few days ago I knew nothing of you or your brothers, or of that period in Elaine's life. Nor wanted to.
CHARLIE	Then what brought you to us?
GORDON	Because, Charles, all my options were closing. As... you... will... see...
CHARLIE	I'm afraid I don't...
GORDON	In your shoes... consider. An old acquaintance – goodness, I nearly said flame – appears on the doorstep. Why?
CHARLIE	Coincidence, I suppose. She happened to see my mother. And you were able to phone us.
GORDON	And on top of that our desperate situation.
CHARLIE	Which needed a telephone.
GORDON	Ye..es... the telephone. That *was* a coincidence.
CHARLIE	Lucky, then.
GORDON	In more ways than you can imagine. Funny how chance events can throw us lifelines.
CHARLIE	When you were 'evicted,' did you have warning of it?
GORDON	I saw it coming, yes.

CHARLIE   And Elaine?

GORDON   Mm… no.

CHARLIE   *(On to something, but floundering)* And it wasn't really
              to do with… money?

> *The telephone rings. Charlie reaches it but Gordon
> snatches it from him*

GORDON   He is… but you can't. Look, ring back in an hour,
              can you… just get off the line, please.

> *Gordon slams down the receiver*

CHARLIE   Who the hell was that?

GORDON   Your mother. I'm afraid I had to…

CHARLIE   My mother? And you…

GORDON   Look, I'm expecting…

CHARLIE   Something might have happened!

> *Charlie reaches for the receiver*

GORDON   Wait, please. I'll try to explain.

> *The telephone rings again. Gordon takes it and
> waves Charlie away. Charlie reluctantly exits to the
> bedroom. As Gordon listens his expression becomes
> increasingly distraught. Nellie enters unseen from
> stairs.*

NELLIE   Just came back for the secat[eurs]…

> *She stands watching him. He is unaware.*

GORDON   Yes?… Oh Christ.

> *He sees her and puts a finger to his lips, then points
> towards the sleeping area. Nellie moves to Gordon and
> momentarily grasps his hand. Gordon slowly replaces
> the receiver.*

NELLIE   Better get Elaine. Can't leave her outside in the
              dark.

> *Nellie quietly exits to stairs. After two or three seconds
> Charlie returns.*

CHARLIE	All well?
GORDON	Earlier I was explaining to Nellie what it's like to approach the brink. But when your toes actually touch the edge – well, it concentrates the mind wonderfully.
CHARLIE	It wasn't an opportunity then?
GORDON	No. No such luck.
CHARLIE	Can I… we… do anything?
GORDON	More than you have? – I don't think so. *(Pause)* Charles, you will not thank us… that is to say, me… Elaine's not…
CHARLIE	You *can* tell, if you want.
GORDON	I know, I know. But that would help neither of us. *(Pause)* I have to go from here, Charles. Amazing how quickly the threads have come together. Matters that once seemed passing irrelevancies suddenly threaten like… masked bandits, demanding… everything. Oh, my God.
CHARLIE	If it's Elaine – and Sarah – they won't be without friends. Does that help at all?
GORDON	It helps beyond measure.
CHARLIE	What do we do?
GORDON	Wait.
CHARLIE	You want a drink. Coffee or something?
GORDON	No.

The doorbell rings three times

	There it is.
CHARLIE	I'll answer it. I'll fetch Elaine and Nellie from the shed.
GORDON	No. No, I'll go. There'll be time to see them on the way out. Think not too unkindly of me – though you undoubtedly will. *(Pause)* Sorry, I'm a bit confused, that's all…

Prolonged ringing of doorbell. Gordon rises and makes for the stairs.

CHARLIE   Gordon… Sarah.

GORDON   Nothing to do with me, old chum. She's your problem now.

              Gordon exits. Charlie looks anxious and bewildered. He picks up the table-lamp and puts it down. Sarah, tearful, enters from the stairs.

SARAH   He's gone, hasn't he?

CHARLIE   He didn't see you?

SARAH   I was hiding on the stairs.

CHARLIE   But you were listening?

SARAH   Heard the end of it. What's the time?

CHARLIE   Does that matter?

SARAH   I'll remember it as the worst moment of my life.

CHARLIE   Eight-thirty.

SARAH   Where are the others?

CHARLIE   In the shed, of all places.

SARAH   He won't have seen them then.

CHARLIE   He said he would.

              Voices of Nellie and Elaine coming up the stairs and entering. Elaine is reluctantly carrying a plant pot with a cutting in it.

ELAINE   Charlie, do you have somewhere for this?

CHARLIE   Here, give it to me.

              Charlie takes the pot and places it in the sink.

ELAINE   Thank you Charlie, you're a sweetie. *(To Sarah)* You're back with us then.

SARAH   Wishing I wasn't.

CHARLIE   She was wondering where Gordon went.

ELAINE   Went?

181

CHARLIE   You didn't see him on his way out?

NELLIE   We've not set eyes on him. Did hear a car, though.

SARAH   I saw it come.

ELAINE   What did he tell you, Charlie? Where is he?

> *Nellie, facing away from them, is crying into her handkerchief. Elaine rounds on her, then turns back to Charlie.*

You're both in on this, aren't you? You know.

SARAH   Mother, calm down. He's always going out. He'll... *(bursts into tears)*

ELAINE   Will he, Charlie? He's running away, isn't he? What's he running away from?

CHARLIE   I don't know. He wouldn't tell me.

ELAINE   If it's money, he's got friends. I can talk to them. I can... fuck the lot of them if I have to.

CHARLIE   I don't think it has to do with money.

ELAINE   What, then? Stop hiding it from me!

CHARLIE   I'm hiding nothing. I can only guess.

ELAINE   Then for pity's sake, *(shouting)* tell me!

CHARLIE   You heard the news, about the defecting agent – Crawshaw – seeking asylum in Moscow.

ELAINE   Crawshaw came to our house. *(Pause)* He's not a spy. Tell me Gordon's not a spy. *(Pause)* He is, isn't he?

CHARLIE   I don't know.

SARAH   *(Icily)* I do. That's what he is and that's why he's gone.

> *The doorbell rings.*

NELLIE   I'll go.

ELAINE   No, I will.

> *Elaine rushes to the stairs, followed by Nellie.*

CHARLIE   *(To Sarah)* You and Elaine will have to be brave. *(Pause)* I'd better go after them.

SARAH	*(Calling after)* Charlie!
	Charlie stops and turns.
SARAH	*(In a whisper)* Last night… something happened.
CHARLIE	I… was awake.
SARAH	Oh, God.
CHARLIE	I've tried not to think about it.
SARAH	And the others?
CHARLIE	Sleeping soundly. *(Long pause)* You've said nothing to Elaine?
SARAH	Mm *(no)*.
CHARLIE	Suspect?
SARAH	Mm *(no)*.
CHARLIE	Perhaps, then… just for the moment… between us, um?
SARAH	All right.
CHARLIE	Trust me?
SARAH	You're the only one I can.
	Charlie puts his arms around her. Nellie re-enters, accompanied by two police officers, one of whom is armed.
	Where's Mother?
NELLIE	They've got her downstairs, with Ruby. Look, can someone please explain?
OFFICER	All in good time. Sit down there, Mrs Westcroft.
NELLIE	Who are you telling…
OFFICER	Sit down!
CHARLIE	Now look, Officer…
OFFICER	And you.
CHARLIE	This is our home.
OFFICER	But it's my bloody country. *(Calmly)* We'll be taking a look around, Sir. Your wife's already told us Mr

	Hogway's been here. When we're done we'll take you all down to the station.
CHARLIE	You missed him then?
OFFICER	Of no consequence, Sir. The car's being tailed to the airport.
SARAH	*(Under breath)* He's not that stupid.
OFFICER	I beg your pardon, young lady.
CHARLIE	She said they'll need to put a zip in it. To catch him.
NELLIE	What's he supposed to have done, anyway?
OFFICER	Got a wireless, have you? Sokolov case? I'd keep tuned in if I was you. If you're back here, that is.

The stage darkens. Short pause.

| RADIO | Here is the nine o'clock news and this is Alvar Liddell reading it. Police are still searching for the missing diplomat Gordon Hogway, who has not been seen since leaving his home in Kensington early yesterday morning. The operation is now concentrating on the West London area following a call from a member of the public earlier this evening. Mr Hogway, who currently chairs the joint committee on international arms deployment, recently came to the public's attention through his links with the defecting businessman Adrian Crawshaw, who surfaced in Moscow two weeks ago. *(Pause)* In the Commons the opposition has tabled a motion of no confidence… *[Fades]* |

ACT TWO

SCENE ONE

[Several weeks later] The room is the same, except that a picture of Red Square (Moscow) and a large calendar now hang on the back wall. Charlie and Sarah are sitting side by side at the table. Charlie's jacket hangs over a chair.

CHARLIE	One more minute. What was *pi* again?
SARAH	Three point one four two. I told you.
CHARLIE	That's not what you told me.
SARAH	What's twenty-two over seven? Work it out.

Charlie scribbles on his paper.

CHARLIE	Three point…
SARAH	Which is?
CHARLIE	What you said.
SARAH	Thank you. Now multiply them.

Charlie completes the calculation.

SARAH	Let me see?

Charlie pushes the paper towards her.

CHARLIE	I'm sure it's not right.
SARAH	*You're* right, *it's* wrong. So that's… six out of ten.
CHARLIE	A good pass, then.
SARAH	So it should be after five weeks.
CHARLIE	At least it's earnt us a drink.
SARAH	Earned *me* a drink, *earnt* gets you nothing.

Charlie rises and goes to the cupboard.

CHARLIE	What would you like? Orange squash?
SARAH	Boring.
CHARLIE	How long have we got?
SARAH	They went shopping at three. Can't possibly be back before five. Four-thirty now, so…

Charlie takes a bottle from the cupboard.

CHARLIE	Apricot brandy. Comrade Jim makes it to sell in the factory.
SARAH	With real apricots?
CHARLIE	I doubt it, knowing Jim.

Charlie pours two glasses.

SARAH	Elaine wouldn't approve.

185

CHARLIE	Will taste all the better for it. If they come, I've only given you a sip, right?
	Voices are heard on the stairs.
SARAH	They *are* coming.
CHARLIE	Damnation!
	Sarah attempts to swallow the brandy in one gulp, resulting in a fit of coughing. Charlie just manages to catch the glass, and stands sheepishly holding both as Nellie and Elaine enter. Nellie appears flushed.
ELAINE	What a pretty spectacle. *(To Sarah)* Let me smell that.
	Elaine sniffs at Sarah's glass.
CHARLIE	I passed Sarah's test… needed celebrating.
ELAINE	*(To Sarah)* How much did he give you?
SARAH	Just a… *(another paroxysm of coughing)*
	Sarah indicates a miniscule amount with finger and thumb.
ELAINE	We can overlook it, can't we Nellie? Just this once?
CHARLIE	Don't like the sound of that.
ELAINE	You might, because the wondrous Nellie has some information for you.
CHARLIE	If you've found another flat, we can't afford it.
NELLIE	Much more exciting than that.
ELAINE	Much more.
NELLIE	I'm pregnant, Charlie. That's where we've been – to the doctor's.
CHARLIE	Why didn't you say…
NELLIE	I wasn't sure. I didn't want to build up your hopes. Elaine came with me.
CHARLIE	Then two more glasses. That's fantastic!
	He embraces Nellie and fills all the glasses.
ELAINE	Congratulations, Charlie.

SARAH	I'm really pleased for you.
	Sarah kisses Charlie.
ELAINE	Sarah, it's Nellie who's pregnant, not Charlie. So, shall we leave the happy couple to celebrate?
SARAH	Don't see why.
ELAINE	*(Under breath)* Because I've an appointment, darling. As you well know.
SARAH	Same time next week, Charlie?
ELAINE	After that her term starts.
CHARLIE	Then of course we must.
ELAINE	And *we* can go looking for baby clothes, Nellie.
NELLIE	Chiswick's not exactly the place…
ELAINE	But Kensington is. And there are those fabulous roof gardens. You'll be amazed.
	Embraces all round and Elaine and Sarah leave.
NELLIE	You are pleased, aren't you, Charlie?
CHARLIE	Over the moon. What we always wanted.
NELLIE	Boy or girl?
CHARLIE	Mm… boy for the first one… then a girl.
NELLIE	I'll see what I can do.
CHARLIE	Got an idea.
NELLIE	Um?
CHARLIE	Practise for the second one?
NELLIE	Now, you mean?
CHARLIE	Can't do any harm.
NELLIE	I'm tired, Charlie. It's been a bit much for me really.
CHARLIE	Later, then?
NELLIE	Perhaps.
	The stage darkens.

SCENE TWO

[Two days later] Charlie and Nellie are sitting in their usual chairs. Nellie is more confident, Charlie more irritable.

NELLIE	Switch on the wireless, Charlie. There's a good boy.
CHARLIE	Why?
NELLIE	It's almost one.
CHARLIE	That means it's lunchtime.
NELLIE	I told you the pie's in the oven. You're nearest – now switch it on.
CHARLIE	Nine o'clock news not good enough? And the *Times*. Do you seriously read that rag? At least I could handle the *Mirror*. Though I admit the *Times* is better for fish and chips.
NELLIE	I like to keep abreast.
CHARLIE	You think mid-morning's a good time for a spy to appear – to catch the news?
NELLIE	It's afternoon there.
CHARLIE	Where's there?
NELLIE	You know where.
CHARLIE	Want to know what I think?
NELLIE	Not particularly.
CHARLIE	I think our chaps will have got him by now. Some dark alley off Red Square.
NELLIE	That's a vile thing to say.
CHARLIE	*(Acting out)* Jab with an umbrella from behind. Scarper. Job done.
NELLIE	I know he's alive.
CHARLIE	How?
NELLIE	Women... sense these things.

CHARLIE	Funny, that's what Elaine said. Except she thought he'd had it.
NELLIE	When did she say that?
CHARLIE	Last time. Ask her when she brings Sarah.
NELLIE	Yes, that's a pointless exercise if ever there was one.
CHARLIE	I find her... well... really helpful.
NELLIE	*(Looking at him pointedly)* How now brown cow. After me now... how now...
CHARLIE	Shut up.
NELLIE	Soon I'll be welcoming you to the middle class.
CHARLIE	You? Middle class?
NELLIE	My father was a Mason! Owned his own business.
CHARLIE	So might mine if he'd lived.
NELLIE	Sorry.
CHARLIE	Anyway, isn't that supposed to be secret – not shouted from the rooftops.
NELLIE	Are you a Mason, Charlie?
CHARLIE	Bloody well not.
NELLIE	Ever likely to be? *(Long pause)* Gordon was.
	They sip their glasses thoughtfully. Charlie empties his.
CHARLIE	I'll see Jim about another bottle.
NELLIE	We'll need to tell Ruby – about the pregnancy.
CHARLIE	Why?
NELLIE	She'll notice.
CHARLIE	That's weeks away. When did the doctor say?
NELLIE	It's on the calendar.
CHARLIE	*(Peering at calendar on wall)* So it is.
NELLIE	And we'll need to tell next door... and your mother.
CHARLIE	I already have... my mother. She said she'd come.
NELLIE	Come for what?

CHARLIE   The confinement. I wouldn't worry. She'd never make the stairs.

NELLIE   Still less squeeze past the pram in the hall.

CHARLIE   Which Ruby's going to love.

             They giggle together.

NELLIE   I'm going next door.

CHARLIE   Tell them, the whole neighbourhood will know.

NELLIE   That's why I'm going.

             Nellie exits. Charlie drains his glass, pours a last drop from the empty bottle, rises and re-examines the calendar.

CHARLIE   Must be right... has to be... *(Cheering up, animated)* You silly, doubting bugger... you're going to be a father. *(Pretending to open an envelope)* Mrs and Mrs Charles Westcroft are pleased to announce the birth of Charles... Spitfire... ha, ha... Westcroft, a brother for... Christ, what am I saying? Where did that come from? *(Pause)* So, Sarah, what would you make of that? A little brother, well half-brother. Oh, this is rubbish I'm talking. *(Pause)* But if it was true, you would be pleased – of course you would – but you must never know... and neither must Nellie. God forbid! *(Looking again at the calendar)* Funny though...

             The stage darkens.

                    SCENE THREE

[The same evening] Charlie is sitting at the table, engrossed in rewiring the plug for the table lamp. Sarah, carrying a large bag, enters silently from the stairs and for several seconds watches him unnoticed.

SARAH   Hello, Charlie. Surprised?

CHARLIE	How did you get in?
SARAH	Ruby.
CHARLIE	I didn't hear you come up.
SARAH	Quiet as a mouse, me. I like to watch you... concentrating.
CHARLIE	Yes, well. Where's Elaine?
SARAH	Oh, I expect at the *Blue Grass*... no that's too early... probably still at Mr Michael's then, having a perm. Or Mr Michael. Not here anyway. I'm sorry you're not pleased to see me.
CHARLIE	I am pleased to see you. It's just... this isn't your usual day.
SARAH	Very pleased... or just pleased.

She sits opposite him, elbows on the table, chin cupped in her hands.

Or not pleased at all?

CHARLIE	Very pleased.
SARAH	That's all right then. *(Pointing)* That's a lucky plug.
CHARLIE	It's just an ordinary three-pin plug. Why?
SARAH	Three times the pleasure. Assuming plugs can...
CHARLIE	You been drinking?

She huffs into his face.

SARAH	Satisfied?
CHARLIE	Benefit of the doubt.
SARAH	Where's Mrs Mouse?
CHARLIE	Sarah, for heaven's sake act your age. *(Pause)* She's gone to her Russian class. I told you...
SARAH	Her...? Zdrastvoyte *[Hello]*, Charlie.
CHARLIE	*(Reluctantly)* Zdrastvoyte, Sarah.
SARAH	Well, at least you two can communicate. *(Distantly, seriously, referring to Gordon)* What that man does to people... without even trying.

CHARLIE	Gordon?
SARAH	Mm. *[Yes]*
CHARLIE	Including you?
SARAH	What do you mean?
CHARLIE	You lived with him.

> *Charlie points at the Red Square poster.*

Nellie only met him once, and look what we've got here.

SARAH	I thought I hated him.
CHARLIE	Why?
SARAH	For what he did to Elaine. But when he'd gone…
CHARLIE	You miss him?
SARAH	No!… but sometimes… *(with hostility)* you wouldn't understand.

> *Charlie puts the plug aside and gives her his full attention.*

CHARLIE	I'm not sure I want to get…
SARAH	Involved? *(Looking searchingly into his face)* What do you want, Charlie… when you look at me?
CHARLIE	When do I look at you?
SARAH	When you think I don't see.
CHARLIE	That's ridiculous!
SARAH	Is it? Ever since Gordon said we looked the same?
CHARLIE	And do we?
SARAH	And ever since you've been wondering what it is.
CHARLIE	Perhaps I… [know what it is]

> *Sarah places her hand across his mouth.*

SARAH	Gordon once taught me an old Russian saying. *[First In Russian, then English]* Vsyo obmancheevo, poetomoo dovol'stvooysya myechtoy. Nothing is what it seems, so be content to dream.

CHARLIE	You frighten me sometimes.
SARAH	Why?
CHARLIE	Because you don't behave like a fifteen-year-old.
SARAH	Is that what Elaine told you? I wonder why? *(Pause)* Older!
CHARLIE	I know.
SARAH	How?
CHARLIE	*(Embarrassed)* I checked.
SARAH	Where?
CHARLIE	Somerset House.
SARAH	Why splash out on the tube fare for that? For someone you hardly know?
CHARLIE	I... can't explain.
SARAH	Can't or won't?
CHARLIE	Really can't.
SARAH	Then I'll have to ask Elaine.
CHARLIE	For God's sake, no.
SARAH	That scared you, didn't it? You know, I don't think we should say anything at all for the next ten minutes.

She begins to stroke his hair.

CHARLIE	This isn't right.
SARAH	*(Seriously)* I'm not your daughter, Charlie.
CHARLIE	*(Long pause; disappointed, then in a hushed voice)* How can you be sure?
SARAH	I am sure.
CHARLIE	*(Ruefully)* Then it was a nice thought while it lasted.
SARAH	*(Resuming challenging tone)* So what can happen in ten little minutes?
CHARLIE	Don't you have a boyfriend?
SARAH	To torment, you mean?

CHARLIE	I'm out of my depth with you.
SARAH	No previous experience of teenagers?
CHARLIE	Absolutely not.
SARAH	No? Really no? Then raise your right hand.
CHARLIE	What game's this?
SARAH	Raise your right hand, Charlie, and say after me:

Charlie reluctantly raises his hand.

I would never, ever, in a million years seduce a sixteen-year-old girl.

CHARLIE	Nor would I.
SARAH	No? Then say it!
CHARLIE	I would never, ever, in a million *(slowing)* years sed… *[recalling childhood]*
SARAH	Why do you stop?
CHARLIE	You witch!
SARAH	*(Gleefully)* And what manner of witch would that be – black or white?
CHARLIE	Dirty-grey.
SARAH	But only white magic tonight, Charlie. Believe me.

The telephone rings. Sarah reaches it first

Hello, this is Chiswick Randy Plugs Limited. *(Pause, looking at Charlie)* Oh! *[In Russian]* Ya doomau vi osheeblees nomyerom. Do sveedanya *[I think you've got the wrong number. Goodbye]*

Sarah laughs at Charlie's bewilderment.

No, not Gordon. I think it was your mother.

CHARLIE	My mother? My mother?
SARAH	Don't worry. She'll think she's got the wrong number and will try again. Like [now]…

The phone rings again. While Charlie answers it Sarah goes to the drawer where Nellie has hidden

Gordon's poem. She finds the envelope and slips it into her pocket.

CHARLIE   *(Into phone)* Mother? I'm just in the middle of something... yes of course I'm pleased... important, yes. A visitor. I'll ring you back *(guiltily)*... in an hour.

Sarah reaches for her bag.

SARAH   Good. *(Pause)* Now, you like doing things for me, don't you, Charlie?

CHARLIE   Depends.

SARAH   Look after something, for me?

She withdraws a large and heavy package from the bag.

Not to look, understand. Promise me.

CHARLIE   Nellie will wonder...

SARAH   Hide it! *(Pinching his cheek viciously between finger and thumb)* Promise me! *(Pause)* That's better.

CHARLIE   Has this to do with Gordon?

SARAH   Don't ask. We're wasting time.

CHARLIE   I'll put it in the shed.

SARAH   She goes there.

CHARLIE   The tool cabinet's always locked.

SARAH   Be quick then.

Charlie exits with the package. Sarah takes the envelope from her pocket and replaces Gordon's poem with what appear to be tickets. She places the envelope in the inside pocket of Charlie's jacket, which is draped over the chair.

SARAH   *(To herself)* Pity I won't be around.

As Sarah moves towards the bedroom the stage darkens.

SCENE FOUR

[An hour later] Charlie, now alone, is hastily putting his tools away. He hears footsteps on the stairs and smooths his hair. Nellie enters, looking angry.

CHARLIE	Hello Nellie. Zdrastvoyte!
NELLIE	Into electrics now, are we?
CHARLIE	Sorry?
NELLIE	Teaching you electricity. You've mastered maths, have you?
CHARLIE	You've lost me.
NELLIE	Your visitor.
CHARLIE	Oh, Sarah. Just left, actually.
NELLIE	So Ruby said.
CHARLIE	I thought you two weren't speaking.
NELLIE	There are times when women can set aside their differences.
CHARLIE	What times?
NELLIE	Times like now. I want to show you something.
	Nellie goes into the bedroom.
CHARLIE	*(To himself)* Oh God in heaven... the bed! Did I, Did I?
	Nellie returns carrying a brown paper bag. She opens it and withdraws a skimpy silk nightdress.
CHARLIE	*(Relieved)* They were selling them in the factory. Jim got me one cheap.
NELLIE	So he might have done. What interests me...
CHARLIE	I had a small win...
NELLIE	I've never known a big one.
CHARLIE	I didn't have to borrow!
NELLIE	For once I don't care. What *interests* me is why you didn't give it to her when you had the chance.

CHARLIE	Oh, now look…
NELLIE	Six-thirty she arrived. Quarter to eight she left. More than enough time to wire a plug, wouldn't you say?
CHARLIE	How do you know when…
NELLIE	Her downstairs.
CHARLIE	Bloody Ruby. You really think…
NELLIE	*(Breaking down)* I don't know what to think.
CHARLIE	Then let me put you straight – I bought it for you.
NELLIE	Then why's it been in the drawer for a week – and under your underpants?
CHARLIE	I didn't want you to see it.
NELLIE	Obviously.
CHARLIE	You really can't guess?
NELLIE	No.
CHARLIE	What is Sunday – or are you so wrapped up in your Russian you've forgotten?
NELLIE	Our wedding anniversary perhaps?
CHARLIE	Bloody right!
NELLIE	*(Sarcastically)* Oh, Charlie. I'm so sorry.
CHARLIE	It's OK.
NELLIE	It's just that… well… she's so pretty.
CHARLIE	You think so? I hadn't really noticed.
NELLIE	You can be switched off sometimes.
CHARLIE	Meaning?
NELLIE	The complexion, the eyes… the dark hair.
CHARLIE	Means nothing.
NELLIE	Then you're not a romantic, are you Charlie?
CHARLIE	I wouldn't say that.
NELLIE	Our anniversary was *last* week, Charlie.

CHARLIE	Oh, bugger. *(Pause)* But Nellie… hang on an moment.
NELLIE	Why?
CHARLIE	You must have forgotten as well.
NELLIE	*(Deadly serious, wearily)* I think it's been getting to both of us.

They embrace momentarily, with affection. The telephone rings. Nellie answers it.

It's your mother's neighbour – she's in a state. Says you promised to ring back and wonders why you haven't.

Charlie taps his forehead in disbelief, then goes to telephone his mother. While he does so Nellie looks in the drawer for Gordon's poem. Not finding it she becomes distraught. Charlie puts down the receiver.

CHARLIE	Why do I bother *[to ring his mother]*?
NELLIE	Where is it?
CHARLIE	Where's what?
NELLIE	It was here this morning. Where is it?
CHARLIE	Nellie, I haven't the foggiest idea what you're on about.
NELLIE	You know what I'm on about because no-one else can possibly… *(To herself)* She couldn't. Did you leave her alone in here?
CHARLIE	Why don't you have a nice lie down. Then, when you've calmed down… Anyway, what is it we're talking about.
NELLIE	An envelope.
CHARLIE	Envelopes are in the cupboard. Help yourself.
NELLIE	This one was for… the laundry.
CHARLIE	You do your own washing.
NELLIE	Sometimes the bed linen get's… well, never mind. It's not something I discuss with you.

CHARLIE	Well, I haven't got it and I'm going out.
	While Nellie continues searching, Charlie picks up his jacket and becomes aware of the envelope Sarah has put there. Nellie sees him take it out.
NELLIE	You *did* have it. You deceitful…
	Nellie grabs the envelope and withdraws the tickets.
	Two tickets for the… Bolshoi Ballet. Next month at the Coliseum. Ah, for my birthday. That's really sweet of you, Charlie, but…
CHARLIE	This time I tried.
NELLIE	So you did. And it's not even your thing, is it?
CHARLIE	I've never been… to the ballet.
NELLIE	And now you shall. *(Pause)* How did you know where to get them?
CHARLIE	*(Hesitating)* Sarah got them for me.
NELLIE	And you put them in there.
CHARLIE	Well… she did. I said she could look for an envelope.
NELLIE	Then what's the hussy done with…
CHARLIE	What?
NELLIE	Just a… a list.
CHARLIE	Of laundry?
NELLIE	Of laundry.
	The stage darkens.

SCENE FIVE

[A few days later] Nellie and Elaine enter, each carrying a large bag. Elaine is jubilant, Nellie less so. During this scene they alternate between hostility (on Nellie's part mostly defensive) and friendliness.

ELAINE	Can't resist another peek.

She withdraws an elegant dress from her bag and holds it against herself.

What do you think?

NELLIE	*(Without conviction)* Oh, perfect.
ELAINE	And if it were yellow with purple spots? Would it still be perfect?
NELLIE	I expect so, on you.
ELAINE	Mm. There. You try it.

She thrusts the dress at Nellie, who reluctantly holds it against herself.

NELLIE	Beautiful. But not quite me. Is it?
ELAINE	You're so wrong, Nellie, do you know that? You're not really a frump. You do know, don't you.
NELLIE	I'm beginning to.
ELAINE	Progress, then. *(Pause)* Lets see what you've brought.
NELLIE	Perhaps later. I'd rather…

Elaine ignores her and begins to draw items from the bag.

ELAINE	Mm, nice. I adore this one. And this.

She withdraws a child's fur hat.

Mm. What's this?

NELLIE	It… just caught my fancy.
ELAINE	For when the chill east wind blows from off the steppes?
NELLIE	I happened to like it.
ELAINE	Nellie, when the child's old enough for this thing those winds will have long since blown themselves out.
NELLIE	As they might be doing for you?
ELAINE	Ouch. That's a bitchy thing to say.
NELLIE	I'm sorry. I didn't mean it that way. It's just that… such a long time has passed without word.

ELAINE	No word, no. But I sense things are happening.
NELLIE	Oh? Like what?
ELAINE	The arrears on my flat were paid off yesterday, and not by me.
NELLIE	Good for you.
ELAINE	In one way. In another it's worrying... signalling a return to the old ways. A poor little pawn on a very big board. Expendable. The message? You can see him – meaning Gordon – if...
NELLIE	If what?
ELAINE	*(Guardedly)* If I comply.
NELLIE	You *can* tell me, if you want to.
ELAINE	It started years ago, Nellie, soon after I met him. 'A little favour to a colleague we're trying to impress.' 'Just an hour of your time. Nothing out of the ordinary, nothing bizarre.'
NELLIE	Are you saying what I think... [you're saying]
ELAINE	Always draw a line between work and home, Gordon would say. And then he'd go away and reappear a couple of days later as if nothing had happened.
NELLIE	And he was never jealous?
ELAINE	Perhaps he was. He just had... other priorities.
NELLIE	Why didn't you just say no?
ELAINE	How naive you are. *(Viciously)* Because it's how I'm made, Nellie. Hormones going in crazy cycles. Or something. Two days without and it's a dull ache, four an intense pain. A week and the search begins in earnest. And it's not difficult, believe me. Bars, clubs. But usually, you see, it wasn't necessary. The envelope would appear under the door... God knows where from. And inside? Just the date, time and place. And they paid, oh yes, they paid.

NELLIE	And Gordon went along…
ELAINE	Ohh, his timing – his absence – was always… perfect.
NELLIE	*(Cautiously)* So who were…
ELAINE	Who?

Elaine sees the copy of the Times on the table.

Give me that – and that pen over there. *(Pause)* I'm saying nothing, right?

Nellie hands her the paper. Elaine turns the pages, frantically circling names she sees, while Nellie looks on aghast.

There. And there.

NELLIE	But these are…
ELAINE	The great and the good?
NELLIE	And Crawshaw was one of them?
ELAINE	No, actually. He was a sweetie, a bit like Gordon. So now you know… *(viciously)* nothing, you understand? I've told you nothing.

Elaine slumps into the sofa, thrashing about and tearful.

It's how it is, Nellie. It's why I look at myself in the mirror, every morning, every evening, following the lines my fingertips. *(Pause)* It's why I'm lost if I don't get him back.

Nellie pours a glass of apricot brandy and gives it to Elaine, who sips it. Then Elaine takes up the dress and thrusts it at Nellie.

Here, take it. I've no need of it.

NELLIE	Are you crazy?
ELAINE	Put it on. Charlie will be back soon. Surprise him.
NELLIE	Now?
ELAINE	This minute.

NELLIE	I'd be embarrassed.
ELAINE	In front of me?

Elaine slips out of her own dress, revealing expensive lingerie.

Now you.

Nellie follows suit, revealing far more basic underwear.

Cover those up. This once… then get rid of them.

While Nellie puts on the dress, Elaine fetches a standing mirror from the bedroom and positions it in front of the sofa.

Now sit.

NELLIE	I don't want to…
ELAINE	Sit!

Nellie sits. Elaine takes a case from her handbag and begins to apply make-up to Nellie's face.

Nose up.

NELLIE	Why are you doing this?
ELAINE	Tell you in a moment. *(Applying the make-up more frantically, then looking at her work approvingly)* Now stand.

Nellie rises.

Uh..um.

NELLIE	Elaine, I asked you a question.
ELAINE	Why I want you to be attractive to your husband?
NELLIE	Yes, if that's what it's all about.
ELAINE	Wait for it then. It's to keep his bloody mind off my fucking daughter.

They glare at one another, then Elaine mellows and puts away her make-up case.

Good-bye, Nellie. If Gordon surfaces maybe we'll meet again. Otherwise we won't trouble you anymore.

Elaine exits and the distant door slams. Nellie preens herself in front of the mirror, trying increasingly provocative stances. She fails to see Charlie enter and stand bemused in the doorway. He is wearing a dapper suit with a flower in the buttonhole. The two are caricatures of their former selves, thinking themselves more desirable, although apparently not for one another.

The stage darkens

ACT THREE

SCENE ONE

[Four months later] Stage in darkness. We hear a Rachmaninov prelude played well on a piano. Lights up on the room more or less as before but with an upright piano against the right partition wall. Nellie, chicly dressed and obviously pregnant, finishes playing and closes her music. A young man (Desmond Finch) with a notepad is sitting on the sofa. He claps as Nellie rises.

FINCH   Bravo, Mrs Westcroft. Beethoven?

NELLIE   Rachmaninov.

FINCH   Well, we reporters don't get many treats like that. And you say the piano just arrived.

NELLIE   Knock on the door – well, the bell went – and there it was. It took two men an hour to get it up here – and a broken toe.

FINCH   And you think there may be a connection.

NELLIE   It *was* quite heavy.

FINCH   No, I meant the piano and Gordon Hogway's…

NELLIE   Teasing you, Mr Finch.

FINCH   Well, our readers appreciate a little humour. Mrs Westcroft, I wanted to ask you…

NELLIE	Call me Nell.
FINCH	Nell then… to ask you about Hogway's…
NELLIE	*Mr* Hogway's…
FINCH	… last day here. When he resurfaced yesterday the Brentford and Chiswick Times was in turmoil. You can imagine. So let's go back to what we were discussing: when he left did you have any inkling that he was a…
NELLIE	*(Romantically)* A spy? None whatsoever. But off the record, Mr Finch, he did confide… we did share… an understanding. I felt something was about to happen. He went as far as he could but…
FINCH	And you don't know where he went?
NELLIE	I couldn't possibly say.
FINCH	Your husband likewise?
NELLIE	*He* had absolutely no idea.
FINCH	And then they lost him on the way to the airport. Can you shed any light on that?
NELLIE	He was too clever for them.
FINCH	Not difficult – but that's also off the record. *(Pause)* Oh, I almost forgot to show you this.

> *Finch hands Nellie a photograph.*

	Released to Pravda yesterday. In his flat in Moscow.
NELLIE	So handsome – and he's grown a beard.
FINCH	No doubt to hide the evil lurking there.
NELLIE	Gordon's as harmless as a lamb.
FINCH	But you don't condone his actions, surely, Mrs Westcroft?
NELLIE	He's been misunderstood.
FINCH	Hm, that's what they said at the Foreign Office. *(Pause)* Before I go, a picture if I may?

NELLIE	Of course.

> *Finch takes out a camera. Nellie poses provocatively, bulge evident, in front of the Moscow poster.*

FINCH	Oh, and one last tit-bit for our readers – boy or girl?
NELLIE	Boy, we hope.
FINCH	Thought about a name?
NELLIE	Ivan.
FINCH	Mm. And if a girl?
NELLIE	Oksana.
FINCH	Oksana Westcroft. Mm. Times must be changing… makes me feel quite old. My regards to your husband, Mrs West… Nell. Really sorry to have missed him.
NELLIE	Bye, Mr Finch. Say boo to the plain clothes man across the street. I think we're under surveillance again.
FINCH	More than a pleasure, Nell. No, I'll see myself out. Goodbye then.

> *Finch exits. As his footsteps on the stairs fade Charlie emerges from the bedroom. Nellie returns to the piano and begins to play.*

CHARLIE	Must you keep playing that piece over and over?
NELLIE	Rachmaninov's music conveys so much.
CHARLIE	Mm. Like why he was forced into exile.
NELLIE	Why don't you just go to the shed and finish making the cot?
CHARLIE	I'll skip my tea then.
NELLIE	Charlie?
CHARLIE	Mm?
NELLIE	You are pleased he's been found?
CHARLIE	As pleased as when he found us.

NELLIE	I think it's fantastic.
CHARLIE	I wonder if Elaine will.
NELLIE	*(Glancing at clock)* God, only two hours and she'll be here. I'd better put the soup on.

The stage darkens.

SCENE TWO

[Two hours later] Charlie and Elaine are seated at the now laid table. Nellie is serving the soup.

NELLIE	Borscht.
ELAINE	*(Amused)* What?
CHARLIE	Nellie's joined a Russian circle – they inflict cooking on one another.
NELLIE	Cuisine, Charlie.
CHARLIE	Chrysants out, red cabbage and beetroot in. I can see it. I started digging yesterday.
ELAINE	I hope you're joking. *(Pause)* The embassy passed me a letter this morning.
NELLIE	Oh?
CHARLIE	That's a turn up for the books.
ELAINE	Isn't it.
NELLIE	Well?
ELAINE	He's okay. A bit tired. They're treating him well. He even has a driver.
CHARLIE	Where'd he been?
ELAINE	They're not saying.
NELLIE	Did he… mention us?
ELAINE	He said regards to all. Sorry. *(Pause)* The FO thinks I might visit, once the fuss has died down.
NELLIE	That will be nice.

ELAINE   Will it? *(Tearfully)* He'll never come back.

CHARLIE   How's the soup?

ELAINE   Red… I'll say that much for it.

CHARLIE   *(Trying to be casual)* So where's Sarah?

ELAINE   I should have explained. She… had extra homework.

CHARLIE   It is term-time.

ELAINE   Yes. Look Charlie, would you mind if she stopped her sessions with you – just for a while?

CHARLIE   People say they were making a difference.

NELLIE   How now…

ELAINE   I know. I'd noticed.

CHARLIE   Well, I'd hoped she'd be with us. Won't mean much to you two but there's something else about today.

NELLIE   Tell us then.

CHARLIE   It's…

ELAINE   *(Softly)*… when your brother died at Dunkirk.

               Charlie and Nellie look at her in amazement.

CHARLIE   That's right, my brother, Tom.

NELLIE   How can you know that, Elaine? If you'd lost contact with the family.

ELAINE   The day I saw your mother in Amberfield.

CHARLIE   *She* told you?

ELAINE   No, of course not. We happened to stop at the church in the village.

NELLIE   I never think of you as being religious.

ELAINE   Gordon thought the churchyard would be a good place for luncheon. Tombstones make good picnic tables, he used to say. Made a thing of it whenever we went anywhere. While he was setting it all out I went inside… and saw the memorial. *(Becoming emotional)* Captain Thomas Westcroft, Royal

208

	Engineers. What a terrible loss.
NELLIE	Charlie never talks about it, except like today.
CHARLIE	I think about him, occasionally.
ELAINE	*(Accusingly)* Only occasionally?
CHARLIE	You know we didn't always get on.
ELAINE	And whose fault was that?
CHARLIE	Um?
ELAINE	At least he managed to better himself.
NELLIE	That's a bit near the bone.
ELAINE	I'm sorry... I'm sorry. I didn't mean it that way.
NELLIE	Then what way did you mean it? *(Pause)* Charlie's never talked much about... that time.
ELAINE	Why should he?
NELLIE	Because I'm his wife, that's why.
ELAINE	Nellie, the war changed everything. It's a great black horrible fog I don't want to look through any more.
CHARLIE	Steady on.
ELAINE	And trying to only distorts everything.
NELLIE	Mm, so. What have I gleaned so far? A tramp of a girl arrives – how old were you, Elaine?
ELAINE	Fourteen, if you must know.
NELLIE	... arrives in Charlie's family. And two years later she's gone. Whoosh, without trace.
ELAINE	There must have been thousands of orphans like me, homeless, displaced by the war – all forgotten.
NELLIE	Obviously not quite all.
ELAINE	Meaning?
NELLIE	I'm not blind, Elaine.
ELAINE	Oh, so what have you seen?
NELLIE	Glances... things shared.

ELAINE   Glances? With Charlie? Ridiculous.

CHARLIE   Nellie, when Elaine arrived she had no proper shoes. That first day with us she clomped around in an old pair of Tom's boots. But what did my mother have? A miserable pension from the Great War. We had to share. It brought us together as a family.

NELLIE   There were tensions, I'll bet.

CHARLIE   Yes.

NELLIE   With your mother?

CHARLIE   Mainly with my mother, yes.

NELLIE   But you boys... took care of the girl.

CHARLIE   We tried.

NELLIE   Like how?

ELAINE   *(Annoyed)* Like making sure I ate enough. Sharing their things with me. A little money sometimes.

NELLIE   For sweeties?

ELAINE   For clothes – what I couldn't make myself.

NELLIE   And how did you repay these... kindnesses?

ELAINE   None of your business.

NELLIE   Sounds as if it should be.

ELAINE   Can't you just accept that the war changed everything?

CHARLIE   Oh! I said I'd ring my mother – to remind her of Tom's birthday. Better do it. Excuse me a moment? Nellie, more soup for me. Elaine?

                Charlie gets up to phone. Nellie and Elaine are silent for a few seconds.

ELAINE   It's a closed book, Nellie. Please.

                Long pause.

NELLIE   Have you replied to Gordon?

ELAINE   One doesn't just 'reply.' The bastard left me, remember?

NELLIE	You sound bitter.
ELAINE	Wouldn't you be? I'd everything to look forward to. A husband. Security for Sarah.
NELLIE	When you do write…
ELAINE	Yes, I'll tell him I've seen you.
NELLIE	Can you also tell him…
ELAINE	That your Rachmaninov's coming along nicely?
NELLIE	Do you have to be so… bitchy. You know he'll be interested that I'm…
ELAINE	Pregnant? Oh, over the moon. Something to brighten up a drab Moscow evening.
NELLIE	Will you then?
ELAINE	What do you think?

Charlie returns from the phone.

CHARLIE	Would you believe? Who was Tom? she says. Oh, oh, oh.
ELAINE	That doesn't surprise me.
NELLIE	Oh?
ELAINE	Charlie was always her favourite
NELLIE	Lucky for her, then.
ELAINE	Why?
NELLIE	Charlie survived.
ELAINE	Not lucky for anyone else, though. Except you. Though looking at you two now I'm beginning to wonder.
CHARLIE	Elaine, have we done something to upset you?
ELAINE	Today the world's against me, and the other way round. *(Crying)* It didn't start well, then that letter came. *(Pause)* I still had hope, you see. That I might one day join him. Fat chance now.
CHARLIE	Elaine, he's not free to write what he feels.
ELAINE	Yes, but something's changed.

CHARLIE   What's changed?

ELAINE   Those Russians from the Embassy who brought it. Oh, didn't they just look the part. *(Pause)* One of them had been drinking with him.

CHARLIE   And he's OK?

ELAINE   Mm. *(Pointedly)* The other one wanted to talk to Sarah.

CHARLIE   Sarah?

ELAINE   Something about youth and Soviet culture. Would you believe, she actually *said* something to them in Russian. Where did she get that from? *(Pause)* Then she went off with them. That's why she's not here. *(Pause)* You know what it's like to be jealous of your own daughter?

NELLIE   Seems jealousy's an occupation.

ELAINE   Meaning you, I suppose?

NELLIE   Pregnancy changes one's whole outlook on life.

ELAINE   Especially when it happens... so conveniently.

NELLIE   So what stopped *you* – you with your face-paint and la-de-da ways? Why aren't we swarming with Sarah's. Can't be that you don't have a taste for it.

ELAINE   I've had more lovers than you've had...

CHARLIE   Hot dinners?

ELAINE   Shut up! *(To Nellie)* What do you know, up in this... prison? Of men... of anything?

CHARLIE   Look, let's stop this. Now.

ELAINE   I won't stop it. This fantasy of hers... sticks in my craw. Charlie, how can you be such a blind fool. She's even marked the bloody calendar.

           She goes to the wall, grasps the calendar and throws it on the table.

CHARLIE   Elaine, there's nothing there.

212

ELAINE	She obviously thinks there is.
CHARLIE	*(Grasping Nellie's arm)* Nellie, what's she saying?
NELLIE	Don't listen to her.
CHARLIE	What's she saying?
NELLIE	Let go. You're hurting me.
CHARLIE	Is she right?
NELLIE	What if she is?
CHARLIE	I don't believe this.
ELAINE	That day at Kew, after we came. There's even a tiny dot.
NELLIE	That's in the paper!
ELAINE	What are the others, then?
CHARLIE	*(Embarrassed)* The pencil dots are me.
ELAINE	Well *that* one looks special.
CHARLIE	*(To Nellie)* Why don't you tell her she's talking rubbish?
NELLIE	*(To Charlie)* And you're so bloody perfect, I suppose?
CHARLIE	I've kept off the horses. For you.
NELLIE	Only because your precious Sarah told you to. It's not the horses, oh no!
CHARLIE	What then?
NELLIE	You think I don't know. Your scriblings.
CHARLIE	What scriblings?
NELLIE	In the loft.
CHARLIE	You've been in the loft. For Christ's sake, why?
NELLIE	That's where you keep them.
CHARLIE	You need a ladder to…
NELLIE	A chair and stool on the table. Not difficult.
CHARLIE	But you're pregnant!
ELAINE	He's right, Nellie.

NELLIE	You keep out of this.
ELAINE	I want to know why you were in the loft.
NELLIE	An informant.
ELAINE	Sarah?
CHARLIE	I told Sarah I kept a diary.
NELLIE	And poems – pathetic they are – and love notes.
CHARLIE	Just notes!
ELAINE	Involving my daughter. That's another bloody fantasy. You two live in dream-land. *(Pause)* What's she been saying?

> *Sarah enters silently from the stairs, having heard much of the conversation.*

CHARLIE	Nothing.
ELAINE	Liar! *(Quietly)* What has she told you?

> *They notice Sarah.*

The prodigal returns.

NELLIE	How did you get in?
SARAH	Ruby was at the door. I had to push past her... the cow.
NELLIE	That's nice.
CHARLIE	We kept some food for you.
SARAH	I don't want it.
ELAINE	Then what do you want? Those Russians – what did they want you for?
SARAH	Oh, my youth and beauty and...
ELAINE	Since when, darling?
SARAH	Took it in turns.
ELAINE	I don't believe you.
SARAH	You wouldn't believe the positions.
ELAINE	Sarah!
CHARLIE	We're trying to be serious.

SARAH	*(Crumbling)* I'm deadly serious. *(Almost inaudibly)* I heard what you said about Nellie and Gordon.
CHARLIE	There's nothing between Nellie and Gordon.
SARAH	Nellie thinks there is. Elaine thinks there is.
ELAINE	Keep out of it, darling. You know nothing about the wiles of men. We are still learning, aren't we, Nellie?
NELLIE	You speak for yourself.
ELAINE	Well, from what I can see *(indicating the picture of Red Square)* and what I understand can be heard *(indicating the piano)*, one of us *(looking at Nellie)* is still walking in the foothills, shortly to come upon a fence with a sign marked 'keep out.'
NELLIE	That's almost poetic, Elaine.
SARAH	Should be. Gordon wrote it.
NELLIE	Did you know that at school I was queen of the high jump?
ELAINE	I can see you crawling under barbed wire, in pig-muck, but leaping over... never! Charlie?
CHARLIE	*(Humorously)* She's never set foot on a sports field, to my knowledge.
NELLIE	No. Well, if Elaine can fantasise, so can I.
CHARLIE	Look, can we please stop this?
SARAH	No, let them go on. Let them enjoy their fun while they can. It won't last.
CHARLIE	I'm sure Elaine and Gordon will eventually... when the time is right.
SARAH	*(Sniggers)*
ELAINE	Despite his eccentricities... and what he's done – which is quite incomprehensible to everybody, including me – Gordon is still loyal to those he loves.
SARAH	As pigs might fly.

ELAINE	I challenge you... little Miss Misfit... to prove otherwise.
SARAH	You mean that?
ELAINE	This time *I'm* deadly serious.
	Sarah produces what appears to be Gordon's poem taken from the drawer and places it on the table.
SARAH	What about that, then?
CHARLIE	What's that?
SARAH	A poem.
	Charlie picks it up and reads.
CHARLIE	To the woman...
	Elaine snatches it from him.
ELAINE	How did you get that? Rummaging through my papers, I suppose... but it just serves to prove my point.
SARAH	*(Looking at Nellie)* Does it?
NELLIE	Actually, Gordon wrote it for *me*... when you were all at Kew. It was so spontaneous, so... direct from the heart.
ELAINE	Utter nonsense...
	Nellie tries to grab the poem but does not succeed.
	I can still see his face in the candlelight. Across the table in Quaglino's when we'd known each other exactly one year – and he'd remembered that. The next morning I found it under my pillow.
CHARLIE	Forget him and get on with your lives.
SARAH	Good thinking, Charlie, but no go. I've got something else for you to fight over.
	Sarah takes a small package from her bag and tosses it onto the table.
ELAINE	What's that?
SARAH	Open it.

Elaine gives it to Charlie.

ELAINE   Charlie, you do it.

                Charlie opens it and withdraws a reel of film.

CHARLIE   What's this?

SARAH   What do you think, Sellotape?

NELLIE   Gordon?

                Sarah nods.

ELAINE   Those men gave it to *you*?

NELLIE   How can we see it?

SARAH   Charlie knows.

CHARLIE   *(To Sarah)* You *knew* this was coming?

                Sarah sniffs in acknowledgement.

SARAH   It took a long time.

CHARLIE   I'll fetch it from the shed.

ELAINE   No, wait! *(To Sarah)* Sarah, have you seen it?

SARAH   *(Reluctantly)* A bit of it.

ELAINE   Where?

SARAH   They said… [I mustn't tell anyone]

CHARLIE   We understand.

ELAINE   Well, I don't. Why all this… subterfuge. Why is my own daughter determined…

CHARLIE   Elaine, calm down.

ELAINE   *(To Sarah)* I always thought there was something going on.

SARAH   Nothing was going on – I *(ambivalently)* hated him.

SCENE THREE

[An hour later] Sarah is setting up the projector with the wall as a screen, with Charlie watching. [In this scene real film could be projected onto the screen or Gordon could deliver his presentation side stage.]

217

CHARLIE   Why won't you tell us anything?

SARAH   Because I swore not to, silly. I told you.

CHARLIE   Only little girls have secrets.

SARAH   And sometimes little girls get themselves into trouble. No compromise, no film.

CHARLIE   Just… concerned, that's all.

SARAH   *(Affectionately)* Don't be, Charlie. *(Pause)* I'm as nervous as you.

               Nellie and Elaine enter from the stairs. Nellie has flowers, Elaine a bottle of wine.

CHARLIE   Vase in the sink, glasses on the table. Give me the bottle.

               Nellie deals with the flowers. Charlie opens the bottle and pours the wine.

ELAINE   Half a glass only [for Sarah].

               Sarah begins to run the film and Charlie turns off the light. Gordon appears on screen, settling himself into a chair behind a desk, bookcase behind. [Although apparently interrupted by remarks from the others, suggesting a dialogue, what he says is actually independent of their responses.]

GORDON   Well, this is my flat, somewhere in Moscow. Fifth floor, south facing – which I'd have you know is a privilege. The view… [To cameraman, in Russian] Mosyem mi pokazat. [Could we just show…?] ['Niet' offscreen] Well, apparently not… but you can see my books. You can also see that I'm fine and reasonably well looked after, as befits a colonel in the KGB. You will be asking – because I know no-one yet has given you a satisfactory explanation – what possessed me. You remember Crawshaw, the first to come over, when he was asked which came first, cause or family – and he said cause. So with me. It's part of my being and has been since, oh, I don't

218

know when. Long before you came along, Elaine, if you're watching.

Elaine rises and approaches the screen.

And if you are I know what's going through your mind – how can that old lecher come to terms with a social life laid waste.

ELAINE   And how can you?

GORDON   There are ways and means. You might also ask if I'm happy here.

ELAINE   *Are* you happy?

GORDON   Whether I am or not is irrelevant. It's an inner drive, unquenchable, unstoppable. One can stand back, like a disembodied soul, watching it do its work. *(He appears to be emotional)* It's not without recompense.

ELAINE   Would I... survive there? If that were possible?

GORDON   But it's no place for a woman, Elaine. There's no Mr Michael, still less a need for one. But the headscarves are not that bad.

ELAINE   Why are you telling me this?

GORDON   It's not my wish to mislead, Elaine. What hypocrisy, I hear you say, after a life of doing just that. There are better things for you, Elaine. Accept. Move on. Use your looks while you can. I cannot stand in the way.

ELAINE   Then I curse you for what you've done to me.

Elaine, tearful, wanders away. Gordon reaches for a bottle and pours something into a glass.

GORDON   Ooph. *(Pause)* And then there's you, Nell. Don't ask me how I know, but I still have long ears, even here.

Nellie approaches the screen.

So I celebrate your good news, your pregnancy *(raises glass and sips)*... to the health of the child...

	but not as a father, you understand. That vista must close.
NELLIE	How can you know…?
GORDON	And make your peace with Elaine, if you can. And then you must learn that there's more to Russian music than Rachmaninov.
NELLIE	It meant nothing then?
GORDON	I'm truly sorry, Nellie.

Nellie, also tearful, is replaced by Charlie.

GORDON	I always wanted to ask, Charles, why you never flew.
CHARLIE	Spitfires?
GORDON	You seemed to have a rapport with *Spitfires*.
CHARLIE	I was invited. But there were family…
GORDON	Commitments, no doubt. So many of our generation *had*… family commitments. Foolishly most could not see the wider picture. And paid the price. But you, you had skills… as a mechanic…

Gordon sips from his glass.

CHARLIE	*(Laughing ruefully)* Cars, motorcycles – anything with an engine.
GORDON	… and were ashamed of that. Well, shame on you. Here, I should tell you, skills such as yours are valued highly. But they go hand in hand with an education, Charles. I understand you've started the climb.
CHARLIE	How can you know about the *[Sarah's]* lessons?

Gordon looks to his side.

GORDON	Aw, they're signalling already. A film in their book – or *their* time – is so short. Would that they could understand the English view that explanations are of right. So I must soon say [farewell]… *(Long pause)*

CHARLIE	You haven't mentioned Sarah.
GORDON	But I've left the most difficult thing to last because it causes me much pain. Maybe you will understand… maybe not. You will be wondering why I haven't mentioned Sarah… my unpredictable, infinitely touchy, hot and cold by turns, *(emotionally)* unbearably absent Sarah. A day doesn't pass without my missing her… and cursing that woman living below in that wretched tenement of yours. Oh, yes, it was she who gave me away… and denied me time for my long-rehearsed expressions of love and affection, and my body a last ecstatic shiver…
VOICE OFF	*(In Russian)* Vi dolsni ostanoveetsa syeychas, tovarishch. *[You must stop now, comrade.]*

> *The film stops abruptly, leaving the room in darkness. Unnoticed by the others Sarah picks up a kitchen knife and leaves the room. Charlie switches on the light. A long pause.*

NELLIE	Now we all know where we stand.
ELAINE	Do we? *(Pause)* Where's Sarah?
CHARLIE	Gone downstairs I expect.
NELLIE	Elaine, what did he mean… about the child?
ELAINE	*(Maliciously)* Didn't you know? But then why should you? Gordon was sterile, Nellie. He couldn't have fathered your child, just as he couldn't father mine.
NELLIE	Then why did you let me go on dreaming?
ELAINE	Whenever I looked at you two, there was a kind of… symmetry… great clouds of ignorance about what you each did not know. It amused me, I suppose. *(Pause)* I'm sorry, that's how I am.
NELLIE	But now the symmetry's gone I'm back to being Sarah's Mrs Mouse, while Charlie…

ELAINE	… is still in a fog of uncertainty. But only for a few moments. Until the symmetry is restored.
CHARLIE	Tell it straight, you…
ELAINE	Devious? Incoherent?
CHARLIE	… bloody woman.
NELLIE	I never believed Charlie had it in him to sow his wild oats… with you.
ELAINE	Oh, but he did. You did, didn't you Charlie? But you see, Nellie, the timing was way, way off. Pity he never kept a diary. Then, anyway.
NELLIE	But if Sarah's sixteen, that means you were still in Amberfield when…
CHARLIE	Who then?
ELAINE	You can't guess?
NELLIE	I can guess.
CHARLIE	You?
NELLIE	Your brother… Tom.
CHARLIE	Tom? *(To Elaine)* You fucked my brother Tom? You bloody whore…
ELAINE	Tom and I were lovers, Charlie. But for the war we would have… *(cries)*. It's why you never heard from me. I'm sorry.
CHARLIE	So Sarah is my…
ELAINE	Niece.
NELLIE	Shush. Something's not quite right – listen!
	Increasingly raised voices are heard from the floor below, followed by a piercing scream.
CHARLIE	Bloody hell.
ELAINE	And that's where she'll end up, that child.
	Charlie rushes downstairs. The noises intensify. Nellie and Elaine grasp hands. After a few seconds Sarah returns, looking distraught, followed by Charlie, who

tosses a bloodied knife into the sink.

ELAINE   *(To Sarah)* What have you done?

                 Sarah looks at them defiantly.

CHARLIE   Ruby's gone.

NELLIE   Not...?

CHARLIE   Out. Fled. Her arm was cut. Not badly, I think.

SARAH   I should have killed her.

ELAINE   You've done enough.

CHARLIE   She'll go to her sister's at Brentford. They'll ring the police from there.

                 Sarah, now composed, goes to the phone and dials.

NELLIE   What are you doing?

CHARLIE   Not the police!

SARAH   *(Into phone)* Hello. Dimitri. I need help – code YF... like now, yes. Immediately, yes! *(Puts down phone)*

ELAINE   *(To Sarah)* Gordon said... Just tell me, for pity's sake, did he ever...

SARAH   Once.

ELAINE   When?

SARAH   That would be telling.

                 Sarah unplugs the projector, waves the plug at Charlie and smiles. She stuffs the projector into her bag.

                 All packed away... uncle.

CHARLIE   You knew... about Tom?

SARAH   Gordon guessed. That day in the churchyard. Elaine always was an open book. That's when it ended for her. With Gordon, I mean.

                 The doorbell rings three times.

SARAH   *(Tearfully)* I have to go.

ELAINE   *(Tearfully)* You can still come home.

                 Sarah curtseys to Elaine.

SARAH	*(To all)* I'll be in touch.
	Sarah exits and runs down the stairs.
ELAINE	Look, will you two be alright if I leave you too?
NELLIE	Strange to say, I feel a weight's been lifted from me.
ELAINE	You Charlie?
CHARLIE	Funny, but the same I suppose.
ELAINE	I'll be at home if anything…
	She exits. A long pause.
CHARLIE	*(Realising)* Ha.
NELLIE	What?
CHARLIE	We've got one loose end to tie up.
NELLIE	What's that?
CHARLIE	To tell my mother she's Sarah's granny. A treat for both of them there.
NELLIE	Charlie, has this really ended?
CHARLIE	We'll have our own family soon. Then bugger them all.
NELLIE	I've been thinking. How about David or Elizabeth – for the baby.
CHARLIE	Definitely not Tom.
NELLIE	Or Sarah. Or Elaine.
CHARLIE	Eelane's not bad.
NELLIE	A bit close for comfort.
CHARLIE	I suppose. You know what I feel like? A spot of Jim's brandy, while we wait to face the music.
NELLIE	There's racing at Kempton tomorrow.
CHARLIE	Well, fancy you telling me that.
NELLIE	No, you're right. Mustn't get carried away. Might not be here.
CHARLIE	As sure as eggs are eggs Mr Plod's going to ring the bell any moment.

They giggle together, then notice Sarah standing in the doorway. Behind her is a man (Dimitri) in a black suit.

CHARLIE   You didn't go?

SARAH   Not yet. *(To Dimitri)* In the sink.

Dimitri steps forward, takes the knife out of the sink, washes it carefully, then rinses the sink.

DIMITRI   *(To Sarah, in Russian)* Gdye eto polozhit'? *[Where do I put this?]*

SARAH   *(Shrugging) (In Russian)* Ya ne znayu. *[I don't know.]*

DIMITRI   *(To Charlie)* Where does this stay?

CHARLIE   In that drawer there.

Dimitri places the knife in the drawer.

DIMITRI   No knife, no attack. That woman – all lies, um?

He nods to Sarah, who follows him out. Sarah, framed in the doorway, turns back to them.

SARAH   Nellie!

Sarah, in profile, places her hand on her abdomen to indicate pregnancy.

NELLIE   You too?

SARAH   You see, Nellie, we do have something in common after all. And you must never, ever, believe anything my mother tells you. Whatever else he might have been, Gordon was never sterile.

CHARLIE   My God.

SARAH   And you, Charlie. You could have what you wanted all along… more or less.

Sarah smiles enigmatically and exits. The stage darkens.

END

225

MELUSINA BALLERINA

Characters:

    Melissa Gray – a young graduate in robotics
    Roberto Malario – MD of *Robotoys*
    Thomas Gray – Melissa's father and an accountant
    Claire Gray – Melissa's stepmother
    Spencer McQueen – a robotics technician
    Bertrand (Bertie) Gray – Thomas' brother and an entrepreneur
    Tariq Al-Khouri – a wealthy Middle Eastern businessman
    Waitress in café

Places – (1) A hidden robotics laboratory adjacent to Roberto's apartment in Kensington; (2) The Grays' family home in Ruislip; (3) A Pimlico café

Time – The present

ACT ONE

SCENE ONE

The stage is dimly lit, with a tall mirror centre rear stage and a single chair right stage. Slumped in the chair is the figure of a presumed teenage schoolgirl (Melissa) wearing a straw hat, blouse and pleated skirt. Dejectedly, she rises, removes her hat, blouse and skirt to reveal a black leotard such as a ballet dancer might wear. She walks slowly towards the mirror, stands in front of it and, back to the audience, raises her arms above her head. She executes several simple, but graceful and perfect, balletic movements, culminating in a 'dying swan' descent to the floor. Only now can the audience see she is in deep distress, becoming tearful and beating the floor with her fists. The lights slowly dim to black.

SCENE TWO

Roberto, Melissa and Spencer sit at a table in a large room containing a jumble of electronic equipment and robotic parts of the human body. Rear stage is a large upright cabinet and a divan-style bed bearing only a mattress. Left stage is a door leading to the main apartment and right stage another door leading to other rooms. On the table is a shoebox-sized black box and a bowl containing several types of fruit. Spencer is holding a robotic animal toy resembling a large caterpillar.

ROBERTO   That's enough heart-searching for today. It's a good idea, Spencer – will sell well – but it's not going to plug the gap. Melissa, what have you got for us. Brighten up my afternoon, please. *(Looking at the box)* Can't see that taking the public by storm.

MELISSA   Not meant to, Roberto. It's what it does. Spencer, choose a fruit from the bowl.

229

ROBERTO   Oh, c'mon. No time for…

SPENCER   For you, my girl, an over-ripe peach I think.

MELISSA   Put it in the chamber and press the button.

Spencer does so. The box lights up.

What does the readout say?

SPENCER   It says a compaction density of nought point seven eight three. Isn't that just dandy?

MELISSA   Press again.

SPENCER   Peach – ripeness index seventy-eight per cent. Bully for you.

ROBERTO   Melissa, since when did we have a stall at Covent Garden? What's this leading up to?

MELISSA   Quantification of the quality of touch. Imagine your finger touching someone's skin.

ROBERTO   Ah! Or lips coming together.

MELISSA   Or other…

SPENCER   And coupled with the motor response mechanisms which we have…

ROBERTO   The caressing hand, the sensuous kiss. But is our figure ready for it?

MELISSA   Spencer says he tried it out yesterday.

SPENCER   It couldn't tell the difference. Human versus robot.

MELISSA   Difference from what though? Your own clumsy appendages? Geeky nerd.

ROBERTO   In the dark perhaps?

MELISSA   *(Giggling)* Otherwise it would have rejected him.

SPENCER   What's that supposed to mean?

Melissa pokes out her tongue at him.

ROBERTO   Look, returning to our earlier discussion. You say the humanoid's ready for trial?

MELISSA   Humanoid? Melusina!

ROBERTO   Perhaps I should test it myself.

MELISSA   To make me jealous?

              Roberto takes her hand, squeezes it and looks into her
              eyes.

ROBERTO   Compaction density – off the scale!

MELISSA   Good.

SPENCER   Should I be watching this?

ROBERTO   Just one question, Melissa.

MELISSA   Fire away.

ROBERTO   You're still the model – for this prototype? Still
              your face? You happy with that?

MELISSA   You pay me extra, remember?

ROBERTO   Okay, then. But give it a different voice. Higher
              pitched – Arabs prefer that.

MELISSA   Absolutely.

ROBERTO   And always in subdued light, eh.

MELISSA   Stop worrying.

ROBERTO   If it can get us out of our financial mess…

MELISSA   It will.

SPENCER   We're done then?

ROBERTO   I think so.

              Spencer picks up his toy and rises.

SPENCER   A good weekend, both.

ROBERTO   You too, Spencer. And thanks for your… discretion.

MELISSA   Bye, Spencer.

              Spencer exits to the apartment left stage.

ROBERTO   Can we trust him?

MELISSA   To stay silent?

ROBERTO   Or with us. We're ahead in the field, the potential's
              enormous. *(Pause)* But sometimes I question
              the…

MELISSA   Morality? Then don't. Isn't it better that men can go home to their wives blameless.

ROBERTO   Without having touched a real woman you mean?

MELISSA   A little white lie, that's all.

ROBERTO   Like getting off a speeding ticket because a branch happened to cover the sign.

MELISSA   And other benefits – health, for one.

ROBERTO   Uhr. Don't spoil my weekend.

MELISSA   Our weekend. Don't forget you're meeting my parents tomorrow.

ROBERTO   Oh, God. I'll have to take them something.

Melissa picks up the black box.

MELISSA   How about this? Help them tell an onion from a potato.

ROBERTO   C'mon, out.

They rise and exit to the apartment, closing the door behind them.

SCENE THREE

[The same evening] The Grays' house in Ruislip. Thomas and Claire are sitting at the dining room table.

THOMAS   If I were a betting man…

CLAIRE   Which you're not, Thomas.

THOMAS   No, dear.

CLAIRE   Go on then.

THOMAS   Well, if I were I would say Melissa has something cooking in that lab of hers. *(Looking at watch)* It's now ten past seven…

CLAIRE   *(Facetiously)* And yesterday it was just five past when she came in.

THOMAS	And the day before that?
CLAIRE	We didn't set eyes on her. *(Pause)* She's twenty-two, Thomas, and entitled to live her life as she pleases… up to a point.
THOMAS	Which is up to our doorstep.
CLAIRE	And inside?
THOMAS	She observes the rules of notification.
CLAIRE	*(Amused)* Is it really that important to you?
THOMAS	That dish there.
CLAIRE	The chicken casserole?
THOMAS	For how many people?
CLAIRE	*(Counting on fingers)* Twelve.
THOMAS	Twelve?
CLAIRE	Portions. Portions in this house equals people. *(Pause)* It's to last for the next three days.
THOMAS	Or *longer* if she doesn't show. You take my point?
CLAIRE	Oh, the advantage of being married to an accountant. *(Pause)* But if she doesn't show at all I agree things could be getting serious. *(Pause)* Have you met this Roberto?
THOMAS	Once. After her interview, when I collected her.
CLAIRE	You didn't tell me.
THOMAS	You weren't interested. Smooth type. Suave.
CLAIRE	A Jacob to your Esau.
THOMAS	*(Mock threatening, waving hands)* Brreeh…
CLAIRE	Quite.
THOMAS	But why's he coming tomorrow? She's never invited anyone for dinner before.
CLAIRE	Something to tell us, perhaps? *(Thoughtfully)* But it is time she left this house, Thomas.
THOMAS	You know he's been ringing here? Three times in one week.

CLAIRE	Is that a calendar week or a continuous series of seven days? Or seven days plucked at random from the last month?
THOMAS	You're being facetious, Claire, and it doesn't become you.
CLAIRE	It's a safety valve, Thomas – where you're concerned – in case I reach the point of exploding, which I'm fast…

Sound of the front door closing.

THOMAS	*(Looking at watch)* Ah, thirteen minutes past.
CLAIRE	Check. *(Pause)* Your opportunity to ask her.

Melissa enters.

MELISSA	Oh, dear. You've got that perplexed look that means something's coming my way. *(Dancing and singing)* Could it be, yes it could… *[West Side Story]*
THOMAS	Oh, for heaven's sake.
CLAIRE	Sit down, Melissa. Your father and I…
MELISSA	*(Without expression)* Yes, Roberto wants me to marry him.
THOMAS	Mm. Won't need the pin, then, to extract that particular winkle.
CLAIRE	Thomas!
THOMAS	Melissa, don't you think it would have been appropriate for you to have…
MELISSA	Introduced him before committing myself? No, I don't.
THOMAS	Why?
MELISSA	*(Flippantly)* Think of the complications. *(Pause)* He's a catholic.
CLAIRE	Really?
THOMAS	And we're so prudish as to think that would make a difference?

MELISSA   Too risky.

CLAIRE   Is he a… practising catholic?

MELISSA   No. But his family is.

THOMAS   Then on Sunday we'll pray for your union.

MELISSA   Why not now?

THOMAS   Now? You mean here and now?

MELISSA   No time like the present. And you can pray for us at tomorrow's dinner.

CLAIRE   Inwardly, Thomas, is sufficient.

THOMAS   A moment's silence then. *(Pause)* Oh my God!

CLAIRE   Thomas! That's excessive.

THOMAS   Do you see who's pulled up outside?

            All peer through the window.

MELISSA   Mm. I love Bertie's plum-coloured jag.

CLAIRE   It's so ostentatious. Whatever can he want?

THOMAS   In short, money.

CLAIRE   Hasn't he got enough?

THOMAS   Apparently not enough for an oil pipeline. I said I'd advise.

CLAIRE   Thomas, I told you not to get involved.

THOMAS   Claire, compose yourself. *(Pause)* He's coming up the path.

CLAIRE   Who's that following him?

MELISSA   An assassin, probably… from the headpiece. *(Pause)* Intriguing… shall I let them in?

            Melissa exits to the front door.

CLAIRE   You knew of this?

THOMAS   Bertie rang this morning. I thought it'd be days away.

CLAIRE   You should know your brother by now.

            Melissa returns with Bertie and the visitor, a

distinguished-looking Arab wearing a traditional headpiece.

BERTIE   Claire, my peach. My heart's desire. *(Kisses)* Mwah, mwah.

CLAIRE   Bertie, trembling though my body might be, you should know by now that your brand of softening up never works.

BERTIE   Try again then. How charming you look, my dear. *(Pause)* I sense Thomas has told you why…

CLAIRE   He didn't need to. Social visits were never your thing.

BERTIE   One day I shall make an exception and you will not even descend to earth.

CLAIRE   I can't wait.

BERTIE   *(Seriously)* But it's good to see you. *(Pause)* Now, it's my pleasure to introduce my good friend Sheikh Tariq Al-Khouri.

TARIQ   So much truth is spoken in jest, Mrs Gray. A peach in parts of our country is of inestimable worth. *(Pause)* And Mr Gray…

THOMAS   Thomas.

TARIQ   … Thomas, whose deep understanding of our country's finances we look to as a lifeline…

THOMAS   You do me too much credit, your… highness.

TARIQ   Tariq.

THOMAS   *(Obsequiously)* Tariq.

CLAIRE   Thomas, why don't you take…

TARIQ   But your beautiful daughter, hovering in the background like a butterfly hesitant over the choicest flower. You haven't properly introduced us.

CLAIRE   Melissa is Thomas' daughter, my step-daughter, at the moment living with us.

Tariq takes Melissa's hand and kisses it.

TARIQ   Your Uncle Bertie has told me much already.

	A first at Keble – and in robotics. A remarkable achievement.
MELISSA	For a woman.
TARIQ	No, for anyone. Melissa, when in Rome… *(Pause)* Now, gentlemen, to business.
THOMAS	I suggest my study.
BERTIE	Admirable. *(To women)* Excuse us. *(Turning to Claire)* Coffee in twenty minutes… Claire?
CLAIRE	Incorrigible.
	The men exit.
	Well, finding ourselves together…
MELISSA	I have to…
CLAIRE	*(Not unkindly)* You'll sit down. You're in my house.
MELSSA	I'm my father's daughter. I have a place here.
CLAIRE	But a defined place. *(Pause)* Now, this Roberto.
MELISSA	Actually, you may like him. Serious, devoted to his work…
CLAIRE	And to you?
MELISSA	*(Enigmatically)* I'm his greatest asset. But I was joking about the marriage.
CLAIRE	I guessed so. Tormenting poor Thomas. *(Pause)* Tomorrow, then. Lasagne alla Napoletana? And Thomas has got in a rather nice Chianti.
MELISSA	Perfect.
CLAIRE	All's well, then.
MELISSA	*(Tentatively)* And between us?
CLAIRE	Of course, naturally… Well, I suppose we've had our ups and downs. *(Pause)* You don't still blame me, do you?
MELISSA	For letting my father destroy my career?
CLAIRE	In ballet, you mean?

MELISSA	It's worked its way through the system. I've flushed the pan.
CLAIRE	I think I just happened to come along at the wrong time.
MELISSA	You could have influenced him.
CLAIRE	I tried to be impartial, but he…
MELISSA	Convinced you I was not good enough.
CLAIRE	How was I to judge?
MELISSA	By coming to watch me – winning my competitions. *(Bitterly)* Which he seldom did.
CLARE	Melissa, if you still harbour such thoughts, speak to him. There may have been other reasons.
MELISSA	Such as?
CLAIRE	The wider picture. His concern for your future. A first at Oxford is a huge deal. Do you deny him credit for that? Resentment doesn't usually breed that sort of success.
MELISSA	Maybe that's because I'd found myself a mission.
CLAIRE	In robotics? I'd like to hear about it.
MELISSA	Ask Roberto tomorrow. *(Wistfully)* It goes back a long way.
CLAIRE	Well, by all accounts you were an…
MELISSA	Unusual child?
CLAIRE	Well, interested in things that seemed more the province of…
MELISSA	Males?
CLAIRE	That sounds very un-pc – but I'd never before heard of a girl wedded to a Meccano set.
MELISSA	Neither had I.
CLAIRE	But when you got your place at Oxford…
MELISSA	*(Suddenly attentive)* How did you feel? About that?

CLAIRE	Immensely proud. To my surprise.
MELISSA	You didn't show it.
CLAIRE	And relieved, because, frankly, with you away there would be time for… well, reassessment of our positions. Reconciliation perhaps.
MELISSA	And has there been?
CLAIRE	Can you recall us sitting, talking like this?
MELISSA	Let's make it work, then.
CLAIRE	After all, we may have common cause in the irascible Thomas. *(Pause)* Oh, I've forgotten the coffee…

> *Claire makes to go to the kitchen but turns at the door. She fights to express her thoughts.*

	Melissa… while we're still alone.
MELISSA	Yes.
CLAIRE	Last night… I heard you crying.
MELISSA	Did you? I don't remember.
CLAIRE	Sometime after midnight.
MELISSA	*(Warily)* Must have been a dream, then.
CLAIRE	But the toilet had just flushed.
MELISSA	Don't worry about it.

> *Claire returns to stand by her.*

CLAIRE	Is anything troubling you?
MELISSA	Why's it important?
CLAIRE	Because it's not the first time. *(Pause)* You *can* tell me… if you want.
MELISSA	*(With a faint smile)* I wouldn't know how.

> *Claire puts her arm around Melissa's shoulders.*

CLAIRE	I'm always around, right? *(No answer)* Right?
MELISSA	Right.
CLAIRE	Good. *(Pause)* Look, don't be alarmed, but there's a wasp crawling up your sleeve.

MELISSA   *(Looking)* Where?

CLAIRE   Behind your elbow.

            *Melissa pulls the sleeve around, sees the wasp and
            brushes it off with her hand; it falls to the floor.
            Seemingly out of character, a look of anger comes into
            her face. Losing control, she takes off a shoe, hits the
            wasp and kills it.*

            Melissa, what's the matter with you?

MELISSA   *(Now repentant, as much for the dead wasp as for Claire)*
            I'm sorry, I'm sorry.

            *She picks up the wasp by the wings as a child might
            and puts it in Claire's outstretched hand.*

CLAIRE   You are a strange one sometimes, Melissa.

            She hugs Melissa, who allows herself to be hugged.

MELISSA   I am, aren't I?

CLAIRE   Come on then, the coffee.

MELISSA   You make it, I'll take it in.

CLAIRE   So long as you don't get involved, eh?

MELISSA   Would I?

            The stage darkens.

SCENE FOUR

*[The following evening] Thomas, Claire, Melissa and Roberto are at the
dining table having coffee after their meal. They are mildly inebriated: Thomas
is overbearing, Claire amused, Melissa sullen and Roberto uncomfortable and
combative. Thomas rises to get more coffee.*

THOMAS   So, as I was saying to Claire only this morning,
            with the impending recession about to…

MELISSA   What recession?

THOMAS   Roberto, you're in business. Explain to my

daughter.

ROBERTO	I'm sorry, Thomas. I'm not sure I know what you're talking about.
MELISSA	*(To Roberto, hissing)* You sure you don't?
THOMAS	The indicators have been there for a while. For those with the nous to see. First go the expendables. Did you follow the summer sales? Tail-end dip?
ROBERTO	Our marketing's been quite steady. We don't rely on sales.
THOMAS	But you'll expect a big leap at Christmas? Or am I mistaken?
ROBERTO	No, you're not mistaken, We're prepared for it.
THOMAS	New products, ahead of the field?
ROBERTO	*(Patiently)* We will have, yes.
THOMAS	Only will have? Should be ready now, my boy.
ROBERTO	*(Now exasperated)* You must be aware, Mr Gray, that our market is susceptible to sudden change. Too early and you can be buggered. Last year we had a robotic parachutist – great hopes for it – then had to withdraw it when that SAS unit was lost in Syria.
CLAIRE	Not lost exactly. Makes me shudder to think about it.
MELISSA	Claire!
CLAIRE	So what *do* you have for us this Christmas, Roberto?
ROBERTO	Robotic caterpillars.
THOMAS	Tell me you're being facetious.
ROBERTO	Far from it. Caterpillar stocking-filler, that's the TV jingle
THOMAS	So what do they do, these… caterpillars?
ROBERTO	They travel the floor consuming lettuce leaves.
THOMAS	*(Looking pointedly at the floor)* Not much use to us here then. *(Pause)* Would they be robotic lettuces?

241

CLAIRE	Thomas, now you're being facetious.
ROBERTO	No, quite stationary.
MELISSA	*(Hardly able to suppress laughter)* So as to conserve caterpillar battery life. If you have two they can compete with one another. Caterpillars, not lettuces.
ROBERTO	That's the *de luxe* box set.
CLAIRE	That's enough sparring, I think. *(Mysteriously)* Now, Roberto. Yesterday Melissa said she had a mission and was too shy to reveal it, and we should ask you.
ROBERTO	*(Taken aback)* I see. Well, so far it's been under wraps.
CLAIRE	Go on, tell!
ROBERTO	*(Reluctantly)* It's a robotic dancer…
MELISSA	A ballerina, actually.
THOMAS	Oh, for heaven's sake. *(To Melissa)* Will you never let it rest?
ROBERTO	An idea she had when she joined us. Stands about seventy centimetres high and can execute all the basic movements, including spins and leaps. Still needs refinement but we think it'll be ready in time.
THOMAS	And what are you going to call it…
MELISSA	Her!
ROBERTO	I wanted it to be Melissa, obviously.
MELISSA	I didn't.
ROBERTO	Then Spencer – our technician – had a brilliant idea. Melusina.
CLAIRE	The legendary lady with the tail of a serpent.
ROBERTO	But only once a week.
THOMAS	Quite often enough I should think. Back end only though, I believe. *(Pause)* I should have thought that was a bit limiting.

MELISSA	You would, wouldn't you.
	For a moment Thomas looks thunderously at Melissa.
CLAIRE	Melissa, what a strange thing to say.
THOMAS	Can you imagine the TV adverts? In prime time. And the packaging.
CLAIRE	But Thomas. That could be something for you. *(To Melissa and Roberto)* Thomas now chairs the local child action group – *Ruislip Against Child Poverty*. Toys at Christmas, Thomas. Help make your mark.
MELISSA	*(Rounding on Thomas)* I didn't know about that.
CLAIRE	Only happened last week.
MELISSA	And *he* knows about children? I don't think so.
CLAIRE	Melissa, whatever's got into you? Calm down.
MELISSA	Don't you need to be screened to work with children?
CLAIRE	Probably not, to control the finances.
MELISSA	If that's all it is.
CLAIRE	Melissa…
MELISSA	*(Rising)* Time for a comfort break, I think.
	Melissa exits hastily.
THOMAS	I know I shouldn't have opened that second bottle. Should I? *(To Roberto)* You sure you know what you're doing?
CLAIRE	She had hardly any.
THOMAS	What's her problem then?
CLAIRE	You touched a raw nerve.
THOMAS	Not that old chestnut again.
ROBERTO	What old chestnut is that?
THOMAS	Melissa thinks…
CLAIRE	Thomas, I'll explain. You see, Roberto – and you may be aware of this already – Melissa wanted to be – of all things – a ballet dancer.

ROBERTO	Cut out for it, I'd say.
CLAIRE	Thomas felt that a good education, in the light of her school record, had priority.
THOMAS	And I stand by that.
CLAIRE	We, Thomas and I – for that was about the time I married him – thought she'd come to accept it. But occasionally, like just now, the old resentment surfaces.
ROBERTO	Yes, she's told me. *(Pause)* But why her reaction to Thomas chairing the child group?
THOMAS	*(Angrily)* Because she thinks I'll stop them all becoming ballerinas. *(More soberly)* Because she's prone to fantasise that as a child she was hard done by.
ROBERTO	And was she?
CLAIRE	After she went to university Thomas cleared her room. An example.
THOMAS	Where else could I put the computer?
CLAIRE	Well, it didn't help. *(Pause)* She's a long time coming back. Think I'd better check she's OK.
	Claire rises and exits.
THOMAS	Highly strung young filly sometimes, our Melissa.
ROBERTO	Must save it for home then.
THOMAS	Well, that's something. *(Pause)* Serious about her, are you?
ROBERTO	That's rather a leading question. But yes, actually. It's just early days.
THOMAS	So it is, so it is. *(Pause)* So what else have you got on the drawing board?
ROBERTO	Eventually, life-size figures. Yesterday I had a request from the Church. Because there were more churches than priests could we develop one to help administer the sacraments? Plop in the wafer, that sort of thing.

THOMAS	You certainly know how to wind people up, don't you?
ROBERTO	No, seriously...

The stage darkens.

SCENE FIVE

[A month later] The robotics workshop. Roberto is sitting at the table, opening an envelope and withdrawing a cheque. Melissa is half-heartedly doing dance exercises.

ROBERTO	Well, look at this.
MELISSA	*(Pausing)* What?
ROBERTO	A cheque for... well look.
MELISSA	Whew. I thought he'd already paid for her... *(sniggers)* favours.
ROBERTO	He wants to buy her.
MELISSA	I'd give him two for that.
ROBERTO	No... no.
MELISSA	Why not?
ROBERTO	Because Melusina – and others to follow – are our future.
MELISSA	Roberto, we make toys – not surrogate prostitutes.
ROBERTO	You call your star ballerina a surrogate prostitute?
MELISSA	Well, isn't she?
ROBERTO	She's the embodiment of technologies others only dream of.
MELISSA	Well, she's beginning to give me the creeps. I look in a mirror. What do I see? Not myself. I see a made up tart that is her.
ROBERTO	You were the one pushing for it.
MELISSA	And still am, but not for that.

ROBERTO   We'll model the next one on someone else – but God knows who. *(Looking at his watch)* Another punter's due – I need to test the thing. *(Pause)* Can you check next door?

Melissa goes to the door right stage, opens it and peers in.

MELISSA   Another world, eh? If they caught sight of in here [the lab] it'd dampen their ardour. Anyway, *(facetiously)* I'll check the bed... and the lighting... and the music.

ROBERTO   The Middle Eastern track, remember.

MELISSA   I'll leave you to your testing. Enjoy!

She makes to exit.

ROBERTO   Melissa.

MELISSA   *(Turning)* What?

ROBERTO   She can't hold a candle to you.

MELISSA   Reassuring to know.

Melissa exits and closes the door. Roberto picks up a remote. He opens the cabinet door to reveal Melusina, dressed in flimsy lingerie [In performance Melusina can be played by Melissa]. Roberto addresses her and she answers seductively.

ROBERTO   Appellation.

MELUSINA   Your excellency.

ROBERTO   Familiar name.

MELUSINA   Hamid Ali.

ROBERTO   Correction – Hamid.

MELUSINA   Hamid.

Using the remote, Roberto gets Melusina to perform a series of responses to supposedly visual, auditory and tactile cues, such a stroking of the cheek, embracing, kissing, sitting on the bed, lying back, etc. Melusina returns to a standing position.

ROBERTO *(Imitating client)* That was fantastic. You were so lifelike, Melusina.

MELUSINA You are a wonderful lover, Hamid.

ROBERTO *(Imitating client)* Am I?

MELUSINA Beyond a girl's wildest dreams.

ROBERTO *(Imitating client)* You almost had me believing you were real.

MELUSINA Next time I will be even better able to anticipate your needs.

ROBERTO *(Aside)* God, that sounds a bit wooden.

MELUSINA I beg your Excellency's pardon?

> *Roberto taps frantically into his remote.*

Next week will be even better. I can't wait for it.

> *Roberto switches off Melusina, who appears to freeze.*

ROBERTO Well, you'll bloody have to, won't you? *(Pause)* Now, back to your cabinet, I think. *(Calling)* Melissa.

> *The door swings open but Melissa remains unseen.*

Melissa, how do you make the thing walk backwards?

MELISSA *(Calling)* That's next month's project.

> *Roberto manoeuvres Melusina into the cabinet and shuts the door.*

ROBERTO Is our receptionist in place?

> *Melissa re-enters.*

MELISSA I just heard her come in.

ROBERTO Client details?

MELISSA Under the blotting pad – where they write their cheques.

ROBERTO And this one is?

MELISSA Another Arab. Curious how this attracts them when money's no barrier to getting the real thing. Conscience, I suppose.

ROBERTO	I'd... have thought not.
MELISSA	What then?
ROBERTO	The quality of the pleasure. Unadulterated by the tackiness of the human body. Muscular movements enhanced. Pheromones spiced up. All in a perfect frame.
MELISSA	Mine?
ROBERTO	Well, I suppose... for the moment. *(Pause)* Now, before we leave, I want you to look at this.

He picks up a robotic arm from the table.

	The sensor is now at the tip of the third finger. See how the arc of the fingers changes according to the pressure. And the other is around the wrist, so that when grasped the forearm moves downwards and the hand rotates.
MELISSA	Who dreamt that up, you?
ROBERTO	Actually, Spencer. I'm coming to realise he's... very innovative.
MELISSA	He's a lemon.
ROBERTO	Maybe. But I'm upping his pay.
MELISSA	To keep him on board?
ROBERTO	Something like that. Anyway, he'll be in shortly to set things up. This one wants Melusina sitting on the edge of the bed. *(To himself)* God knows how she'll finish up, though.
MELISSA	In submissive mode before they've even started.
ROBERTO	Who are we to argue? *(Pause)* Drink before you go home?
MELISSA	Pratchett's next door?
ROBERTO	Right.

They switch off the main light and exit stage left. As soon as the front door to the apartment has closed, Spencer enters from the door stage right. He searches for Melusina's remote, then goes to her cabinet and opens it. He presses the remote. Melusina moves forward stiffly and stops. As Spencer places his arm around her waist the lights dim to blackness.

SCENE SIX

[Several days later] The Grays' living room. Melissa is on the sofa, idly flicking through the pages of a magazine. Thomas is at the table doing paperwork. They are not comfortable together and throughout Melissa speaks in a tone suggestive of recrimination. As Thomas starts to speak Melissa looks at her wristwatch.

THOMAS   Melissa...

MELISSA   Twenty-two minutes and thirty-five seconds.

THOMAS   For what?

MELISSA   Since you last spoke to me.

THOMAS   What? I'm sorry then. These demands get more and more pressing. Once you could set them aside for weeks. Now, they're down on you in a fortnight.

MELISSA   Is that why you've seemed so... detached?

THOMAS   Partly.

MELISSA   Only partly? *(Pause)* Ah, it's me, isn't it, not paying my way. I said I'd contribute.

THOMAS   It wouldn't make much difference if you did.

MELISSA   What then?

THOMAS   It's just that I... sometimes worry about you, Melissa.

MELISSA   Why?

THOMAS   I wish I knew. Gut feelings. A promise made to your mother before she died. To involve myself more.

MELISSA   Well, there's news. *(Pause)* About Roberto, then?

THOMAS	He seemed a nice enough young fellow.
MELSSA	But?
THOMAS	I suppose it's that – in my work – I pigeon-hole people. A fault, I know, but it's how I see my way through difficult negotiations. A bit like navigating across a chessboard. Rigidly. Limited pieces, some powerful. I know life's not really like that.
MELISSA	So much for the subtly calculating financial wizard.
THOMAS	Thing is though, I'm seldom wrong.
MELISSA	OK. So how did you get in the mess you're in?
THOMAS	Where?
MELISSA	There. On the table.
THOMAS	Oh, because they're all unseen. Names, not faces. And some of the names – like this one: Peaching and Pixter, for heaven's sake – are fabrications. Bogus companies set up just to claw back your money.
MELISSA	Golly. And that's where you put Roberto.
THOMAS	Of course not. But in my mind he's someone for whom money takes precedence over ideals. And that's next to a box labelled: money takes precedence over all else.
MELISSA	Meaning relationships.
THOMAS	Look, Melissa, I've gone too far. I'm sorry. I must have sucked on a lemon at breakfast. I'm sure you're both well suited.
MELISSA	Meaning you could still be right. *(Pause)* Actually… I think you might be right.
THOMAS	Oh?
MELISSA	Mm.
THOMAS	And that doesn't worry you?
MELISSA	I'm not committed to anything. At least yet. And what he has – his business – gives me what… I once dreamed of.

THOMAS	A robotic ballerina… but not a toy?
MELISSA	*(Surprised)* Roberto told you that?
THOMAS	You left sketches lying around.
MELISSA	You've been in my room!
THOMAS	I put two and two together.
MELISSA	Huh. Imagine. If you go to the ballet…
THOMAS	Which I never do.
MELISSA	… what you see is talent, sure, but what you don't see is perfection. Poor timing, ungraceful movements. Over-developed thighs. Ugliness where there should be beauty. Expressions of pain on their faces because of the hell it is… that's real for sure.
THOMAS	You can eliminate them?
MELISSA	Yes… and take it further. Leaps higher than you thought possible, movements graceful beyond compare. Differences the human eye can appreciate.
THOMAS	Sounds far too clinical to me. Besides, would people pay? I think half the time they go to criticise. They're waiting for the leap that doesn't come off, or the principal ballerina falling into the orchestra pit.
MELISSA	Forget it. It's years away.
THOMAS	But Roberto would support it.
MELISSA	If it pays.
THOMAS	But first a toy at Christmas.
MELISSA	A toy at Christmas. The first hurdle.
THOMAS	And development costs are covered?
MELISSA	Mm… no.
THOMAS	Do you think he'll ask me direct… for help?
MELISSA	He might… but I've told him not yet. Because you were addicted to an oil pipeline.

THOMAS   If it comes off I'd be better placed to help. Though whether I would or not...

The stage darkens.

SCENE SEVEN

[A week later] Melissa and Spencer are working at the bench in the laboratory.

SPENCER   Don't you think Melusina's got class?

MELISSA   She's very classy.

SPENCER   I meant her background, if she had one. Where'd you put her, classwise, if she was real?

MELISSA   Not like me?

SPENCER   Mm. No. I'd put her higher. Seeing as who she mixes with.

MELISSA   You patronising little twat. Remind me, then, where you were brought up.

SPENCER   Mile End Road.

MELISSA   Which end?

SPENCER   Stratford.

MELISSA   So as a child you'd always be looking back towards the city, wondering if you could make it? And you didn't. Why no uni?

SPENCER   No parents, no money. Not like you.

MELISSA   You think that helped?

SPENCER   Didn't it?

MELISSA   It might have done if my mum hadn't died.

SPENCER   *(Mock sympathy)* Ahh. Father not up to much?

MELISSA   Love, hate, all that jazz.

SPENCER   Hate? You're capable of that? *(Sarcastically)* You seem such a nice girl.

MELISSA   Sometimes.

SPENCER	That's scary.
MELISSA	Oh, God, I'm sorry. It's not true.
SPENCER	*(Pause)* If you ever wanted a shoulder to cry on…
MELISSA	Sweet of you, but I'm in a relationship, remember. *(No response)* Spencer, why are you looking at me like that?
SPENCER	So all in the garden's lovely?
MELISSA	Not always, no. Is it that obvious?
SPENCER	He hardly ever looks at you. I think you're just an asset – useful now, gone tomorrow.
MELISSA	So what's all this leading up to?
SPENCER	I wondered if you'd like to come for a meal tonight?
MELISSA	Why would I want to do that?
SPENCER	Because I think you need…
MELISSA	What?
SPENCER	Some… *(highly embarrassed)* some affection.
MELISSA	From you?
SPENCER	Why not?
MELISSA	Because you're…
SPENCER	Just a little squirt of a technician? Whereas you, high and mighty…
MELISSA	I don't think that.
SPENCER	You implied it. *(Pause)* Forget what I said. I've got work to do.

> Spencer gets up and goes to the cabinet containing *Melusina.*

MELISSA	Must you keep touching that thing? Why not have her splayed out on the bed or something. Save you time.
SPENCER	You tell me you're sick of her company. I'm just obliging.
MELISSA	Wish I believed you.

SPENCER	Know what I think? I think you're jealous.
	Spencer opens the cabinet to reveal Melusina dressed in a simple tunic.[Could be either a life-like model or played by another actor, for example with hair covering the face.]
MELISSA	Of that? Ridiculous.
SPENCER	Tell me then, which of you has the more exciting life?
MELISSA	If I were jealous of that there'd be no need for her, would there? I'd just spend my life next door, satisfying the punters.
SPENCER	Or yourself. *(Pause)* OK. If they had a choice. Who do you think they'd go for? Assuming they could tell the difference.
MELISSA	Look, I really don't care.
SPENCER	Of course you care. Half your day's spent honing the opposition.
MELISSA	So, what's the answer to your question?
SPENCER	*They'd* go for her, whereas I…
MELISSA	Give me strength. Am I hearing right? What makes you so different?
SPENCER	Seeing things they don't see.
MELISSA	In me? Now I've really got a problem. Should I fight off this idiot flattery, or should I just be worried?
SPENCER	*(Hurt, embarrassed)* It's not idiot flattery.
	Melissa sits beside him.
MELISSA	Don't pursue this, Spencer, right? I've heard that same tone before in others.
SPENCER	Where?
MELISSA	At college. Before even. And let me tell you, it's not productive. Never once.
SPENCER	Christ!

MELISSA	Just be pleased we share the same mind-set. Jobwise. *(Pause)* You find the work rewarding, don't you?
SPENCER	I'm not sure there are rewards. It's all never-ending refinement. One idea after another, each smothered by the next.
MELISSA	That's just technology.
SPENCER	I suppose.
MELISSA	But the toys we make at the factory. For the children, at Acton. They get pleasure. Isn't it worth it?
SPENCER	Except that's not what we're about, is it?
MELISSA	What's driving us, this project, you mean?
SPENCER	Don't say you haven't thought about it.
MELISSA	Not really. It's Roberto's pigeon now.
SPENCER	We just go along. Um? For Roberto it's simple. Getting out of a financial mess. If he wasn't doing this he'd be selling fruit machines. Or guided missiles. Anything. Equally happy.
MELISSA	You think he's just a glorified car salesman?
SPENCER	No. He's deeper than that. *(Long pause)* Your affair's serious, right?
MELISSA	That's my bloody business.
SPENCER	Is it? If it threatens my job?
MELISSA	Why should it do that?
SPENCER	Because, geeky nerd that I might be, we share something that he doesn't. He sees that. I know.
MELISSA	Spencer, I said don't go there. I see how your mind's working. You think that if I don't go for you at the emotional level you can... bloody get me on an intellectual one. So I say, go back to your precious Melusina, give her a different face, not mine, and fuck her till the cows come home when none of us is around. Got that?

255

Spencer, now in tears, walks away, then turns maliciously.

SPENCER   Got any friends, then, with faces to match, willing to stick them in the mould?

MELISSA   I don't have any friends. Full stop.

SPENCER   *(Desperately)* You could have had.

Melissa shakes her head negatively and the stage darkens.

SCENE EIGHT

[Several days later] The Grays' living room. Claire is sitting at the table. In front of her is the black box seen in Scene One. She is cautiously placing an apple in the chamber. Thomas enters.

THOMAS   Have you fathomed out how to work it?

Claire lifts the apple out, shows it to him, and replaces it carefully.

CLAIRE   It's asking for... sensitivity range. Narrow, intermediate or broad?

THOMAS   Try broad.

CLAIRE   Eating apple, semi-ripe tomato, engorged pen... penis?

THOMAS   Must mean pear, dear. Try narrow.

CLAIRE   There we are – it is apple. Want to know the coefficient...?

THOMAS   Claire, switch it off.

CLAIRE   He was such a nice young man, Melissa's Roberto.

THOMAS   Mm. Not a shade too old for her?

CLAIRE   It's said women age earlier.

THOMAS   They enter a phase of suspended greyness so as to die later. That's if their husbands run true to form.

CLAIRE	Oh, you will dear.
THOMAS	Claire, I take particular care. Clean living, exercise, no sugar, no salt.
CLAIRE	Except in the dinners provided by me, every night, which you invariably relish whilst protesting otherwise. *(Pause)* But back to Roberto. *(Pause)* Is he really Italian?
THOMAS	If he is, he's been exposed to Gateshead at some stage of his career.
CLAIRE	Gateshead?
THOMAS	Was surprised myself. He was looking at the sports page and I asked him to read from the match report. He must have got carried away and the mask slipped for an instant.
CLAIRE	That was underhand, Thomas.
THOMAS	Don't we have a duty to our daughter?
CLAIRE	Your daughter.
THOMAS	Splitting hairs. Yesterday I saw you deep in conversation, heads together. Commonality of purpose.
CLAIRE	Plotting, you mean?
THOMAS	Conspiring.
CLAIRE	Against you? Whatever next?
THOMAS	For wanting to safeguard her future.
CLAIRE	Think that if you want to. *(Pause)* You know, she told me about her first interview – with Roberto. You know what clinched it?
THOMAS	Tell then.
CLAIRE	Her dancing. Those years you spent ferrying her to classes. Must have paid off.
THOMAS	Cost me a fortune... and for what?
CLAIRE	Bonding, Thomas.
THOMAS	It kept the puppy fat at bay. That I'll admit.

CLAIRE	So when Roberto asked her to dance…
THOMAS	At an interview for a technician?
CLAIRE	They there and then hatched up the project she's been involved with since.
THOMAS	Melusina.
CLAIRE	Melissa applied those little luminous discs…
THOMAS	I think they were transmitters, dear.
CLAIRE	… to various parts of her anatomy and then danced. The robotic model is based on Melissa's measurements. Isn't that exciting?
THOMAS	A full-size Melusina, then.
CLAIRE	Something like that.
THOMAS	Then that must be the new idea Roberto was talking to me about. 'Still under wraps, Mr Gray, because it could be big!' I got the feeling there was an urgency about…
CLAIRE	What?
THOMAS	Well, funding something big. I offered to advise. On the financial front, obviously.
CLAIRE	Obviously. But too early in the relationship, Thomas. And besides, he doesn't need an old fuddy-duddy like you…
	The voices of Bertie and Melissa are heard in the hall. Melissa enters, followed by a jubilant Bertie.
MELISSA	I found him kerb-crawling. *(Pause)* He gave me a lift.
BERTIE	Hardly crawling. I was driving max. vitesse to deliver the news, Thomas. Want to hear it?
THOMAS	Tell, then.
BERTIE	The deal's on. Tariq phoned from… guess where.
THOMAS	The embassy.
BERTIE	The FO. They've agreed the export licences. So it's over to you to handle the cash – if you want to.

Melissa exits to the kitchen.

THOMAS   Bertie, let's not be too hasty, shall we?

CLAIRE   Why ever not, Thomas? You promised me my own car – which has been on the way for the last eighteen months.

THOMAS   My dear, the model's become obsolete.

CLAIRE   This is not the Republic – is it a republic? – of North Korea, dear. Don't we have alternatives in the UK?

BERTIE   We do. There may even be a plum-coloured jag seeking a new owner if you're patient. Because I've been promised…

    Melissa appears from the kitchen with a sherry bottle and glasses on a tray. She begins to fill the glasses.

CLAIRE   Not too much for Thomas.

BERTIE   Indeed not.

THOMAS   Why?

BERTIE   Because the ambassador is welcoming us to a small celebration. In fact, Tariq is picking us up… *(looking at watch)* in about five minutes.

CLAIRE   But I can't be ready in five minutes.

BERTIE   Ah. My dear Claire. Mea culpa. Mea maxima culpa. How inconsiderate of me not to have anticipated… But you see, it's the custom of the embassy only to invite the, well, active participants.

CLAIRE   Who happen not to be women.

MELISSA   *(Quoting Tariq)* When in Rome…

BERTIE   Ah, right, technically the embassy's on national soil.

CLAIRE   Then make sure you don't step outside it. If you do I shall certainly hear of it. *(Pause)* My spies!

BERTIE   *(Mock alarm)* Can she be serious, Thomas?

    Thomas looks momentarily perplexed, then brightens.

THOMAS She'd need time to organise things.

BERTIE That's the spirit. *(Pause)* Just a small top-up for me then, thanks, Melissa.

   Melissa obliges. The phone in the hall rings. Melissa puts down the bottle and exits to answer it.

THOMAS Work again. You can bet your life.

   The stage darkens.

SCENE NINE

[An hour later] The robotics laboratory. Melusina is lying on the bed, her head away from the audience. Roberto is tapping frantically on the remote, but the body remains 'lifeless'. He tosses it aside, picks up his mobile from the table and taps that too. Melissa enters from the door to the apartment.

MELISSA I passed Suzanne in reception. A full evening she says. *(She notices Roberto's anxiety)* Problems?

ROBERTO *(Pointing at Melusina)* Not a dicky-bird.

MELISSA *(Chanting)* Press escape and start again.

ROBERTO I'm not an imbecile.

MELISSA *(Continuing chant)* Count to ten, to ease the pain.

ROBERTO Please!

   Melissa goes to Melusina and lifts a flap in her back to expose the control module.

MELISSA Pass me the probe on the shelf there.

   Roberto does so. Melissa applies the probe to the control module. A red light flickers, followed by a low moan, but no movement.

   Poor sod. Can feel but can't respond. The motor mechanism's died. But it's modular. Got a replacement?

ROBERTO Not here.

MELISSA	*(Surprised)* Why not?
	Roberto shrugs, embarrassed.
	Where then?
ROBERTO	The store at Acton. Would take hours to locate it.
MELISSA	So?
ROBERTO	*(Abashed)* There's a client in an hour.
MELISSA	Can't he wait?
ROBERTO	Not this one.
MELISSA	Why?
ROBERTO	A plane out, apparently. And…
MELISSA	And?
ROBERTO	He's not alone.
MELISSA	Not… The protocol says only ever one… [at a time] Not money again?
ROBERTO	The offer, this time – almost beyond belief.
MELISSA	You fool. You fool. *(Pause)* Have you tried Spencer?
ROBERTO	He told me where the replacement was.
MELISSA	He lives nearby. Can't he fetch it?
ROBERTO	He's on holiday, he says.
MELISSA	Two hours ago he was here to test it.
ROBERTO	What?
MELISSA	Melusina!
ROBERTO	Well, now he's halfway up the M1.
MELISSA	And she was working when he left?
ROBERTO	He says so.
MELISSA	My philosophy is that when there's no choice you accept what's coming with good grace.
ROBERTO	Oh yes?
MELISSA	Yes. Plan for that.
ROBERTO	So what are the options?
MELISSA	Tell Suzanne…

ROBERTO	That there's no fury like an Arab scorned? Too right. She's not up to that, I can tell you.
MELISSA	Then give him a voucher for six more sessions.
ROBERTO	Great after he's flown home.
MELISSA	Then sell her.
ROBERTO	What?
MELISSA	Sell her. Promise to ship her out when she's working.
ROBERTO	How would we get another?
MELISSA	Spencer and I would help.
ROBERTO	You'd model again?
MELISSA	I told you I never would.
ROBERTO	No. So easier to find other clients than keep this one.
MELISSA	Tell you what. I'll do the apologies. When he comes. Promise something for the future. He's never met me.
ROBERTO	Melissa, he knows you like the back of his... fucking hand. *(Pause)* Wait a minute though.
	Roberto stares at Melissa, who realises that he is thinking about a substitution.
MELISSA	You pervert. I'm leaving. Sort it yourself.
ROBERTO	The consequences are as great for you as for me.
MELISSA	My job?
ROBERTO	Your life, I think – if we go under. Which we will. *(Pause)* Sit to talk?
	They sit together at the table.
	The issue, then: all we stand to lose against the – relatively modest – moral objections you may have.
MELISSA	Modest? I've never behaved in...
ROBERTO	You did at college.
MELISSA	I didn't *have* any relationships at college.
ROBERTO	Not what I've heard.

MELISSA	What have you heard?
ROBERTO	Star bird in your year. That sort of thing.
MELISSA	Who said that?
ROBERTO	Never mind.
MELISSA	I do mind.
ROBERTO	Why?
MELISSA	Because I'm not like that.
ROBERTO	Now, maybe.
MELISSA	Never!
ROBERTO	Once a…
MELISSA	That's a hateful thing to say.
ROBERTO	I'm sorry, I'm sorry. I take it all back. *(Long pause)* Alright. Try another tack. Why are you here?
MELISSA	To fulfil a dream.
ROBERTO	Melusina?
MELISSA	What she could become. With others. *(Tearfully)* What she was supposed to become.
ROBERTO	The Royal Ballet, stage alive with swirling Melusinas. Is that your great dream?
MELISSA	As good as any.
ROBERTO	So how do you propose to realise it? *(Pause)* I thought we had a relationship. That doesn't count?
MELISSA	We do have a relationship. Isn't that the problem?
ROBERTO	Stronger through overcoming adversity together.
MELISSA	Balls.
ROBERTO	You know that if we go under your dream dies.
MELISSA	*(Staring into the distance, wistfully)* I suppose. *(Pause)* You know. After one of our competitions, and I was standing there with a silver plate or something in my hand, which this celebrity'd given me, and he said, to us all, when life throws up opportunities, take them, regardless of cost.

ROBERTO   Right then, what would the cost be?

MELISSA   Humiliation, remorse…

ROBERTO   For what?

MELISSA   For the indignity of having to flush out my vagina. What do you think?

ROBERTO   Hardly necessary I would have thought.

MELISSA   You think they wash, knowing it's a machine?

ROBERTO   *(Amused)* Come on.

MELISSA   So you really wouldn't mind? No qualms for the future? For us?

ROBERTO   Like you I have a dream – for this company, which is on the fucking rocks. *(Pause)* We're not so different, Melissa.

MELISSA   And my image, in your eyes, will be…

ROBERTO   Unblemished.

MELISSA   And in the wider world?

ROBERTO   Our punters will never know.

MELISSA   *(Softly)* And if I agree, to impersonate her?

ROBERTO   Keep the lights very low. Music up a bit. Don't say too much. You know the routines.

MELISSA   And the responses?

                 Roberto fetches a volume from the shelf.

ROBERTO   In the manual. You've half an hour to digest them. Believe me, it's the only way. *(Pause)* Please, Melissa.

                 Melissa gingerly fingers the manual.

MELISSA   Just one question.

ROBERTO   Mm?

MELISSA   You had this in mind from the beginning, didn't you? *(Pause)* I wonder who put it there.

ROBERTO   Spencer, you mean? You're getting bloody paranoid about him, aren't you? Next you'll be suggesting he deliberately sabotaged…

MELISSA   I wouldn't put it past him.

ROBERTO   Then I give up.

              The stage darkens.

ACT TWO

SCENE ONE

[The following morning] Same set as in the last scene. Melusina is lying prone on the bed as if she has not been moved. The flap on her back is open, as it was. Roberto is at his desk. He looks with disgust at Melusina over his shoulder. He picks up a cheque from his desk, smiles and waves it in the air.

ROBERTO   Solvent. *(Hint of despair)* But what a price to pay.

              He rises, goes to the coffee machine and fills a cup. The
              door opens. Spencer enters and sashays across the room.

SPENCER   Get yourself a thinking, walking, sleeping, talking, fucking doll.

ROBERTO   For heaven's sake, Spencer.

SPENCER   *(Seeing Melusina)* No joy, eh?

ROBERTO   On the desk... the control module. Can you fit it?

SPENCER   No Mel?

ROBERTO   Rang in with a headache.

SPENCER   Wonder why. *(Peering at module)* No probs.

ROBERTO   So why wasn't it here? Had to pick it up myself on the way in. Know what the North Circular's like, at 7.30?

SPENCER   Tell me about it. *(Pause)* Sorry. I'd meant to bring it over.

ROBERTO   *(Sarcastically)* You do still go there then? The factory we have – remember it? *(Pause)* You want a coffee? *(Pause)* Good trip north?

SPENCER   So-so… yes please. You managed to fend them off, did you?

ROBERTO   Who, exactly?

SPENCER   *(Mysteriously)* The gentlemen of the night. I take it they turned up.

ROBERTO   Gentlemen? You mean Hamid…

SPENCER   Him, yes. *(Fishing)* Wasn't there another?

> *Roberto looks at Spencer with fleeting suspicion but does not pursue the matter.*

ROBERTO   Let's say he went away… satisfied.

SPENCER   Oh?

ROBERTO   *(Lying)* I… capitulated, Spencer. I had to promise something. I said we'd make him a copy.

SPENCER   You did what? Of Melusina?

ROBERTO   I know. We'll have to cut back on your development programme for a few weeks. All hands on deck and all that. I'm sorry.

SPENCER   So who'll we model it on? Have you thought about that?

ROBERTO   A problem there?

SPENCER   Melissa won't exactly want to go public, will she?

ROBERTO   Hadn't thought that far.

SPENCER   Perhaps our Arab friend knows a porn star who fancies her face being pushed into a bowl of hot wax.

ROBERTO   Quite likely, but…

SPENCER   There's something else?

ROBERTO   Yes.

SPENCER   You're getting cold feet, right?

ROBERTO   Been thinking about it all last night. It's a wake-up call, Spencer. To concentrate on what we should be doing.

SPENCER   Children's toys?

ROBERTO	Children's toys.
SPENCER	At Acton.
ROBERTO	Afraid so.
SPENCER	The Arab... what you've promised him. You're stalling, yeah?
ROBERTO	Something like that. I told him there might be technical problems.
SPENCER	Thank God he's on the plane out.
ROBERTO	*(Surprised)* You knew about that?
SPENCER	Know about everything, my master.

The stage darkens.

SCENE TWO

[Contemporaneously with the last scene] The Grays' house. Claire is just finishing laying out the breakfast table. She opens the door to the hall and calls upstairs.

CLAIRE	Thomas! *(No answer)* Thomas, your toast is getting cold.
THOMAS	*(Offstage)* Down in a moment.
CLAIRE	Thomas, you have an appointment at eleven.
	Thomas enters dressed for the office, but with signs of haste. His shirt is improperly buttoned and his tie does not match his shirt.
	Your taxi's due in fifteen minutes and your eggs are under the napkin.
THOMAS	No time for eggs. Pour me some coffee?
	Claire takes no notice, then sits opposite him. Thomas nibbles a piece of unbuttered toast.
CLAIRE	Just what time did you crash in?

THOMAS	Oh, about three.
CLAIRE	Four twenty-eight! You've had just three hours sleep. *(Pause)* Good, was it?
THOMAS	Could have done with longer.
CLAIRE	Don't stall!
THOMAS	What was…
CLAIRE	Good? Where you went.
THOMAS	The embassy, you mean. Yes, very jolly. Most welcoming they were.
CLAIRE	And then?
THOMAS	Can't remember.
CLAIRE	So you've been walking the streets in a state of amnesia?
THOMAS	Just a drink in a bar.
CLAIRE	Why?
THOMAS	Discuss a new irrigation project.
CLAIRE	Was Bertie there?
THOMAS	Mm. I think so.
CLAIRE	Then I'll ask him.
THOMAS	Not advisable.
CLAIRE	Why not?

> *Sounds of a vehicle pulling up outside.*

THOMAS	Because… *(Looking at watch)* My heavens, the taxi.

> *The doorbell rings. Claire fetches Thomas' briefcase and umbrella.*

CLAIRE	Here's your case. And umbrella.
THOMAS	It's not raining.
CLAIRE	Thomas, just go.

> *Thomas lurches out of the door. As Claire begins to tidy the table a bleary-eyed Melissa enters and slumps onto a chair at the table.*

CLAIRE	Thomas' eggs are under the napkin. I can put them back into boiling water.
MELISSA	Don't like hard eggs.
CLAIRE	I can do you another.
MELISSA	Got a Disprin?

Claire takes a packet from a drawer, puts the tablets in a glass, adds water from the tap and gives it to Melissa. She sits opposite her.

MELISSA	What are you staring at?
CLAIRE	Turn your face to the light.
MELISSA	Got your oil paints handy, then?
CLAIRE	Hardly a beauty this morning, are we? That's a bruise under your eye.
MELISSA	Uh? Must have fallen somewhere.

Claire rises, stands Behind Melissa and pulls back the collar of her dressing gown. Melissa snatches at her hand.

CLAIRE	There too. Who were you with last night?
MELISSA	No-one. I was working late.
CLAIRE	So you were. Was Roberto there?
MELISSA	To start with.
CLAIRE	Did he do that?
MELISSA	He'd gone when I fell.
CLAIRE	So who…
MELISSA	I fell. Standing on a stool which collapsed.
CLAIRE	Like your explanation.
MELISSA	I fell, right?
CLAIRE	Wrong.
MELISSA	Why?
CLAIRE	Because those marks on your neck are love bites.
MELISSA	Shit!

CLAIRE	You know you can tell me.
MELISSA	I know. But I can't. *(Emotionally)* I wish I could. Please understand. *(Pause)* But it wasn't Roberto.
CLAIRE	That's something, I suppose. So who else... *(Reconsidering)* I'm around if you want me. *(Pause)* You haven't touched your Disprin.
MELISSA	*(Drinking it down, crying)* Thank you.

The stage darkens.

SCENE THREE

[The following Saturday] The Grays' living room. Thomas is on the sofa reading a newspaper. Claire is fussing around the room, ready to go out.

CLAIRE	Move your bottom, Thomas. You're sitting on my magazine.
THOMAS	Sorry, dear.

She puts the magazine on the coffee table and taps it.

CLAIRE	Should read it. Food article. Help you lose that stubborn last ten kilograms. *(Pause)* Now, what did I tell you?
THOMAS	I don't know.
CLAIRE	The oven? Putting the pie in? What time?
THOMAS	Oh, eight-thirty.
CLAIRE	At?
THOMAS	Ten, Denison Gardens?
CLAIRE	Try again. Tem..per..at..ure.
THOMAS	Isn't it on the packet?
CLAIRE	I give up. 180, and my pies don't come in packets, as you well know. I take it I can trust you to lay the table. Remember Bertie's coming. That makes four of us.

THOMAS	Pie in at 8.30.
CLAIRE	That's it, then. See you at nine.
THOMAS	Oh… yes.
CLAIRE	At ten, Denison Gardens.

> *She exits and the front door slams. Bertie enters from the kitchen, looking glum. Thomas motions him to sit.*

BERTIE	Hid in the garage till she'd gone.
THOMAS	Very wise.
BERTIE	Look, Thomas, what's all this about?

> *Thomas takes two photographs from his inside jacket pocket and hands them to Bertie.*

THOMAS	These came in the post.
BERTIE	Mean nothing to me, old chap – just a couple if figures lying on a bed. Difficult to make out. Not even titillating.
THOMAS	Okay, then. The chair in the corner.
BERTIE	Clothes draped over it… *(Pause)* Ah. I see what you mean.
THOMAS	Hardly a tea towel is it?
BERTIE	Tariq's headpiece? Come on!
THOMAS	That him – on the bed?
BERTIE	You can't see… Could be anyone, anywhere, anytime.
THOMAS	There's a clock on the table.
BERTIE	Can't read it though.
THOMAS	Don't have to.
BERTIE	*(Long pause, now concerned)* What happened, Thomas… after I left you?
THOMAS	A club – don't remember which. A drink or two. Another taxi, I think.
BERTIE	Home?
THOMAS	No.

BERTIE	Something in your drink?
THOMAS	Maybe.
BERTIE	But you remember the room?
THOMAS	I... think so.
BERTIE	Should I ask more?
THOMAS	No... no, not just yet.
BERTIE	OK, so why has this come?
THOMAS	No idea.
BERTIE	Could be political, I suppose.
THOMAS	Thought of that. But why, if he caught the plane home? Off the scene. *(Pause)* Assuming he did.
BERTIE	Sandra from our office saw him off. Perky as a parakeet, apparently. *(Pause)* Look Thomas, there's nothing incriminating in those photos.
THOMAS	Isn't that the problem?
BERTIE	More to come, you think?
THOMAS	Well, won't they? This a warning shot?
BERTIE	OK. First thing, where the hell is it? I'll get someone onto it.
THOMAS	How?
BERTIE	Contacts in the press. You wouldn't believe. May need a bit of cash, though.
THOMAS	But you know what happens when I give you...
BERTIE	If you can't trust your own brother, who can you...

> Sound of the front door opening. Bertie motions Thomas to be cautious. Melissa enters looking glum. She immediately senses the atmosphere.

MELISSA	Someone died or something?
BERTIE	Pregustatory expectation. Nothing more. And you? No balletic movements for your old uncle?

> Melissa performs a perfunctory bending of the knees.

	Remind me – how's our Christmas ballerina coming along?
MELISSA	Production's started at Acton.
BERTIE	Acton? How romantic. Remind me of her name, your dancer.
MELISSA	Melusina.
BERTIE	Ah, yes, the beautiful Melusina. As a child I was quite drawn to that sexy lady. *(Pause)* Used to keep snakes. Loved them. So thought about her every Saturday evening. You know, once I put one in Thomas' bed and you know what he...
THOMAS	Bertie, calm down a bit, please.
MELISSA	Uncle Bertie used to tell me that excitability was a front for a pricking conscience.
BERTIE	Shrewd little minx, aren't you? *(Sniffing)* Thomas, what's Claire cooking up for us?
THOMAS	*(Looking at his watch)* Hell and damnation, the pie.

Thomas rushes to the kitchen.

BERTIE	*(Seriously, sympathetically)* This Melusina... does she... it... fill the void?
MELISSA	*(Amused)* A toy won't do that.
BERTIE	And a scaled-up version? If you had lots of them?
MELISSA	It's crossed our minds. Truly. We shall see.
BERTIE	But you still have regrets.
MELISSA	About not taking up ballet?
BERTIE	I just wish I'd been around.
MELISSA	*(Outburst)* He was so cruel, my father.
BERTIE	Shhh. Not so loud. Maybe it's still not too late.
MELISSA	Oh, it is. Every evening I see the youngsters from the academy pouring out onto the pavement. Leaner, prettier, better legs. Already I feel old.

BERTIE   Not prettier, Mel, and as for the legs... And at twenty-two? Fonteyn was still going at seventy.

MELISSA   And started at fourteen. I never even started – thanks to him. *(Pause)* What were you looking at, when I came in?

BERTIE   *(Lying)* Oh, just some pictures relating to the oil pipeline. *(Bluffing)* Want to hear?

MELISSA   Boring. I've better things to do.

            She makes to exit but encounters Thomas returning from the kitchen.

THOMAS   Not so fast. I heard what you said.

MELISSA   About being unreasonable, unkind? Well, you were. *(Menacingly)* And it wasn't only that, was it?

BERTIE   Urgent call to make. Leave you both to it. Back when the next pie is ready.

            Bertie exits.

THOMAS   I've never said this before, but all those years I ferried you to dancing classes. All those competitions you seldom won, in spite of you being the prettiest.

MELISSA   Surprised you noticed.

THOMAS   Your teachers, your friends even. Don't think I didn't know what they were thinking.

MELISSA   They were just jealous.

THOMAS   And wasn't I right? Haven't you done well for yourself? Surely. Oxford? A good job? *(Pause)* You'd have traded all those away?

MELISSA   Yes!

            Melissa makes to flee the room.

THOMAS   Melissa!

            She stops in the doorway.

            Turn around.

She does so, glaring at him while he stares at her. She adopts a provocative pose.

MELISSA   Seen enough?

She goes out. Thomas looks bemused, as if he has realised something. He sits and runs a hand through his hair. Claire enters.

THOMAS   Bloody Bertie.

CLAIRE   Why, Thomas?

THOMAS   Opening old wounds – between her and me.

CLAIRE   Want to tell me?

THOMAS   No.

CLAIRE   It'll fade, with time.

THOMAS   I was so proud of her. Still am. More than ever, but... *(Alarmed)* The pie...

CLAIRE   Not important. *(Pause)* Thomas, is there something else between you two?

THOMAS   What do you mean?

CLAIRE   Only that since your escapade last week you've... well... avoided each other.

THOMAS   Your imagination, Claire. Which is apt to run away with itself. Actually, we've just had a very frank discussion.

CLAIRE   Well, I hope that's all it is. And that if it isn't you'd tell me.

THOMAS   Don't I always?

CLAIRE   Tell me things? No.

The stage darkens.

SCENE FOUR

[Two days later] The Grays' living room. A soft knock at the door. Claire rises as Bertie opens it and enters.

BERTIE	My peach.
CLAIRE	Be careful you don't choke on the stone.
BERTIE	Aw. A seedless grape, then. *(Pause)* No Thomas?
CLAIRE	Gone to… correction, sent to… Waitrose…
BERTIE	Does he usually…
CLAIRE	He does what he's told.
BERTIE	But surely…
CLAIRE	You'll get your dinner, Bertie. But first some questions.
BERTIE	I do so admire assertive women.
CLAIRE	*(Pointing to armchair)* Sit!

He sits and she follows, facing him.

BERTIE	My guard's down, soft belly exposed, what now?
CLAIRE	I warn you, Bertie. If you're not going to be serious… It's about Thomas and Melissa. I'm worried.
BERTIE	Why?
CLAIRE	They've scarcely spoken these last few days. I think they're avoiding each other.
BERTIE	Since when?
CLAIRE	Apparently since you led Thomas astray.
BERTIE	Now wait a minute. I left him…
CLAIRE	In the care of your very dubious friends.

She takes a photograph from under a book on the coffee table.

Why's he been hiding this?

BERTIE	*(Laughing)* Surely you don't think that's him in the picture?
CLAIRE	I can see it's not – no beer belly. It wouldn't have crossed my mind. Except that earlier this evening someone rang to speak to Thomas. Male, estuary English. A young voice.

BERTIE	And?
CLAIRE	He asked if I'd seen the photos. Before I could reply, he rang off. Then I searched for them.
BERTIE	That's rather untrusting. You've told Thomas?
CLAIRE	I'm telling you.
BERTIE	Is that fair?
CLAIRE	There's a link, isn't there. Your dealings with the Arabs. I knew he should have kept his nose out of it.
BERTIE	So what concerns you? Indiscretion? Blackmail?
CLAIRE	The effect on his daughter. I think he must have told her something, from her behaviour.

The front door slams as Thomas returns.

Find out for me, Bertie, so I know how to play it. *(Pause)* I'm away to the kitchen.

Claire exits. Thomas enters and sees Bertie.

THOMAS	Back already?
BERTIE	She suspects.
THOMAS	How?
BERTIE	An anonymous call.
THOMAS	Blackmail?
BERTIE	Could be, except you're probably not important enough. Sorry. *(Pause)* She thinks you've told Melissa something. Hence her behaviour of late.
THOMAS	That's ridiculous.
BERTIE	Perhaps Melissa's also been contacted. Want me to find out?
THOMAS	I suggest you keep your prying nose out of it. *(Pause, contrite)* Sorry, sorry. You're my brother, I know.
BERTIE	Sounds as if I've touched a nerve.

Melissa enters and stares at them.

Not even a pirouette for your favourite uncle?

MELISSA   My only uncle.

            She turns once and flops into an armchair.

            Satisfied?

BERTIE   Melissa, Claire had a very strange phone call earlier
            this evening. *(Casually)* Anything come your way
            too?

MELISSA   Why, should it?

BERTIE   No, then.

MELISSA   No.

BERTIE   Forget I mentioned it. *(Pause)* Oh, Claire was
            asking for help in the kitchen. Completely forgot.

            *Bertie exits hastily to the kitchen. Thomas and
            Melissa look guardedly at one another as the stage
            darkens.*

SCENE FIVE

*[A week later] The robotics laboratory. Melissa and Spencer are working at the
table. There is tension between them. Spencer holds out a robotic part.*

SPENCER   Hold that for me, while I tighten the screw?

MELISSA   What is it?

SPENCER   The multiplex server for the lower leg. I've changed
            the activators that work the toes.

MELISSA   Why?

SPENCER   So that as the foot rises the big toe can initiate a
            spin.

MELISSA   I thought all the balletic stuff was on hold.

SPENCER   Roberto's had second thoughts. He's coming
            round to your way of thinking. *(Confidingly)* Don't
            know what your problem was but I think he's
            trying to win you back.

MELISSA	Big of him.
SPENCER	We all do and say things we don't always mean. Don't we?
MELISSA	Spencer, are you fishing?
SPENCER	*(Feigning innocence)* Why, has something happened?
MELISSA	Nothing that need concern you. *(Cunningly)* Or maybe it should. Did Roberto mention photos that were sent to my home?
SPENCER	Punters taking selfies you mean?
MELISSA	To send to me?
SPENCER	I smell… blackmail!
MELISSA	Um, could be. Or someone wanting to draw attention to themselves.
SPENCER	Know any rich Arabs that might want to do that?
MELISSA	Or maybe not so rich. *(Pointedly)* Or even Arab.
SPENCER	Can't help you there.
MELISSA	Didn't expect you to. *(Casually)* Where do you think they placed the camera?
SPENCER	Oh, easy. There's a clamp mark on the shelf across from the bed.
MELISSA	Clever of you to find it.
SPENCER	Yes, wasn't it. Actually not so clever, really.
MELISSA	Just a small feat of memory.
SPENCER	Pretty much, I imagine.
MELISSA	We'll never know then, will we? For sure?
SPENCER	Probably not. So why don't you just hold the multiplex, while I tighten the screw?

SCENE SIX

[A week later] Bertie and Thomas are drinking coffee in an otherwise deserted café. Thomas has his back to the door.

BERTIE	You think I'm poking my nose in.
THOMAS	Without your interference…
BERTIE	You wouldn't be in this mess. I know, and I'm contrite. *(Pause)* But look, Thomas, you need to see it, the paper.

Bertie produces the London evening paper.

THOMAS	I don't want to see it.
BERTIE	Thomas, things have gone too far – there could be consequences.
THOMAS	Read it then.
BERTIE	OK. *(Pause)* It's the same scene as before, but more – how shall we say – complete. It shows a second figure – well, third if you count…
THOMAS	Me, I suppose.
BERTIE	No way of knowing, but it's probably from a film and who knows what else is on that. But listen to the captions. The shape of things to come? Technology in the service of lust. No longer do husbands need to lie – provided they are not too explicit with the truth. And so on. Thomas, it seems you fucked a bloody robot.
THOMAS	No. No way.
BERTIE	Why not?
THOMAS	Because… she felt… real.
BERTIE	It was dark, you said.
THOMAS	Very.
BERTIE	Did she move?
THOMAS	Oh yes.
BERTIE	Speak?
THOMAS	Not much. A few words, maybe.
BERTIE	Answer questions?
THOMAS	Look, I can't remember, right?

BERTIE	What can you remember?
THOMAS	A perfume. Very faint... but somehow familiar.
BERTIE	That's a big help.
THOMAS	But I'm off the hook. aren't I? Who'd want to blackmail me on the basis of that? I'm a nobody *(Pause)* Let me get you another coffee.
BERTIE	Thomas, it's not that simple.
THOMAS	No?
BERTIE	Emphatically no. You see, the press know the location.
THOMAS	How do they know?
BERTIE	Doesn't matter. Maybe they've tried it, even. Don't worry about it.
THOMAS	*(Pause, hesitantly)* Where is it then?
BERTIE	A flat in Kensington. Expensive, very respectable, apparently.
THOMAS	Owned by?
BERTIE	Are you ready for this? It's the tipping point, Thomas. *(Pause)* Roberto's apartment... Melissa's Roberto.

Melissa appears in the doorway. Bertie sees her and rises. Then she sees Thomas and realises there has been a set-up. As she turns to leave Bertie strides across the room and clutches her arm.

MELISSA	You said you'd be alone.
BERTIE	Something's changed.
MELISSA	Why's it your sodding business anyway?
BERTIE	*(Angrily)* Because I can see further ahead than you. There's something you need to sort with your father. I'd hoped it would have stayed buried, but it hasn't. And it won't, now it's in the paper. *(Pause)* Sit down.

Melissa reluctantly sits opposite Thomas, but Bertie remains standing.

Best without me. I won't be far. I've got my mobile.

Bertie exits.

WAITRESS   *(With a cup on a tray, to Melissa)* Coffee, black, no sugar.

MELISSA   What?

THOMAS   It's Bertie oiling the wheels. Just accept it.

MELISSA   *(To waitress)* Thanks.

THOMAS   *(Pointing to the paper)* Bertie's found out – don't ask me how – where those photos were taken.

MELISSA   *(Aggressively)* You know or you want me to tell you?

THOMAS   Tell if you want.

MELISSA   Roberto has an apartment…

THOMAS   In Kensington.

MELISSA   In Kensington. And next to it are a lab and a workshop where…

THOMAS   Robotic figures are constructed?

MELISSA   Right. Life-size robotic figures.

THOMAS   And you've had a hand in that?

MELISSA   Is that why we're here? You want to *reprimand* me?

THOMAS   I thought you were into toys, not humanoid prostitutes.

MELISSA   That was Roberto's idea, not mine. It just happened that our ballerina…

THOMAS   Melusina.

MELISSA   … lent herself… I'm sorry…

THOMAS   You could never let your obsession rest, could you?

MELISSA   I'm sorry. I'll have nothing more to do with it. It won't happen ever again. *(Rising)* Can I go now?

Thomas puts his head in his hands, near to tears.

THOMAS   But this isn't why we're here. Is it?

MELISSA	Then what is? *(Maliciously)* Why we're here? *(Pause, nervously)* Why are we here?
THOMAS	Do you ever have the feeling that something's terribly amiss and you daren't admit it to yourself?
MELISSA	Sometimes.
THOMAS	You know, you find yourself in a situation that could be horrendous but you don't know for sure, and because of the uncertainty you don't risk taking a step to find out. In case… *(Pause)* Once, when Bertie and I were young, I found my pocket money missing. If I'd said to him 'have you seen it?' it would have amounted to an accusation. Irreparable damage.
MELISSA	What did you do?
THOMAS	I said nothing, then found the two pound coins had fallen from my pocket between the cushions.
MELISSA	And were glad you never mentioned it.
THOMAS	Exactly.
MELISSA	But that's not where we're at, is it?
THOMAS	I'm praying for deliverance.
MELISSA	*(Viciously)* So. Did you enjoy her?
THOMAS	*(Looking up)* Uh?
MELISSA	Our tarty Melusina? Super-bitch, doyenne of the technical age.
THOMAS	It was like… something I'd… never experienced before.
MELISSA	Great! Not with my mother? Or Claire?
THOMAS	Pale imitations, both.
MELISSA	Christ, are you telling me you think it was human?
THOMAS	Of course it was bloody human. I'm not that much of a fool, even pissed as a newt.
MELISSA	Then now we have a problem.

THOMAS	*(Desperately)* We could stop here. Forget everything. Go our separate ways.
MELISSA	*(Pointing at newspaper)* But this won't let us, will it? They know about you, no-one bloody cares about that. But what about me?
THOMAS	You mustn't say it.
MELISSA	If I don't, the press will.
THOMAS	For God's sake, don't say it.
MELISSA	There's no escape and it's all your doing.
THOMAS	I wasn't in control, and even if I had been I'd no idea they would take me there, to that place. *(Pause)* Besides, even if it hadn't been me, would that have made it so different for you? Can you ask yourself that?
MELISSA	*(Shouting)* It wouldn't have been with my father.
THOMAS	*(Quietly)* OK. Let's put morals to one side. Was it such a disaster?
MELISSA	You wonder why I've been so neurotic since it happened? You want to know why?
THOMAS	I can't imagine why.
MELISSA	No?
THOMAS	Can't we stop this?
MELISSA	No?
THOMAS	Melissa!
MELISSA	I'll tell you. Because it unlocked something from the past. Something I'd blocked out, all these years, because I didn't dare face it. When people said I was a dream, with my odd ways, I took refuge in that, and blocked it out still more. Now. You and that brother of yours, through your stupidity, released – God knows how – something I thought I'd buried.
THOMAS	Go on.

MELISSA   My great sin, in that bed, in Roberto's flat, peeled away those years. Sleepless I heard again the footsteps in the corridor and the door opening and – do you know what – *(snarling)* I was waiting for it. So when it came again – like a jolt of electricity – it all came flooding back. No Arab's companion, that, the other night.

THOMAS   You could have stopped it.

MELISSA   I didn't know who it was.

THOMAS   Why didn't you stop it?

MELISSA   You really want to know?

THOMAS   No, yes, go on.

MELISSA   Because I relished it!

THOMAS   But that would never come out. Not now. So why?

MELISSA   *(Losing control)* Because I may want it to.

THOMAS   You can't be serious.

MELISSA   Try me!

            The waitress, who has been listening, comes forward to take their cups. Thomas, seeing her, flees to the door and exits.

WAITRESS   Got him right where you want him, eh Miss. Mine was the same. Never forgotten it. He got ten years.

            Melissa gets up to follow Thomas.

MELISSA   Excuse me.

WAITRESS   What about the bill?

            Melissa scrabbles in her pocket, draws out a note and throws it down. When she is midway to the door there is a crash outside consistent with a vehicle striking a pedestrian.

MELISSA   Christ, what was that?

            The waitress races to the window.

WAITRESS   It's that man you were with. You better look. The other bloke's with him.

Melissa races to the window. For a few seconds she remains frozen, then sinks into a nearby chair.

WAITRESS   I'll ring for an ambulance. *(Pause)* Aren't you goin' to see to him?

Melissa nods, rises slowly and makes for the door, bumping into Bertie.

BERTIE   Melissa, you have to come. Your father's…

He stops abruptly, seeing Melissa's expression of confusion, anger and sorrow.

I think he may be… beyond help.

The stage darkens.

SCENE SEVEN

[Several days later] The Grays' living room. Bertie and Roberto are sitting on the sofa. Bertie leans towards Roberto.

BERTIE   Are the good ladies out of earshot, do you think?

ROBERTO   Still going through Thomas' papers upstairs, I imagine.

BERTIE   Remarkable thing, that.

ROBERTO   What, bringing them together?

BERTIE   I don't think the old reprobate tried very hard, do you?

ROBERTO   Too tied up with his finances. Everything done by numbers.

BERTIE   But he did deliver on the pipeline – getting that off the ground. When I told him, he was sitting right there, where you are. You know what he said? A bit of cash, then, for Melusina. Melusina, note – not Melissa.

ROBERTO   Pull the other one. A joke, surely.

BERTIE   No, he meant it. Didn't do humour, my brother.

ROBERTO   A sight too serious, him. Do you think that's why…

BERTIE   He ended up under a white van? Accident or deliberate? We'll never know.

ROBERTO   A bloody mess though.

BERTIE   Eh?

ROBERTO   I mean, what went before. Can you make sense of it?

BERTIE   I've tried. But no. It wouldn't surprise me if what happened in your flat was his first experience of… well… you know… encounters outside marriage. Even as boys – students even – he seemed…

ROBERTO   Repressed?

BERTIE   Maybe. Unsure of women, maybe. So it all got magnified. Let's not go there, eh? No, what I don't understand is why he suddenly rushed out of the bar. After all, he already knew the score, even before he talked to Melissa.

ROBERTO   You think he did… really know the score?

BERTIE   Why are you looking at me like that?

ROBERTO   Trying to work out what you know.

BERTIE   Look, man. He fucked one of your robots. Bizarre, but coincidences happen.

ROBERTO   In that case, surely, the shame would be less, not more.

BERTIE   Than with a real person? Some other factor, then?

ROBERTO   Best leave it there, don't you think?

BERTIE   If there's more it will come out at the inquest. Who else knows anything?

ROBERTO   (Shrugs) Spencer, possibly.

BERTIE   The technician chappie?

ROBERTO	A very bright young man with a very big chip on his shoulder. Hopelessly infatuated with your niece.
BERTIE	So why haven't you sacked him?
ROBERTO	Vital to the project.
BERTIE	But why's he relevant?
ROBERTO	A potential witness? But let's tread carefully, eh? He won't admit it – and this is just supposition – but I believe it was he who sent Thomas those photos.
BERTIE	But how would he have known it was Thomas in that room? He'd never met him.
ROBERTO	I don't believe he did know. It was Spencer's way of getting back at Melissa. Pure and simple. Embarrass her in front of her father for not succumbing to his charms. Easy to mislead, as the figure in the photos resembled her. Nothing at all to do with blackmail.
BERTIE	But hold on. You just said 'witness.' Witness to what?
ROBERTO	Witness is perhaps too strong…
BERTIE	Stop prevaricating, man. Witness – or whatever you want to call it – to what?
ROBERTO	You'll have to ask Melissa. But I'd advise you not to.
BERTIE	Why?
ROBERTO	Because she's distraught. And I care for her. It's not just Claire who's suffering.
BERTIE	So what are your intentions towards Melissa? We've all been wondering.
ROBERTO	I hope we shall marry, in due course. *(Pause)* I know that's not what Thomas wanted for his daughter.
BERTIE	He felt your financial situation was precarious.
ROBERTO	But not only that?

BERTIE	*(Amused)* No, he thought you were a complete imposter. He even checked birth records. Robert Malario, from Gateshead.
ROBERTO	Middlesborough, actually. But to an Italian father, also Roberto. *(Hesitantly)* Robotoys was his, you see, and nothing to do with robotics. To begin with. He's dead now. Both parents are.
	Melissa appears in the doorway.
BERTIE	*(Raising glass)* Well, here's to your future together.
MELISSA	What future?
ROBERTO	Ours, love.
MELISSA	With me as spoilt goods? I should be lucky.
BERTIE	What does that mean?
ROBERTO	Come on, sweetheart. Come and sit down.
MELISSA	*(Blurting out)* You want to go upstairs. See what's on his computer, his photos. *(Crying)* Hundreds of them.
BERTIE	Where's Claire?
MELISSA	Still upstairs. Needing help, I should think.
BERTIE	Why have you left her, then?
MELISSA	Because I'm going out.
BERTIE	Why?
MELISSA	*(Viciously)* Because I've got a job to do.
	Melissa leaves the room. The front door is heard to slam shut. The stage darkens.

SCENE EIGHT

[An hour later] The robotics laboratory, dimly lit and empty. The door left stage opens and Spencer enters cautiously. He switches on the light, goes to the cupboard, unlocks it and stands confronting Melusina. He eases her forward out of the cupboard, draws her to him and kisses her fervently.

SPENCER　　You know, don't you my love, that this could be our last time? But don't be sorry. No, no need to answer. I'll leave the switch off for a moment. There'll be plenty of time to say good-bye. *(Pause)* Wait though, I'll put it just on movement. Remember what I taught you? You do, don't you?

Against the languorous music of a waltz they dance slowly around the room. As they pass the bed he pushes her gently onto it and stands contemplating her figure. He begins to undo his belt.

On second thoughts, a quick piss I think, before… so everything's perfect.

He rebuckles his belt and exits right stage. Melissa enters cautiously from the apartment left stage. She is dressed in a tunic exactly like Melusina. She contemplates the supine figure, lifts it off the bed and pushes it underneath with her foot. She sees a knife on the table, picks it up and places it under the pillow. She lies exactly in Melusina's original position on the bed. Spencer returns and stands at the foot of the bed.

The above paragraph relates to performances in which Melissa and Melusina can be played by different actors. If 'Melissa' plays both parts the following modification is appropriate:

He rebuckles his belt and exits right stage, turning off the light as he does so. [The momentary darkness enables Melissa to exit and the stage crew to replace Melusina (on the bed) with a figure of similar appearance.] Melissa enters cautiously left stage and switches on the light. She contemplates the supine figure, lifts it off the bed and pushes it underneath with her foot. She sees a knife on the table, picks it up and places it under the pillow. Then she switches off the light and lies exactly in Melusina's original position. Spencer re-enters, switches on the light and stands at the foot of the bed.

SPENCER   I'm sorry my films never did you justice. But when the police come again – as they will you know, because of what happened to Thomas Gray – prying and poking your body… So this has to be the end for us. You do know that, don't you?

MELISSA   I shall be sorry, too, Spencer. It has been wonderful.

SPENCER   You mean that? You really mean that?

MELISSA   I cannot lie, Spencer. You know that.

SPENCER   Then I shall reward you as I've never…

He kneels down and begins to caress Melissa's thighs, slowly moving up her body. As he does so Melissa slowly extends her arms above her head and grasps the knife. Spencer begins to climax. Melissa responds, but in an agony of indecision.

MELISSA   Now you've got what you always wanted, haven't you, Spencer?

SPENCER   *(Puzzled)* Is something different?

MELISSA   Are you satisfied?

SPENCER   Deeply.

Melissa plunges the knife into his back. For many seconds both figures lie inert. The door left stage bursts open and Bertie and Roberto enter. They contemplate the figures.

BERTIE   *(To Melissa)* Are you real?

MELISSA   Yes.

BERTIE   Stay still, then.

He sees a pair of rubber gloves on the bench, puts them on and removes Melissa's fingers from the knife. He rolls Spencer's body to the edge of the bed, freeing Melissa. Together they manoeuvre Melusina back onto the bed, roll Spencer's body on top of her and place Melusina's fingers around the knife handle. Roberto, meanwhile, looks on aghast, making no move to help Melissa.

BERTIE	Scrub yourself till you're black and blue. *(Pause)* Well, did he die happy?
MELISSA	I really think he did.
BERTIE	Leave her switched on then, eh. Remote beside him.
MELISSA	Right.

> *They look carefully around the room, then walk towards the door left stage, leaving Roberto still standing motionless. At the door Melissa turns and looks at him reproachfully.*

MELISSA	Don't you want to comfort me?
ROBERTO	When you've destroyed everything.
BERTIE	*(To Roberto)* Be that as it may, you know nothing and this was how you found it, right? *(Pointing to Melissa)* You still have a duty towards her.

> *As the stage darkens, Melissa and Bertie exit.*

SCENE NINE

[An hour later] The Gray's living room. The room is dark, but for the light of a standard lamp. Bertie is sitting, holding a glass. Melissa enters carrying a plastic bag.

BERTIE	You've included everything?
MELISSA	Even my underwear.
BERTIE	Put it down, then. I'll get rid of it.

> *Melissa places the bag by the door and sits opposite Bertie. They stare at one another.*

MELISSA	Yes. You can look. Must be interesting, facing a murderess. A new experience for you.
BERTIE	I suppose it is. Yes. Never had to think about it before.
MELISSA	Too sharp to get into such a ridiculous situation?

BERTIE   One reaches an age when such things… become
                unlikely. That's true.

MELISSA   (Beginning to cry) You must have words for me.
                Questions. You wouldn't have come back with me
                otherwise.

BERTIE   The protective uncle.

MELISSA   You have been. Sometimes.

BERTIE   In the background, always. Except that this time I
                screwed up.

MELISSA   You couldn't see it coming?

BERTIE   Killing Spencer? No. I wouldn't have believed you
                capable of that.

MELISSA   Nor me. Until from the doorway I saw what he
                was doing with that… that thing.

BERTIE   Melusina?

MELISSA   Me! Melissa. That's who she was, to him.

BERTIE   Yet you let him…

MELISSA   Enter me. Yes!

BERTIE   Why?

MELISSA   Because it heightened my satisfaction, that's why.

BERTIE   In stabbing him?

MELISSA   Yes!

BERTIE   Melissa, that can't all be Spencer's doing, however
                objectionable he may have been to you.

MELISSA   You think there's something else? Would make me
                do that?

BERTIE   Mustn't there be?

                Melissa rises and pours herself a drink.

MELISSA   How well did you know your brother?

BERTIE   Thomas? We were very different…

MELISSA   Thankfully for you.

BERTIE   Eh?

MELISSA	Those photos we found – on his computer.
BERTIE	Many men have pornography hidden away.
MELISSA	Of that kind? *(Pause)* You stayed with us sometimes, when I was little.
BERTIE	Of course.
MELISSA	Were you ever awake at night? You never heard soft feet padding down the corridor, the click of my door? With my dying mother drugged up to the eyeballs.
BERTIE	Melissa, stop! We're stepping into quicksand. I beg you, don't go on.
MELISSA	You're quick on the uptake, aren't you?
BERTIE	He's dead, Melissa. Your father, is dead. Isn't that retribution enough?
MELISSA	No, it's not enough. I need to tell you more. To make the link.
BERTIE	Link with what?
MELISSA	With Spencer.
BERTIE	O…kay.
MELISSA	You see – and you won't be prepared for this – like with Spencer it was not entirely… one-sided.
BERTIE	Oh my God.
MELISSA	I could have locked my door. Fought him off. Told someone. *(Pause)* It was only afterwards… I felt…
BERTIE	Remorse?
MELISSA	Wretched. It blighted my childhood. *(Pause)* So Spencer became… suffered… what inwardly I'd wished for my father. In those few moments of opportunity.
BERTIE	But hold on. You couldn't have thought that through before you got there.

MELISSA	No.
BERTIE	So… why did you go?
MELISSA	Just to confront him, only that. With the misery he caused, leading to my father's death.
BERTIE	Which was an accident, Melissa.
MELISSA	Really? You think that?
BERTIE	Don't you?
MELISSA	No.
BERTIE	Then what did you say to Thomas? At the café, to make him run out like that?
MELISSA	What we've been discussing.
BERTIE	But you were both adults. You'd lived with the shame of it all these years. Surely you could have weathered it now.
MELISSA	Ah. But those photos in the paper. Too tempting for a journalist not to follow up, wouldn't you say?
BERTIE	The past can still be buried, Melissa. We have to draw a line. Look only to the future.

They clasp hands.

MELISSA	It can never go away, Bertie.
BERTIE	Why?
MELISSA	Witnesses.
BERTIE	Me and…
MELISSA	Exactly. Roberto. What he'll tell the police.
BERTIE	He promised he wouldn't…
MELISSA	You don't know him like I do. He'd do anything for money, to keep his company afloat. And there's a bloody good story there.

Bertie takes Melissa's hand and raises her up.

BERTIE	Come on, I'll take your clothes.
MELISSA	And Roberto?

BERTIE	I'll see what I can do. The test for him is how quickly the police get here. Lets go.

They exit and the stage darkens.

SCENE TEN

[Several days later, after Thomas' funeral] The living room of the Grays' house. Claire and Bertie, still in black, are discussing the funeral.

CLAIRE	Who were all those people? The church was packed.
BERTIE	Thomas had many… contacts.
CLAIRE	Even that Arab…
BERTIE	Tariq.
CLAIRE	… was there.
BERTIE	Which reminds me. I suggested he call by… on the way back to the airport.
CLAIRE	He flew over specially?
BERTIE	Apparently. Says there are one or two financial matters to clear with you. Thomas' consultancy fees and the like. Greatly to your advantage, I understand. With the oil pipeline going ahead.
CLAIRE	As if I cared.
BERTIE	You will. *(Pause)* Now, where is that girl of yours?
CLAIRE	Melissa's hardly mine.
BERTIE	*(Softly)* Surely you've resolved your differences, eh? She needs your help.
CLAIRE	Of course.
BERTIE	Splendid. She did look beautiful, you have to grant her that.
CLAIRE	Black suits her.
BERTIE	I saw Tariq making a bee-line. Her other admirers looked quite put out.

CLAIRE	Roberto seemed to be keeping his distance.
BERTIE	A lot on his mind, I think. With Spencer's inquest next week.

Sound of a vehicle drawing up outside, then the front door slamming. Melissa enters, twirls and flops into an armchair.

No Roberto?

MELISSA	He's following behind.
BERTIE	Aren't you going to take your coat off?
MELISSA	In a moment. *(Pause)* What are you two discussing? Apart from me.
BERTIE	Don't flatter yourself. Mainly that a horrendously ill-wind may have blown Claire some cash.
MELISSA	Pity it didn't come sooner then. Could have bailed out Roberto's company.
BERTIE	Melissa, I'm truly sorry. That was thoughtless of me. Still no white knight for *Robotoys*?
MELISSA	Into the receiver's hands. With Christmas sales buggered.
CLAIRE	And Spencer's accident.
BERTIE	Let's change the subject.
CLAIRE	No. Don't let's change the subject. With the funeral out of the way there are things I want to know.
BERTIE	Oh? Such as?
CLAIRE	What was troubling Thomas? To such an extent that he had to meet Melissa secretly…
BERTIE	Hardly secret. I was there.
CLAIRE	… in a café in Pimlico?
BERTIE	He was concerned about her job. The direction her work was taking. What she'd got herself into.
CLAIRE	Thomas believed that on the night in question he visited what we now know was Roberto's apartment.

BERTIE	Did he tell you that?
CLAIRE	I'm not stupid.
BERTIE	And why would he have thought that? Being in a drunken stupor.
CLAIRE	Why otherwise would the photos have been sent to him? The police seemed convinced Spencer was setting up a blackmail.
BERTIE	Do you still have the photos?
CLAIRE	I… scanned them in before the police took them. I'll get them.

She takes a sheet of paper from a drawer and hands it to Melissa.

	Now, for the last time, is that Roberto's apartment or not?
MELISSA	Is.
BERTIE	I suggest the chequered headpiece over the chair clinched it for him. Had to be Tariq's.

Sounds of a car drawing up, footsteps and the doorbell ringing. Claire looks out of the window.

CLAIRE	It's him. We'll confront him.
BERTIE	Look, Claire. There are other issues at stake. For me.

Bertie rises to go to the door, but Claire is ahead of him.

CLAIRE	Stay where you are. He's brought some flowers.

She exits. Melissa checks that she is out of hearing distance.

MELISSA	Bertie, where's Roberto? He said he would follow us.
BERTIE	The traffic is rather heavy.
MELISSA	But he was right behind us. *(Pause)* He's not coming, is he?

BERTIE	Perhaps with Spencer's inquest only days away he felt…
MELISSA	He's going to tell, isn't he?
BERTIE	We don't know that.
MELISSA	He hates me. During the service, I could see it in his eyes.
BERTIE	He sees himself as a ruined man, Melissa. *(Pause)* I can try to influence him.
MELISSA	I thought you had. *(Pause)* A murder charge? You an accessory? *(Pause, losing control)* And it's your doing, isn't it. If you hadn't arranged that meeting in Pimlico, I'd never have confronted my father and he'd never have run out into the road.
BERTIE	You'd still have had your conscience to live with, for… what went before. That's been my impression.
MELISSA	And you're right about that. Even with two deaths on my hands…
BERTIE	Melissa, that's not true.
MELISSA	Hear me out. Even with those two deaths, do you know what's kept me awake at night? Not those. It's dream after terrible dream, night after night – things dredged up from the past. *(Crying)* It wasn't Spencer I killed. It was my father. For what he'd done to me. *(Composing herself)* So, what to do?
BERTIE	We've little choice.
MELISSA	No? Really no choice? *[Implying suicide]*
BERTIE	Listen, they're coming.
	Tariq follows Claire into the room.
CLAIRE	I've put Tariq's wonderful flowers in the kitchen. *(To Tariq)* Please do take a seat.

TARIQ   I hope I'm not intruding.

BERTIE   On the contrary, old chap. You're about to become the life and soul of the party.

TARIQ   *(Sitting)* I don't quite understand.

             Claire shows him the photo.

CLAIRE   A straight question and you'll oblige me with a straight answer – were you ever in this room?

TARIQ   Ah. That's a challenging supposition.

             Melissa quietly gets up unnoticed and leaves the room.

BERTIE   The headpiece on the chair.

TARIQ   Ah, I see. What suspicious minds you must have. The chequered pattern is quite different. Not mine, I assure you.

CLAIRE   That Saturday night, after the embassy. Where did you take Thomas?

TARIQ   Personally, nowhere, Mrs Gray. But since it will come out sooner or later, to my eternal regret, I have to tell you that my diplomatic colleagues do sometimes favour an establishment in... Knightsbridge.

BERTIE   Knightsbridge?

TARIQ   ... of impeccable reputation I assure you. If Thomas went anywhere – and I make no assertions in that respect since I was not there – that is where he would have been taken.

BERTIE   You're saying Thomas was never in that room, never encountered Roberto's humanoid... companion.

TARIQ   That I cannot say. But I see no evidence for it. *(Pause)* Now, Mrs Gray, with that out of the way let me be the bearer of more gladsome tidings. A sum of fifty thousand pounds will be deposited in your account...

Bertie notices that Melissa has left the room.

BERTIE   Where's Melissa?

CLAIRE   Couldn't face more of the truth, I suppose.

BERTIE   But for God's sake, Claire, she doesn't know the truth. I ought to follow her.

CLAIRE   Nonsense. You're to make your peace with Mr Al-Khouri. And hear what he has to tell me. Then we'll see how she is.

SCENE ELEVEN

[A few moments later] Melissa's room, exactly as it was in Act One, Scene One, except that further stage right is a bedside cabinet on which stand a glass of water and a school straw hat (the bed itself is not necessarily visible). [The action in that scene will be interpolated exactly in what follows.] Melissa, still in her black coat, enters in a state of distress, moving about the room, touching objects as if in farewell, and standing in front of the mirror.

MELISSA   Fulfilled and happy. That's all I wanted to be.

She contemplates the straw hat, then picks it up and puts it on her head. As if on an impulse she tears off her coat and throws it aside, revealing the blouse and pleated skirt of a schoolgirl. She kicks off her shoes, bends down beside the cabinet, opens the drawer and takes out a bottle containing tablets. She tips the tablets into her hand and swallows them with water from the glass, then flops into the chair. [From now on the action is exactly as in Scene One] She rises, removes her hat, blouse and skirt to reveal a black leotard. She walks slowly towards the mirror, stands in front of it and, back to the audience, raises her arms above her head. She executes several simple, but graceful and perfect, balletic movements, culminating in a 'dying swan' descent to the floor.

Tearful and in deep distress, she beats the floor with her fists. As the movements lessen Bertie and Claire enter the room. They move towards her and the stage darkens.

END

SUMMARIES AND NOTES

Beyond the Red Curtain

This one-act play is set in the near future, after the passing of a new law permitting physician-assisted suicide. It concerns the decision of an elderly and terminally ill couple to die together. The action takes place in real time, according to a clock on the wall, beginning at 7.30 (or when the performance starts), with the doctor arriving at 9.00.

Teddy is a retired chief executive and Alice, his wife, a retired librarian. They live in a suburban apartment found for them by their daughter Sarah and her husband Richard after Teddy had been diagnosed with terminal lung cancer six months previously. More recently Alice developed uterine cancer, which has now spread; though outwardly healthy, she has been given only a few more weeks to live. Teddy's condition, worsening by the day, has led the couple to seek to die together and the two doctors involved have acquiesced.

Alice and Teddy decided that immediately before this happened they would share a farewell meal with Sarah and Richard and their two other children, Eric (the eldest) and Pamela. They have chosen to do this on the occasion of their fiftieth wedding anniversary, much as they did for their fortieth. Sarah and Richard have undertaken arrangements for the meal.

The play begins with Teddy and Alice entering the dining room, part of which is separated by a wall to wall red curtain behind which the lethal administrations will take place. Eric, a petty criminal and the black sheep of the family, has telephoned to excuse himself and the pregnant Pamela is about to give birth prematurely. Pamela's unplanned pregnancy has been kept from her parents and, the contractions having started, she has persuaded her children, Robert (16) and Amelia (15), to take her and her husband Martin's place.

Unfortunately she fails to tell them the true reason for the meal and they arrive believing they are celebrating a wedding anniversary.

Teddy is not only seriously ill but is suffering from dementia. Not knowing the circumstances, the teenagers engage in trivial repartee. Teddy, his condition worsening, is taken from the room. Then Alice informs the teenagers that Teddy is to die later that evening. Amelia, as a result of a class exercise at school, knows about assisted suicide; she is firmly against it, while her brother Robert takes a more compassionate stance. When Alice leaves to tend Teddy, the teenagers discuss the situation with Richard. They recall their childhood days and Amelia hints that she was once abused by Teddy while on holiday in the country. Thus a different atmosphere prevails when Teddy re-joins them. They are further challenged when they learn of Teddy's professional life in the construction business and his part in influencing the suicide of a householder pressurised to sell to the company. Alice then recounts her early career as a nightclub hostess and her meeting with Teddy, which ended it. The scene ends with Richard telling Sarah about Teddy's alleged misdemeanour.

The second scene follows without a break. Amelia and Robert are toying with their mobile phones and discussing the situation. Eric arrives unexpectedly. In spite of some robust dialogue he has clear rapport with the teenagers, who have admired him as young children. His criminal past is hinted at. When they appear, Alice is delighted to see him but Teddy is dismayed. It seems that Eric's motivation in coming may have something to do with being excluded from Teddy's will, should Teddy die after, rather than before, Alice. Alice takes Eric aside to reconcile their positions. When the family regathers Richard dims the lights and Sarah lights candles so they might all reflect on the situation. Alice explains how she and Teddy had gained the agreement of the two doctors. Amelia, while grudgingly supporting Teddy's position, again asserts that Alice's case is defective, while Robert is more understanding and Sarah believes Alice's decision to die with Teddy is a beautiful thing. They then hear from Martin that Pam is to undergo surgery and discuss the possibility of delaying Dr Metcalfe to await the outcome of the delivery. At this point Eric accuses Richard of having influenced the couple's decision through his (up until now unrevealed) social acquaintance with Metcalfe. Having arrived, Metcalfe leaves the room to allow everyone the opportunity to exchange final thoughts. Alice then tells them of her visit to a local church to take communion, and how the disapproval of the priest was disregarded when she saw a picture of Jesus and realised that he, too, chose his time to die. Metcalfe returns to find Teddy in distress because of his guilt concerning Amelia who, having persuaded Eric to fetch Teddy's cat Bumble, is able to forgive him.

Teddy and Alice then go behind the red curtain. Unheard by them, the telephone rings – it is Martin to say that Pam has given birth to a boy. Robert, ignoring the others, rushes into the dining room to tell Alice. Metcalfe appears through the curtains to reprimand him. It is clear that Teddy has died, but unclear about Alice, who then emerges clutching her glass of lethal fluid. Alice, initially remorseful at having 'failed' Teddy but thankful at seeing the family at last united and pleased about the baby, passes back through the curtains. At this point it is uncertain whether Alice has returned to follow Teddy in death or is there just to be with him, intending to re-join the others later. Believing Alice has died with Teddy, Eric leaves, concealing his sorrow from the others. Metcalfe emerges to tell them that Alice is sleeping, but then she too appears, having decided to live. First the teenagers and then Sarah and Richard go behind the curtain to see Teddy, leaving the stage empty. Eric then returns and, after a few moments of contemplation, joins them.

Shadow of a Queen

The play has as its background two historical events for which the year 1290 is best remembered: the death of Queen Eleanor (Eleanor of Castile, wife of King Edward I) and the first major expulsion of Jews from any country in Europe.

Alicia, a companion of Queen Eleanor and governess to the young Prince Edward, has been brought up by her supposed uncle, Sir Richard de Redwell, lord of the manor of Easingbourne. The manor has long been coveted by the Queen, who is known for her rapacious acquisition of manors, especially from impoverished knights in debt to Jews.

The play begins with a flashback to the year 1273, soon after the recently crowned Edward and Eleanor have taken up residence in the Tower. Eleanor has summoned both Hagin of Northampton – a Jew with whom she has had business dealings – and Redwell, with whom she is on intimate terms. Meeting Hagin at Easingbourne, Redwell admits to an infatuation with Eleanor, and explains that his refusal to sell his manor is in order to preserve his only link with her. Hagin offers to waive Redwell's debt to him – he is an inveterate gambler – if he would agree to substitute Hagin's illegitimate new-born child for his sister's baby, which has just died. Redwell being freed from debt, Eleanor is thus denied the opportunity to acquire the manor. The child – Alice – is brought up believing Redwell is her uncle.

It is now late summer in the year 1290. At Easingbourne, Redwell and Hagin await the appearance of Alice who, now known as Alicia, is a companion of Eleanor and governess to the six-year-old Prince Edward. The Edict of Expulsion of Jews from England has recently been enacted. When she arrives Alice is friendly towards Redwell but cold towards Hagin, and unsympathetic to his wish to convert to Christianity, being ignorant of the reason for it – his wish to remain near to his daughter. Redwell and Hagin agree to petition Eleanor.

At the Royal Hunting Lodge two weeks later Eleanor and de Berewyk, her treasurer, receive Redwell and Hagin. An offer for Easingbourne is again made and again refused, and Redwell declines a challenge by Eleanor to resolve the matter by completing a game of chess. However, he suggests he might be more amenable if she were to facilitate Hagin's application to convert. Eleanor is sympathetic but after the visitors have gone suggests to Alicia there may be other reasons for Redwell's change of position. Alone now, Alice is confronted by the Dowager Queen, now a nun, who chides her for flirting with the King.

At the Royal Hunting Lodge a week later, Friar Benedict appears with plans for Eleanor's memorial chapel at the church of the Dominican Friars at Blackfriars. As she walks away to see her pet wolf, Gretel – which is about to give birth – de Berwyk chides Alice for not looking after young Edward, who then appears with a kite. Using the kite as a metaphor, Berewyk explains to the uncomprehending Edward his fears concerning the demise of the queen. They then observe that in the distance Eleanor has lost her balance and fallen.

The following scenes see the King flirting with Alicia and Alicia teasing de Berewyk, who, she claims, is infatuated by her.

Alicia tells Eleanor that Gretel has produced thirteen pups, comparing this number to that of Eleanor's children. Alice not being able to name the thirteenth prompts Eleanor to recount the trauma of her first childbirth and her early memories of Castile – and the emotional constraints of being a queen. Eleanor asks Alicia to arrange for her to visit Redwell's manor house at Easingbourne that evening, their last at Geddington.

At Easingbourne, in an intimate exchange, Eleanor tells Redwell she is terminally ill, and recounts her experience as a girl when, at a tournament in Castile attended by her future husband, one of the knights had shown an interest in her and as a consequence was blinded, not so much as punishment but as a warning to her. Possibilities of further intimacy are stifled when Alice appears, looking for the young Edward. Redwell refuses to reveal the secret of Alicia's parentage to Eleanor and she leaves in anger. Back at the hunting lodge Eleanor chides Alicia for obstructing her meeting with Redwell and accuses her of impropriety with the King. The antisemitic Dowager Queen persuades Alicia to intercept letters from Eleanor supporting Hagin's conversion. Meanwhile, in the chapel, Eleanor anticipates her death and shows remorse for her avarice.

In November Eleanor dies, at Harby, near Lincoln. About the same time Hagin, his petition having apparently failed, is put with his family on a ship for deportation to France. The passengers are cruelly set upon a sandbank in the Thames estuary and all but Hagin are drowned. Hagin reaches shore and, to seek his daughter, with great hardship walks to Geddington where, coincidentally, the body of the dead queen is brought as her funeral cortège journeys to London. There he is recognised, set upon by angry bystanders and fatally wounded. Alicia, at Redwell's instigation, reluctantly tends to him, but refuses to acknowledge that he is her father.

Just before Hagin dies Alicia enters the chapel to mourn the dead queen. There she is joined by the King. The enebriated Redwell enters the chapel and hears in his mind that Eleanor's apparent affection for him was only because he resembled the knight blinded after the tourney. His infatuation with her becomes apparent to Edward, sealing his fate. The King learns not only that Alicia is bearing his child but also that she is Hagin's daughter and therefore Jewish, which places her in mortal danger. After the King's departure and finding the murdered Redwell's body, Alicia is at last reconciled with her dying father.

The following morning the funeral cortège prepares to depart. Now knowing that he will father the child of a Jewish mother, the King gives Alicia the option of death or the surrender of the child, after birth, to the wife of de Berewyk, who is barren. She accepts the latter course, finding herself in the much the same situation as the father she had once rejected, the wheel having thus turned a full circle.

Historical note

The historical context is broadly authentic. The royal entourage did visit the hunting lodge at Geddington in the autumn of 1290 on its way to a parliament at Clipstone (although, unlike in the play, the stop would have been brief), by which time Eleanor was clearly unwell. Following the parliament the party slowly made its way its way towards Lincoln but, before reaching there, Eleanor died, at the nearby village of Harby, probably during the night of 28 November. Following her death her body was brought to London. The places at which the funeral cortège stopped were later to be marked by the famous 'Eleanor crosses', of which that at Geddington – where the bier rested on 6-7 December – still survives. Eleanor's body was buried at Westminster but her heart was taken to a memorial chapel at the Dominican church of the Black Friars, where plans for the heart tomb had been made at least several months before her death. Eleanor's compulsive acquisition of manorial lands through taking debts to Jews in exchange for relief from taxation is almost the sole known blemish on her character; in this regard it has been suggested that her final journey while living may in part have been linked to overseeing her widespread manorial holdings.

The expulsion of all Jews from England resulted from the Edict of Expulsion, passed during the summer of 1290. The abandonment of deported Jews on a sandbank in the Thames estuary was an historical event in which there were no survivors. In this regard Eleanor of Provence (the 'Dowager Queen'), an antisemite who had banned Jews from her own estates, was undoubtedly influential with respect to the King. At the time of the action she was a nun at Amesbury, having taken the veil following the death of her husband, Henry III.

The involvement of Queen Eleanor, King Edward, the Dowager Queen, de Berewyk and the young Prince Edward (the future Edward II) as players in this story is wholly fictional and the author has taken great liberties with their characters and actions, painting them – in retrospect with some misgivings – in far darker tones than they deserve. In fact historians are generally agreed that the love of Edward for Eleanor that found expression in the construction of the Eleanor crosses was both genuine and profound. Alicia, Richard de Redwell, Hagin of Northampton, Friar Benedict and the Manor of Easingbourne are, of course, wholly fictional.

Court life is here portrayed as being quite simple. Although outwardly there was clearly magnificence, in private the informality between characters as suggested in the play may not have been wholly inconsistent with reality.

The Woman Below

The fragile relationship of an impoverished and childless couple is tested by the sudden appearance of a childhood acquaintance whose partner is about to defect. The action takes place entirely in the couple's west London attic flat, in the early 1950s and over a period of about six months.

Nellie Westcroft contemplates a telephone, just installed, while waiting for her husband Charlie to return from work. After he appears the telephone rings. It is not Charlie's mother, as expected, but Elaine, a woman who, as a child, was sheltered by Charlie's family before the outbreak of the Second World War. She arrives accompanied by her partner, Gordon, and her sixteen-year-old daughter Sarah. They appear socially superior to the Westcrofts, but claim to be destitute, seeking shelter. They stay in the cramped attic accommodation for one night.

During this time Gordon charms Nellie, but also finds an unlikely affinity with Charlie on account of his left-wing political views. Maliciously, though, he hints at a likeness between Charlie and Sarah, leading Charlie to suppose that he might be Sarah's father. During their stay there are suggestions of improper intimacy between Gordon and Sarah. While the others visit Kew Gardens, Gordon learns of Nellie's unrealized talent as a pianist – and that her piano had been sold by Charlie to support his gambling. Gordon leaves Nellie a poem, apparently written just for her, which she hides away.

In a frank discussion with Charlie, Gordon reveals that he was once a Cambridge Apostle (communist sympathiser) and claims, without any justification, to have been a fighter pilot. Mysterious telephone calls suggest that Gordon is about to defect. To Elaine – and Nellie's – consternation he leaves in haste without saying goodbye. Security police descend on the flat in response, as is later revealed, to a tip-off from Ruby, who occupies the flat below. As the stage darkens we hear on the radio the voice of Alvar Liddell reading the news. Gordon's defection is confirmed, although his whereabouts are unknown.

Several weeks after Gordon's disappearance it is clear that Nellie is pregnant. Charlie and Nellie celebrate but Charlie, studying the calendar, has doubts about being the father. Later, when Nellie is attending an evening class in Russian, Sarah appears unannounced and 'seduces' Charlie, towards whom she is both tender and aggressive. Unseen by Charlie, she finds the envelope containing the poem that Gordon has given to Nellie and replaces the poem with tickets for the Russian ballet. When confronted by Nellie, Charlie claims they are for their wedding anniversary, but Nellie further suspects Charlie's infatuation with Sarah.

Four months later Gordon resurfaces in Moscow. A reporter from the local paper comes to interview Nellie and hears her playing on a recently acquired piano that, presumably, was sent to her though the influence of Gordon. He observes that she is pregnant, a condition that she appears to relish, to the extent of proposing Russian names for the unborn child. Later, Elaine appears, having at last received a letter from Gordon; but she is jealous of Sarah on account of the interest in her shown by the Russian embassy. Elaine then explains that Sarah is the daughter, not of Charlie, but of his deceased brother Tom, with whom she had a secret affair.

Sarah then produces a film given to her by the embassy that shows Gordon in his Moscow flat blandly explaining his situation. He apologises to Elaine for terminating their relationship, disillusions Nellie concerning the supposed parentage of her unborn child, chides Charlie for his lack of ambition and admits to a passion for Sarah. Finally he reveals that Ruby – the 'woman below' – was responsible for revealing his location to the police. Sarah, distraught and resentful, confronts Ruby and stabs her superficially. She and Elaine depart.

While waiting for the inevitable appearance of the police, Charlie and Nellie agree that weights have been lifted from their shoulders. However, Sarah re-appears with a Russian agent who cleans the knife and advises silence. As she leaves it is obvious that she too is pregnant. Sarah tells Nellie not to believe anything her mother has said, re-opening the possibility that Nellie is bearing Gordon's child and hinting that her own child could indeed be Charlie's. The doubts (though perhaps unfounded) will remain with Nellie and Charlie, mutual suspicion being their penalty for the fantasies each has rashly entertained.

Melusina Ballerina

Melissa Gray is a twenty-two-year-old Oxford graduate in robotics working for a company that makes robotic toys. *Robotoys* – headed by Roberto Malario – has a factory in Acton, but also a hidden laboratory adjacent to Roberto's flat in Kensington dedicated to producing humanoid figures. Melissa's obsession with ballet has sparked the development of a children's toy for Christmas that has also morphed into a life-sized figure of a ballerina – Melusina – which Roberto has begun exploit as a surrogate prostitute for rich Middle Eastern diplomats and businessmen.

Melissa is resentful that her accountant father, Thomas Gray, blocked her career as a ballet dancer, which he unjustly attributes to the influence of his second wife Claire. Nevertheless, Melissa still lives at home. Partly because of Melissa, Claire has an uneasy relationship with her weak, religious and bigoted husband, whom she dominates.

One day Thomas' brother Bertie introduces the Grays to a Middle Eastern businessman, Tariq Al-Khouri, who recruits Thomas as a financial adviser for a project to build an oil pipeline. In anticipation of Thomas' efforts, the embassy of the country concerned invites him to a reception, after which he is taken to night clubs and, eventually, to a brothel, of which he has only a vague recollection. He believes, however, that some sexual activity took place there.

Earlier the same day, Roberto's Melusina developed a malfunction that could not be rectified because the technician, Spencer, had failed to appear. In desperation because of the financial plight of his company, Roberto persuades Melissa to stand in for Melusina. Unknown to everyone else, Spencer has set up a camera in the bedroom and, though not himself present and not anticipating anything 'unusual', films what takes place there.

In order to embarrass Melissa, who has repeatedly rebuffed his advances, Spencer sends her father, anonymously, a photograph of activity in the bedroom. Thomas, thinking in terms of blackmail, wrongly assumes that the indistinct photographs are of his own exploits.

Sometime later the London evening paper publishes one of the photos in an article on robotic prostitution. However, the location is not divulged. Thomas, seeing it, discusses his presumed predicament with Bertie and both assume (erroneously) that Thomas has in fact visited Roberto's apartment and by implication availed himself of Melusina. As the 'truth' seems likely to come out Bertie advises

Thomas to come clean with Melissa. Following the evening in question both Melissa and Thomas have behaved in ways suggesting guilt.

To help resolve Thomas' plight Bertie arranges a meeting with Melissa in a Pimlico café, then leaves them together. Thomas 'confesses' to having visited Roberto's flat. Father and daughter now both believe they have committed incest. But it also emerges in the heated discussion that Thomas abused Melissa as a child, recollections of which both have hitherto chosen to suppress. Thomas, in remorse, flees the restaurant, only to be struck by a passing vehicle and killed. Melissa comes to believe her father's death was intentional.

Believing that Spencer was the cause of her tribulations, Melissa goes to the Kensington laboratory to confront him. Unseen, she observes him about to engage in a sexual act with Melusina. While he is temporarily out of the room she places Melusina under the bed and takes her place. As Spencer begins to make love to her she stabs him to death. Helped by Bertie, who has followed her, she replaces Melusina under Spencer's body, with the knife in her hands. In the immediate aftermath it is generally assumed that the robotic Melusina killed Spencer. Roberto, however, has been a witness and could be untrustworthy.

Bertie accompanies Melissa home. She reveals the abuse she suffered as a child at the hands of Thomas. They agree to conceal the truth about Spencer's death.

After Thomas' funeral a few days later, Tariq, who has flown in for the occasion, visits the Gray's home to tell Claire that she is entitled to Thomas' consultancy fees. Melissa, in a disturbed state – and still believing that she committed incest with her father – leaves the room. After she has gone Tariq makes clear that the establishment to which Thomas had been taken was in Knightsbridge, not Kensington, and had nothing to do with Melissa or Melusina.

Meanwhile Melissa enters her bedroom in deep distress. She removes her coat to reveal her schoolgirl dress, presumably worn during the funeral. She swallows an overdose of sedative pills, then removes her clothes to reveal her ballet leotard. She stands in front of the mirror performing balletic movements. As the potentially lethal drug takes effect, she sinks to the floor. It is not revealed whether Bertie and Claire are in time to save her.

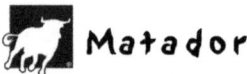

Matador

For exclusive discounts on Matador titles,
sign up to our occasional newsletter at
troubador.co.uk/bookshop